Gendering Government

Louise A. Chappell

Gendering Government: Feminist Engagement with the State in Australia and Canada

UBC Press · Vancouver · Toronto

09 08 07 06 05 04 03 02   5 4 3 2 1

Printed in Canada on acid-free paper ∞

National Library of Canada Cataloguing in Publication Data

Chappell, Louise, 1966-
  Gendering government: feminist engagement with the state
  in Australia and Canada / Louise Chappell.

  Includes bibliographical references and index.
  ISBN 0-7748-0965-5

  1. Feminism – Political aspects – Canada. 2. Feminism – Political aspects – Australia. 3. Women in politics – Canada. 4. Women in politics – Australia. 5. Comparative government. 6. Canada – Politics and government – 1993- 7. Australia – Politics and government – 1945- I. Title.
  HQ1236.5.C2C43 2002   320.9/0082'0971   C2002-911078-5

Canadä

UBC Press gratefully acknowledges the financial support for our publishing program of the Government of Canada through the Book Publishing Industry Development Program (BPIDP), and of the Canada Council for the Arts, and the British Columbia Arts Council.

This book has been published with the help of a grant from the Humanities and Social Sciences Federation of Canada, using funds provided by the Social Sciences and Humanities Research Council of Canada, and a grant from the School of Economics and Political Science, University of Sydney, Australia.

Printed and bound in Canada by Friesens
Set in Stone by Brenda and Neil West, BN Typographics West
Copy editor: Joanne Richardson
Proofreader: Deborah Kerr
Indexer: Annette Lorek

UBC Press
The University of British Columbia
2029 West Mall
Vancouver, BC V6T 1Z2
604-822-5959 / Fax: 604-822-6083
www.ubcpress.ca

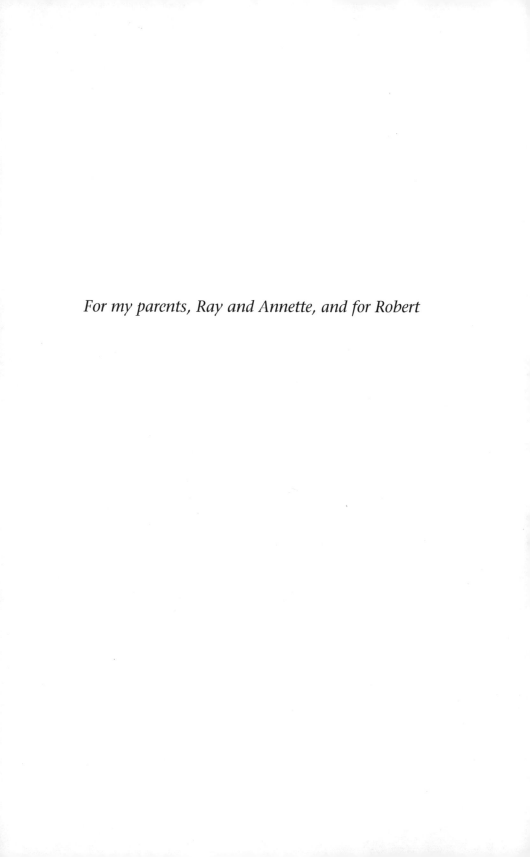

For my parents, Ray and Annette, and for Robert

Contents

Acknowledgments

This book has been a long time in the making, and I am grateful to many people for their assistance in helping me see it to fruition. Colleagues Martin Painter, Bob Howard, and Deborah Brennan have given me guidance and support. Jill Vickers has always been generous with her time and has provided me with helpful comments and suggestions on all matters Canadian. Thanks also to Emily Andrew and the staff of UBC Press, who have been a delight to deal with and who provided me with a smooth passage through the publishing process. I have enjoyed the patience and good humour of many friends, especially Liz Kirby and Lisa Hill, and the encouragement of Trevor Matthews and Lye Yang. The members of my family have been unflagging in their love and support, which I could not do without. I am indebted to Helen Nelson, who has given me the benefit of her analytical mind, good humour, and hospitality. Without Helen's influence, this book would never have been written. Finally, thanks go to Robert Ridley, who every day teaches me something new about the most important things in life. Of course, any errors contained in this book are my own.

Acronyms

AD	Australian Democrats
AEC	Australian Electoral Commission
ALP	Australian Labor Party
ALRC	Australian Law Reform Commission
BC	British Columbia
CACSW	Canadian Advisory Council on the Status of Women
CC	Constitutional Convention
CCP	Court Challenges Program
CEDAW	Convention on the Elimination of All Forms of Discrimination against Women
EEO	Equal Employment Opportunity
FFQ	Fédération des femmes du Québec
HoC	House of Commons
HoR	House of Representatives
HRC	Human Rights Commission (Canada)
HREOC	Human Rights and Equal Opportunity Commission
LEAF	Legal Education and Action Fund
LPA	Liberal Party of Australia
NAC	National Action Committee on the Status of Women
NAFTA	North American Free Trade Agreement
NAWL	National Association of Women and the Law
NDP	New Democratic Party
NSW	New South Wales
OSW	Office of the Status of Women (Australia)
OWD	Ontario Women's Directorate
PC	Progressive Conservative Party
PCO	Privy Council Office
PIAC	Public Interest Advocacy Centre
PM&C	Prime Minister and Cabinet Department (Australia)
POS	Political Opportunity Structure

PR   Proportional Representation
QLD   Queensland
RCAGA   Royal Commission on Australian Government Administration
RCERPF   Royal Commission on Electoral Reform and Party Financing
RCNRT   Royal Commission on New Reproductive Technologies
RCSW   Royal Commission on the Status of Women
SA   South Australia
SDA   Sex Discrimination Act (Australia)
SOS   Secretary of State Department
SWC   Status of Women Canada
WA   Western Australia
WAGE   Women Advocates for Gender Equity
WCC   Women's Constitutional Convention
WEL   Women's Electoral Lobby
WLM   Women's Liberation Movement (Australia)

Gendering Government

1
Gender and Political Institutions in Australia and Canada

Feminist activists cannot avoid the state. Whether feminists are pursuing equal pay, anti-domestic violence laws, or refuge or childcare centres, they must engage with state institutions at some level. The nature of this engagement can range from accepting minimal financial assistance to being employed in a state institution. What determines the extent and nature of this engagement? Why are some feminists willing to engage with some institutions but not others?

Feminist engagement with the state has become a key area of research for feminist scholars. Conventional debates have tended to cast the relationship between gender interests and the state in either/or terms; that is, between those who see the state as either inherently patriarchal and oppressive of women or as gender-neutral and beneficial to women's emancipation. This book provides a new dimension to our understanding of this relationship, suggesting a mid-position that sees the interaction between gender interests and the state as dynamic and co-constitutive. This approach to feminist engagement bypasses the usual normative debate about whether or not feminists *should* engage with the state and, instead, considers what effect political institutions have on shaping feminist claims (and, in turn, what effect these claims have on the nature of these institutions). It raises a number of new questions about the gendered nature of the state, such as: To what extent do gendered political institutions shape feminist strategies? Can feminists challenge established structures and gender patterns within institutions in order to make them more amenable to feminist demands? To what extent are political institutions gendered? And to what extent does this vary across the institutional spectrum?

Gendering Government argues that, alongside ideology, political institutions are central to shaping feminists' strategic choices. It does this by comparing the engagement of feminists with political institutions in Australia and Canada during the contemporary period. This comparison is illuminating because it shows that, despite some important similarities between Australian and Canadian political institutions, feminists in each country have found that these institutions present them with quite different opportunity and constraint structures. As a result, they have adopted divergent strategies to advance their objectives. Whereas Australian feminists have looked primarily to bureaucratic institutions, Canadian feminists have emphasized lobbying through a peak umbrella organization – the National Action Committee on the Status of Women (NAC) – and, in recent years, have focused some of their efforts on using the Charter of Rights and Freedoms to pursue their claims.

It is not only the 'top-down' influence of political institutions on feminist activists that is important in this analysis. A second, equally important, point involves demonstrating how, through their strategies, feminist activists have themselves influenced the nature of political institutions. In doing this, *Gendering Government* engages with the structure-versus-agency debate. Rather than coming down on one side of this debate or the other, it demonstrates that the relationship between feminists and political institutions is *co-constitutive,* with agents and structures continuously informing one another. Perhaps the best example of this reciprocal relationship involves the interaction between Canadian feminists and the Canadian Charter of Rights and Freedoms. Although the charter channelled some of the efforts of the Canadian women's movement towards litigation, it also enabled them to have a direct influence upon how it has come to be understood. Not only did feminist involvement in charter debates ensure that equality clauses were included in the final document, but, since the charter's entrenchment, it has also ensured that feminist legal experts have directly influenced charter interpretation.

In sum, *Gendering Government* has two central objectives. The first is to explain, from an institutional perspective, the differences between feminist activism in Australia and in Canada. It provides a comprehensive comparative account of the role of institutions in shaping feminist strategies. Its second aim is to add to the knowledge of institutions – to gain a better understanding of the interaction between social actors (in this case feminists), gender norms, and political institutions. It rejects both purely structural and purely agential explanations of the engagement of activists with institutions and suggests, instead, that the relationship between them needs to be seen as a two-way street, with feminists involved in shaping the political opportunity structures (POSs) open to them.

The Role of Ideology and the Importance of Institutions
To the extent that feminist scholars have paid attention to the question of what influences Western feminists' strategic choices, ideology has often been cited as the key variable. Many analyses have suggested that their

strategies are influenced by a commitment to one or other of two foundational tenets of Western feminist thought. For some scholars, the key to feminist engagement with the state has rested on the extent to which feminists perceive the state to be patriarchal. The more radical or socialist strands of the feminist movement (that emphasize the *inherent* patriarchal character of the state) are more anti-statist and, consequently, less willing to engage directly with the state. This line of argument has been used to explain why feminists in the United Kingdom and the United States have eschewed direct engagement with the state (see Watson 1992; MacKinnon 1989; Brown 1995).

Other commentators have suggested that feminist strategies have been shaped by an ideological opposition to hierarchical forms of organization. For many feminists, such structures represent masculine forms of organizing and are to be eschewed. A resistance to hierarchies has been used to explain why Australian feminists have failed to develop an institutionalized feminist organization (Sawer and Groves 1994) and why Canadian feminists have emphasized external lobbying rather than bureaucratic 'entrism' (Findlay 1987).

Although ideological explanations go some way to illuminating the choices of feminist activists, they are limited. Ideology is better able to explain why feminists have not attempted certain strategies than why, in many instances, they have engaged with the state and created hierarchical organizations. For instance, feminist ideology does not explain why many radical feminists who view the state as patriarchal have chosen to work as bureaucrats, politicians, or legal advocates. Nor does it reveal why certain activists remain hostile to hierarchical structures yet nevertheless create hierarchical organizations. Such a phenomenon has occurred in Canada, where feminists opposed to hierarchical structures have established and maintained the peak organization known as NAC.

Those relying solely upon ideological explanations treat these activities as instances of liberal feminism at work – liberal feminism being the most benign form of feminism, which sees the state as able to operate as a neutral body once women achieve equal representation within its institutions. However, feminists who argue from this position, such as Kaplan (1996) and Burgmann (1993), usually refer to liberal feminism in a pejorative sense; to their minds, liberal feminists are blind to the true nature of the state and will, in time, be co-opted into its patriarchal structures. One limitation of the logic of this argument is that it sees patriarchy as being functional to the operation of the state: one is necessary in order for the other to exist. It also fails to explain the numerous instances in which feminists committed to more radical or socialist perspectives have successfully engaged with state institutions to bring about greater equality for women.

Others looking at feminist strategies from an ideological perspective have preferred to use the term 'pro-statist' to refer to all feminists who are willing to engage with the state in order to advance gender-equality objectives (see Sawer 1990; Vickers 1992; Eisenstein 1996). This is a broad and useful term in that it does not infer that those engaging with the state necessarily see it in benign liberal feminist terms. It thereby encompasses feminists from radical and socialist perspectives. Even this term, however, leaves us with the problem of relying solely on ideology to explain feminist action. It does not tell us why, in those instances in which feminists share a pro-statist position (as in Australia and Canada), they choose different strategies.

Although, by itself, feminist ideology is a relatively weak tool with which to understand feminist strategies, it cannot be discounted altogether. However, when discussing the role of ideology, it is important not to isolate it from feminist praxis. As *Gendering Government* demonstrates, the two are interlinked and reinforce each other. Ideology, within the broader political context, also appears to have some explanatory value for political activists (including feminists). Ideological concepts, especially those held by political parties concerning the role and nature of the state, have been a significant factor in shaping the available POS open to feminist activists across the institutional environment. As will be detailed throughout the following chapters, political parties representing different ideological perspectives have operated as an intervening force to shape the openings and obstacles within political institutions.

An additional explanation for feminists' choice of political action has to do with the influence of political institutions. These institutions provide openings and constraints that operate to encourage feminists to pursue particular avenues in order to advance their political agenda. Its particular structural and normative features will influence whether an institution is closed or open to the demands of political actors. For instance, as the following chapters demonstrate, in Australia a tolerance for, and culture of, advocacy in the bureaucracy has encouraged Australian feminists to focus on a 'femocrat' strategy, whereas in Canada a constitutionally enshrined equality guarantee has provided the opportunity for Canadian feminists to focus on litigation. Other opportunities have been influenced by political parties intervening in institutions. More frequently, parties have operated together with other institutions to shape the prevailing POS.

Gendering Government adopts an institutional approach to the state and, in doing so, represents an overt attempt to bring a stronger institutional focus to bear on feminist political science. This is not to suggest that the literature has entirely ignored institutions. However, where feminist scholars in the field have taken feminist engagement with the state seriously (rather than seeing it as a form of false consciousness), attempts to incorporate an institutional analysis have been limited in a number of respects. First, much of the existing research has tended to adopt a micro view, focusing on specific institutions within a given polity. The role of women, the legislature, and political parties has been extensively researched in the United Kingdom (Norris and Lovenduski 1995), Australia (Sawer and Simms 1984), and Canada (Bashevkin 1993; Arscott and Trimble 1997). Women and the bureaucracy has been another favoured topic in Australia (see Sawer 1990, Yeatman 1990; Eisenstein 1996) and, to a lesser extent, in Canada (Findlay 1987; Andrew and Rodgers 1997).

Moreover, while there is some work that addresses the influence of a single institution – such as the legislature or bureaucracy – across polities (see Randall 1987; Lovenduski and Norris 1996; Stetson and Mazur 1995), little work has been done on the influence of a *range* of political institutions across states. Joyce Gelb's *Feminism and Politics* (1989) and Sylvia Bashevkin's *Women on the Defensive* (1998) are seminal comparative studies that include institutional differences in their analyses, but neither study gives a comprehensive account of the institutional structures in the countries under review. In their study of gender and social policy in Australia, Canada, the United States, and Britain, O'Connor, Orloff, and Shaver (1999) suggest that the different institutional contexts of each country is a key variable influencing the representation of gender issues. Yet they pay only cursory attention to this context in their account (see O'Connor, Orloff, and Shaver 1999, 202-2). Work is only now beginning to emerge on certain institutions, especially federalism, and, in Australia (at least until the recent republican debate), the constitutional and legal system.

This study examines feminists' engagement with institutions at a macro level, outlining how they have engaged with the full range of political institutions in two polities. It not only considers feminists' engagement with the legislature, political parties, and the bureaucracy, but also with the less well-studied constitutional and legal institutions, as well as the institutions of federalism. Using this overarching approach, it is possible to assess the impact of institutions, operating individually and in combination with each other, on feminists' choices. It enables us to identify the arenas where feminists face the most positive POSs and where their efforts have been blocked. Furthermore, when one looks across the spectrum of political institutions, the extent of feminist influence on institutional structures becomes more evident. The analysis avoids the trap that many who focus solely on one institutional arena risk falling into – adopting either an overly optimistic or an overly pessimistic view of feminists' ability to use political institutions to their own ends. Where feminists may be frustrated with their efforts in one institution, they may be able to make advances in another. This broad perspective allows us to examine the wide range of strategies open to these activists and allows us to provide a comprehensive account of feminist successes and failures.

Neo-Institutionalism

In emphasizing institutions as a major determining variable shaping feminist strategies, my argument falls under the rubric of neo-institutionalism. Using this approach to understand feminist strategies towards the state stems from a broader effort to 'bring the state back in' to political science. The most well-known exponent of this effort, Theda Skocpol (1985, 21), explains that states matter

> not simply because of the goal-orientated activities of state officials. They matter because their organizational configurations, along with their overall patterns of activity, affect political culture, encourage some kinds of group formation and collective political actions (but not others), and make possible the raising of certain political issues (but not others).

Neo-institutionalism in its broadest sense is interested in examining the way institutional arrangements shape political behaviour.

There are many 'new institutionalisms' – in economics, organization theory, political science and public choice, international relations, history, and sociology. The variant used in this book is the historical-institutional approach to the state, which suggests that the role of actors within a political system can be understood only by investigating, over time, the nature of the institutions within that system (Keman 1997, 12). The basic argument is that initial choices about policy, or institutional forms, shape subsequent decisions; that policies and political actors are 'path dependent'; and that, once launched, political actors will follow a particular path until 'some sufficiently strong force deflects them from it' (Peters 1999, 19). Historical neo-institutionalism can be seen to have four defining features: it disaggregates the state into separate institutional arenas; it provides a broad definition of political institutions, including the political party system; it stresses the importance of the interaction between institutions within a given polity in influencing the relationship between the state and social actors; and it allows for an embedded and dynamic view of the state.

The point about the relations between various institutions, made forcefully in the work of Thelen and Steinmo (1992), is particularly important in the following argument. The influence of single institutional variables on the behaviour of social actors often does not capture the whole picture. What is required, and what neo-institutionalism offers, is a framework that highlights the independent effect that *the pattern of interaction between various institutions within a given polity* can have on the behaviour of social actors. In interacting with each other, it is possible that one institution can bring about a change within another, thereby prising open, or foreclosing, opportunities for the advancement of the objectives of a particular social group. As will become obvious throughout this book, not only do individual institutions operate to shape feminist strategies, but the interaction of institutions in a given polity (notably, in this case, the interaction between political parties and other institutions) has an independent influence on feminist activities.

Political Opportunity Structures

The neo-institutionalist approach to political institutions provides a dynamic and interactive way of understanding the state. However, it does not explain the strategies chosen by the Australian and Canadian women's movements. It has two key problems: (1) it fails to take into account the gendered nature of institutions; and (2) although it provides for a disaggregated and dynamic understanding of the state, its emphasis is more on the policy outcomes of political institutions than on the relationship between institutions and policy practitioners and policy activists. *Gendering Government*, therefore, supplements neo-institutionalism with an additional 'tool' for understanding political behaviour – the concept of political opportunity structure (POS). According to Tarrow (1998, 77), a leading proponent of POS, the concept refers to 'consistent – but not necessarily permanent – dimensions of the political environment that provide incentive for collection action by affecting people's expectations for success or failure.' The POS approach to political behaviour is interested in how political actors can both take advantage of existing opportunities and create new ones. In this sense, it provides a dynamic view of the interaction of social movements and political structures.

At its core, the POS approach suggests that social actors are not just influenced in their choices by endogenous factors, such as the 'resources' at their disposal, but also by external political forces (see McAdam, McCarthy, and Zald 1996, 3; Tarrow 1998, 77). There is, however, some debate about which forces are to be included under the definition. Banaszak (1996, 30-1) provides a useful synthesis of POS factors and suggests that they have three key dimensions: (1) the formal political rules and institutions that provide challengers with points of access; (2) the constellation of political actors involved, including political parties, interest groups, and social movements; and (3) the informal procedures of decision making and the strategies of those in power.

The first two factors are particularly relevant to this study. In both Australia and Canada, formal political institutions have provided a range of openings (as well as constraints) to feminist activists. What the following chapters reveal, and where *Gendering Government* makes a contribution to the POS literature, is that these openings cannot be presumed to exist in similar institutions; rather, they can vary between institutions across polities. For instance, the multiple access points offered by federalism have advantaged the Australian women's movement, allowing it to enjoy a system of 'dual democracy,' but the same openings have not always been available to Canadian activists. The importance of the interplay between political actors, especially the alliance between feminists and political parties in the Australian case, is also illustrated throughout this study.

In recent times a range of feminist scholars have come to appreciate and to utilize the POS approach to explain feminist political actions (Dobrowolsky 2000; Katzenstein 1998; Banaszak 1996; Staggenborg 1991). The primary attractions of POS for these scholars include its emphasis on the political context in shaping feminists' strategies and its ability to provide a dynamic account of the interaction between the political context and feminist activists. Feminist work has looked particularly at how the POS influences feminists, and at how feminists create opportunities for themselves (see Banaszak 1996, 29). Aware that opportunities are, as Tarrow suggests, 'fickle friends,' these studies have sought to identify those factors that can increase them.[1]

A common feminist critique of the POS approach to political behaviour is that it has failed to take adequate account of the culture and norms that underlie political structures. As Banaszak (1996, 40) argues: 'Political opportunity structures are more than mere "reality" about which political actors must be informed; they also generate a set of values that supports the maintenance of these structures.' Katzenstein (1998, 32), in her impressive study of feminist activism in the military and the Roman Catholic Church, emphasizes the importance of norms as a variable influencing the POS. In her analysis, she shows how the law provides (and withholds) opportunities for 'claims making' as well as how it shapes the way activists define themselves and prioritize their agenda (165).

Katzenstein presents an additional challenge to the POS literature by offering a normative approach to the nature of protest itself. She argues that protest can occur inside as well as outside formal institutions. The key to protest is not the form (such as a sit-in or street march) but the content, which must be 'disturbance making.' Included in her definition of protest actors are feminists who enter traditional institutions in order to challenge and disturb 'long-settled assumptions, rules and practices' (7). The subjects of *Gendering Government* – feminists who have chosen to bring about change through institutions, including the bureaucracy, political party structures, Parliament, and legal structures – fit neatly within Katzenstein's definition of protest activists.

Gender Norms, Institutions, and Opportunities

Gendering Government shares much with the work of Katzenstein and other feminist adaptations of the POS concept in that it suggests that institutions, and the POS available to feminists, can only be understood by taking into account the normative context within which they operate. It is unique in that it accounts for how gender norms operate within institutions and the influence they have had on the opportunities open to feminist activists in Australia and Canada. It takes up the point of key institutionalists March and Olsen (1989); that is, that there is a 'logic of appropriateness' within institutions that guides the behaviour of those operating within them. At the same time it demonstrates that, underlying this 'logic of appropriateness,' there are well-defined guidelines about how men and women should act and the value that is ascribed to masculine and feminine behaviour. It is one of my key objectives to 'undo the taken-for-grantedness' of institutions (Stivers 1993, 5), to show how much of what is presented as 'neutral' is in fact gendered. Each chapter examines how gender norms influence the political opportunity and constraint structures faced by feminists, and each illustrates when and how feminists can unsettle the entrenched norms in order to use institutions for their own ends.

An emphasis on a gendered view of institutions does not imply that one should conceive of the state as being inherently patriarchal. This book rejects the proposition put forward in some feminist theories – notably radical and socialist feminist analyses – that the state is a monolith that always operates to oppress women (for examples of these approaches see MacKinnon 1989; Ferguson 1987; Eisenstein 1993; Brown 1995). One problem with the view that the state represents only male interests is that, as Franzway, Court, and Connell (1989, 29) warn, 'this approaches a conspiracy theory. One is left searching for Patriarchal Headquarters to explain what goes on.' Another problem is that it reifies the state and elides the differences that exist between the various institutions that form it. As Hester Eisenstein (1996, xvii) notes: 'To speak of "the state" is misleading. "The state" means the entire apparatus of government, from parliaments, cabinets, and bureaucracies administering programs for health, welfare, education, and commerce to the judicial system, the army and the police ... Each has a different relation to women.'

Rather than viewing the state as inherently patriarchal, it is more useful to see the individual institutions that comprise it as 'culturally marked as masculine' and as operating largely as the 'institutionalisation of the power of men' (Franzway, Court, and Connell 1989, 41). Nevertheless, the institutionalization of gender values is not 'fixed'; gender norms can manifest themselves in different ways within different institutions and can fluctuate across time and between states. Furthermore, gender operates within institutions at both a *nominal* and a *substantive* level. This point is well made by Savage and Witz (1992, 37, emphasis added), who argue:

> it is not the gender of state actors which renders the state patriarchal, but
> the ways in which the competing political interests of gender are displaced

onto or 'distilled' through the state. A *nominally* patriarchal state is not necessarily a *substantively* patriarchal one, although it is clear that, if the legislative, administrative and policy making arenas are in male hands (i.e., nominally patriarchal) then the more likely it is that the state will be substantively patriarchal.

Although the political opportunities open to all activists are shaped by existing gender norms, they are especially important to feminists who seek to challenge and destabilize them in order to create new avenues for reform within institutions.

If it is accepted that institutions are gendered and that this shapes the opportunities open to feminist activists, then the question becomes: what constitutes a positive or negative outcome for feminist activists in their engagement with political institutions? In this book, the mark of feminist success or failure is measured by the extent to which they are able to take advantage of existing political opportunities or to create new opportunities through which to pursue 'women's issues.' But how are these issues to be defined? The feminist literature is alive with debates surrounding whether there are, indeed, specifically women's needs, interests, and issues. Given the challenge presented by women from various identity groups about what constitutes a 'woman,' feminist scholars and practitioners are increasingly reluctant to hold on to universalist concepts, which suggest that there is one identifiable set of women's issues. Women, like men, have widely diverse interests and cannot be treated as a monolithic block. Women's diversity presents a dilemma for those arguing for increasing women's representation, whether in a corporeal sense or in terms of 'interests' in political institutions such as Parliament or the bureaucracy. As Anne Phillips (1991, 26) points out, 'the representation of women *as women* potentially founders on both the difficulties of defining shared values of women and difficulties of establishing mechanisms through which these interests are voiced.'

Through their practice it is possible to identify two levels at which feminist activists have understood and operationalized the concept of women's interests. The first relates to women's unique and common biological characteristics, or what could be defined as sex-based commonalities. The fact that women share a similar reproductive system and potential has provided the basis for feminists, politicians, bureaucrats, lawyers, and lobbyists to argue for specialist reproductive and health services, including access to abortion, assisted reproductive technology, maternity services, and the like. However, even this seemingly straightforward understanding of women's interests is problematic with different categories of women. Certain groups of women, those deemed 'most desirable,' have found the state more willing to encourage and support their reproductive needs, while others, such as those from Aboriginal back-grounds, have faced direct discrimination in terms of access to services. For example, while White women in Australia were benefiting from par-ticular aspects of the welfare state, such as mothers pensions and child custody rights, Aboriginal women were not only denied these rights but, until the 1970s, many were forced to suffer state-sanctioned removal of their children (see Lake 1999, 83). In Canada, First Nations women suf-fered similar trauma in relation to the absence of rights over their children as well as, until 1985, being discriminated against under the Indian Act (see Weaver 1993).

The second sense in which the term 'women's interests' has been under-stood and applied by the feminist community relates to those specific interests that arise from women's particular historical and social position (see Vickers 1997b). In this view, women have a set of common interests because of the historical fact of women's relegation to the private sphere and men's predominance in the public sphere. This historical, patriarchal division between the public and private spheres resulted in women being economically and emotionally dependent upon men as well as being less educated. Moreover, it has meant that women have been underrepre-sented in all areas of the public realm, including corporate and political life. These historical distinctions, and the ongoing attitudes and norms that stem from them, are not founded in any natural biological difference between men and women but, rather, are gender-based; that is, they are socially constructed and are, therefore, able to be challenged. Feminist activists have attempted to do this through legislation, constitutional and common law, and public policies and practices within all forms of politi-cal institutions. The introduction of childcare facilities, girl's and women's education programs, equal pay and affirmative action in employment, and anti-violence against women measures are all examples of these efforts.

Arguments about the existence of common women's interests, especi-ally those related to gender-based distinctions between men and women, have been controversial. Challenges have come from a number of direc-tions. Some feminists, particularly those outside the majoritarian strand of the movement, have argued that the analysis of women's specific needs has failed to incorporate the division between women based on race, class, and sexuality. Efforts to redress these socio-historical imbalances have also presented a broad challenge to the social status quo. Many men and women wanting to uphold traditional roles have, therefore, been highly critical of feminist activists' assessment of 'women's issues,' claiming that feminists do not speak on behalf of all women.

Despite the controversies around the notion of women's interests, the con-cept has been an important discursive tool for activists. The extent to which feminists have used this concept, in both its sex-based and gender-based variants, is a focus of this book. I am interested in evaluating the extent to which majoritarian feminist activists have been able to take advantage of, or to create, political opportunities to enter institutions and then to advance what they define as women's interests.

A Comparative Perspective

As discussed above, the theoretical basis of *Gendering Government* is grounded in a historical neo-institutionalist approach. A key tenet of this approach is the importance of comparing the influence of institutional forces across both time and place. The temporal element is important in showing how changes in the institutional landscape are reflected in social actors' choices within a given polity. I focus on the influence of institutions on feminist activists' choices in Australia and Canada since the resurgence of feminism in the late 1960s to the late 1990s. This thirty-year time span provides an opportunity to plot the effect of the creation of new institutions (such as the entrenchment of the Charter of Rights and Freedoms in Canada) and the reform of existing institutions (such as changes to political party pre-selection processes) on feminist strategies in each polity.

The comparative method also has a spatial dimension. It examines differences and similarities in the institutional settings of Australia and Canada in order to make some generalizations about the influence of institutions on feminist activists across place. To what extent do differences in the operation of similar institutions in Australia and Canada – including the legislature and political party system, the bureaucracy, federalism, and the legal and constitutional system – explain the variations in the choice of strategies pursued by feminists in the two polities? What is the effect on feminists of differences between individual institutions (and of the interaction between them)?

I have selected Australia and Canada as the sites of comparison because these two countries are extremely similar to one another. By holding many variables more or less constant, it is possible to identify unexpected and interesting differences between these countries in order to develop 'a more refined account of national attributes and peculiarities' (Alexander and Galligan 1992, 1). Both Australia and Canada have a large landmass with relatively small multicultural and multiracial populations. Both are settler societies with Aboriginal populations. The two countries share a British colonial heritage as well as strong ties to the United States, the influences of which are reflected in similar economic, cultural, and political structures. Both are capitalist countries with residual welfare states. And each has blended a Westminster parliamentary and common law tradition with federal structures to create a hybrid political system.

Despite these similarities, interesting differences between Australia and

Canada are evident at a number of levels. In Canada, cultural, linguistic, and regional cleavages are more pronounced than they are in Australia. To a large extent this can be explained by the existence of Quebec, a province that differs from the rest of the country in terms of its heritage, culture, and language. The pressure stemming from Quebec separatism, or, at the very least, the demand by the province that the rest of Canada acknowledge its 'distinct society status,' has long had a major impact on the Canadian political scene. With the resurgence of Quebec nationalism in the 1960s, the province has been a particularly potent political force throughout the contemporary period.

The cleavages dividing Australia have taken quite a different form from those dividing Canada. Although regionalism has occasionally been a factor, cultural and linguistic divisions have been much less obvious. Historically, religious sectarianism and class have set the parameters around which social and political battles have been fought. The latter has declined in significance during the past three decades only to be replaced by the increased significance of the urban/rural divide. Nevertheless, class has remained an enduring organizing force in Australian political life. In terms of political culture, it appears that Canadians have seen the state as an instrument for accommodating and recognizing minority rights, whereas Australians have traditionally perceived the state in utilitarian terms.

The differences between the two countries do not stop here. It is also possible to identify significant variations between what are outwardly similar political institutional structures in Australia and Canada. For instance, both countries have a system of responsible government in place, yet there are key differences in how parliamentarians are elected to office, the level of partisanship within Parliament, and the composition and operation of the Senate. Important differences are also apparent within the two bureaucracies, especially in their levels of internal politicization and their interaction with the political executive. The federal structures of both countries also diverge from each other in terms of the level of political and fiscal autonomy of the constituent units, crucial aspects of any federal state. Finally, in relation to the Constitution and legal system, Canada has an entrenched bill of rights, whereas Australia has no express rights protections. These institutional differences are not superficial, especially when we consider them from the point of view of social actors. In the following chapters I argue that these differences have influenced the opportunity structures open to political activists in the two countries and, as a result, have shaped their choices in relation to strategies and structures.

Gendering Government also contributes to existing comparative feminist literature. Other comparative feminist works, such as that by Joyce Gelb (1989) and Sylvia Bashevkin (1998), have developed arguments about the importance of institutions by analyzing political systems that differ from each other in important respects. Gelb considers the corporatist Swedish system, the federal congressional regime in the United States, and the unitary parliamentary system in the United Kingdom. Bashevkin compares the American, British, and Canadian federal parliamentary systems. These studies are interesting in that, for feminists, they advance contrasting conclusions about the advantages and disadvantages of these divergent institutional settings. For Gelb, the American-style congressional system most benefits feminists because it enables them to operate as independent, autonomous activists. Bashevkin's (1998, 10) study produces somewhat different conclusions, arguing that the parliamentary systems found in Canada and Britain are not as constraining as Gelb has assumed. While these studies provide valuable comparisons of the influence of different political systems on feminists, they cannot explain why feminists within similar institutional settings – in this case, parliamentary and federal – vary in their strategic approaches to the state. *Gendering Government* is the first book to undertake such a comparison. In providing such an account, it argues, alongside Gelb and Bashevkin, that institutions matter; however, it refines the argument to illustrate how differences within similar institutions influence feminist activism.

I limit myself to providing an account of the strategies of majoritarian feminists in Australia and Canada; that is, the predominantly White, middle-class movement in Australia and the Anglophone strand of the movement in Canada. In doing so, I omit other important feminist actors, including those from minority groups (e.g., Aboriginal activists and those from non-English speaking backgrounds and, in the case of Canada, a second majoritarian movement made up of Francophone feminists in Quebec). The various elements of feminist activism in both countries have not been completely isolated from each other. At various times they have cooperated on a range of issues. Nevertheless, the variations between these activists in terms of strategies and structure make it necessary to differentiate between them.

The same political opportunity and constraint structures cannot be assumed for all women in any single state; rather, we need to acknowledge that the racial aspects of the state have meant that women from different backgrounds have faced different opportunities and constraints. The Anglo-majoritarian feminist movements that are the focus of this book have been in a relatively privileged position compared to their Aboriginal and non-Anglo contemporaries vis-à-vis political institutions. The focus on Anglo-majoritarian elements of the movements in Australia and Canada prohibits broad generalizations about the experiences of all feminists in these two countries. Activists from Aboriginal communities, non-English speaking groups, and Francophone backgrounds all have different stories to tell about the nature of the political and constraint structures that are open to them and the strategies they have developed in response. It is not my purpose to tell these stories, nor is it my intention to make generalizations about all feminist engagement with the state.

The data for *Gendering Government* are derived from three main sources. They draw upon a significant body of secondary literature related to political institutions, gender politics, and feminist intervention in the state in Australia and Canada. They are also based, to a significant degree, on primary research undertaken in Australia and Canada during the period between 1995 and 2000. I consulted government documents, feminist activist archives, and newspaper reports in each country. I also conducted a number of open-ended interviews with key feminist activists and politicians in Australia and Canada. In Australia these included former heads of the key Commonwealth 'femocrat' agency, the Office of the Status of Women (and the equivalent state agencies in New South Wales and South Australia), feminist activists from the Women's Liberation and the Women's Electoral Lobby strands of the women's movement, and a former minister assisting the prime minister for women's affairs. In Canada, I conducted interviews with former and current bureaucrats in women's agencies, feminist activists from NAC, and feminist academics. To enable interviewees to be as frank as possible, it was agreed that their identities would be protected in any published work arising from this research. Although not referred to by name in the text, these interviewees provided invaluable information that enabled me both to cross-check and clarify information I had gathered from other sources. They also enabled me to open new lines of inquiry. Where direct quotes from interviews are used in the text, the position of the person is noted so long as her anonymity is protected. A list of when and where interviews took place is included with other references.

The following discussion takes up the issues outlined here and extends the current debate about gender interests and the state on three levels. First, it broadens existing feminist analyses by highlighting the importance of institutions, and the opportunities they afford, for shaping the strategic choices of feminist activists. It does this through examining Anglo-feminist engagement with the electoral, bureaucratic, legal, and federal institutions in Australia and Canada. Second, it bridges the structure/agency debate to show how feminists are both shaped by and shape the POSs open to them. Third, it expands the current neo-institutionalist and POS literature by examining how gender norms operate within institutions.

2
Feminist Actors in Australia and Canada: Identities, Ideas, Strategies, and Structures

When viewed from a macro perspective, the Australian and Anglo-Canadian women's movements share a number of characteristics. Both are diversified, encompassing a range of identities and ideas.[1] In addition, both have a varied strategic repertoire that operates inside and outside political institutions.

When viewed from a micro level, however, some important differences between the two movements come into focus. In relation to strategies, Australian feminists have focused primarily on bureaucratic 'entrism' (which has entailed some alliance with the Australian Labor Party) as well as mainstream lobbying techniques. Anglo-Canadian feminists have also used lobbying but 'with a difference' (Dobrowolsky 2000), combining it with more militant direct action and mass mobilization protests. Recently, under the Charter of Rights and Freedoms, some Anglo-Canadian feminists have also come to use litigation as a form of political action. Other differences exist at a structural level. While Australian feminists have eschewed formal organizational forms, their Canadian counterparts have created and maintained a peak women's organization as well as numerous other permanent organizations.

Why is it that Australian and Anglo-Canadian feminists operating within such seemingly similar institutional settings and pursuing similar goals have chosen to adopt different strategies and structures? This chapter considers this question first by examining the salience of ideological explanations and then considering the role of institutions.

Ideology

Ideology is a common explanation for differences between feminist activists across polities. Other comparative analyses, including Watson's (1992) study of why Australian feminists have and British feminists have not entered bureaucratic institutions and Sawer's (1994) account of differences between the Australian and Canadian women's movements, consider ideology to be the key variable. In both cases, differences in feminist views of the patriarchal nature of the state and the degree of tolerance for 'masculine' hierarchical structures have been seen to underpin feminist strategies. Sawer's study, which is most pertinent here, suggests that 'in Canada the women's movement has been ... more suspicious of state initiatives than the Australian women's movement' (65). This distrust of the state has made Canadian feminists less inclined to enter state institutions – particularly the bureaucracy – than their Australian counterparts (65).

Sawer's argument takes this point too far. Although there is no question that ideological differences exist, there are more points of ideological convergence than difference between the two movements. On the fundamental issue of whether Australian and Canadian feminists are prepared to engage with state institutions to advance their objectives, the two movements are in accord. Both the Canadian and Australian women's movements have included radical elements that reject engagement with the state. Overall, however, both share an overarching pragmatic and pro-statist operational code. This code can be understood as feminist 'ideology-in-practice.' Canadian feminists may be less willing than their Australian counterparts to enter the bureaucracy, but, as this chapter shows, they have nevertheless engaged with other areas of the state, and this has included intervening in the legal system and lobbying politicians. Within the broad political context, it can be argued that Canadian feminists are not more suspicious of the state than are their Australian counterparts, only that they have targeted different institutions. In other words, their 'pro-statism' has manifested itself in different ways.

Similarly, it cannot be assumed that ideology fully explains the differences between the structures of the two movements, as has been suggested in some studies (see Sawer and Groves 1994). Although Australian and Canadian feminists have shared a general distrust of hierarchical forms of organization, there are important differences between the structural aspects of the two movements. On the one hand, the Canadian movement has created a highly institutionalized movement through the National Action Committee on the Status of Women, which has a powerful executive and which, since its inception, has operated according to Robert's *Rules of Order*. On the other hand, the Australian movement has resisted all attempts to encourage it to become better organized, even though greater institutionalization would likely enhance the femocrat strategy.

In both the Australian and Canadian cases, ideas have had some influence on the nature of feminist orientation towards the state, but they do not explain why, in each country, activists have chosen to adopt different structures or strategies. To fully explain these phenomena it is necessary to look both at ideas as well as at the political environment within which each of the movements operates. An institutional lens makes it possible to show how political structures influence feminist strategies. It draws attention to the fact that changes in the political opportunity structure have had a direct bearing on the strategic choices made by feminist activists.

Similarity in Difference: Diversity in the Australian and Canadian Women's Movements

The Australian and Anglo-Canadian women's movements share certain characteristics. One of the most noticeable is that they are both extremely diverse. Diversity is evident both in the range of identities encompassed by each movement as well as in the variety of ideological positions that they embrace. Although there exists a range of ideas within the two movements, both have adopted a very similar operational code – one that can be described as pro-statist and pragmatic. Understanding how the two movements are alike makes it easier to then understand how and why they differ.

Identities

One of the most obvious parallels between the contemporary Australian and Anglo-Canadian women's movements is that they both incorporate a variety of identity groups. Women who belong to both movements come from different classes, races, sexual orientations, and age groups, and they vary in their degree of 'able-bodiedness.' Moreover, all these identities overlap. While this work focuses on the Anglo strand of the Canadian movement, it is important to note the existence of the Franco-Canadian movement (another majoritarian feminist movement in Canada), which distinguishes itself from the former according to language and cultural orientation.[2]

Although it is correct to speak of each movement as being diverse, it is an exaggeration to call either of them inclusive. What both movements share is a history within which women from White, middle-class, heterosexual, and able-bodied backgrounds have been in the foreground and within which other women have been marginalized. This dominant/subordinate relationship has been especially apparent since the time of the emergence of these contemporary movements at the end of the 1960s and throughout the 1970s. While, during this period, feminists within the movement in both countries were very keen on the rhetoric of inclusion and 'sisterhood,' in neither case did this involve embracing women in all their difference; rather, attempts were made to assimilate all women. Huggins (1994, 71) outlines the process for Aboriginal women in Australia: 'In their enthusiasm to be anti-racist, white women simply invited Aboriginal women to join their movement with little apparent recognition of the horror of racism in australia [sic], nor of how it continued to damage Aboriginal men as well as women.' And a disabled woman filmmaker in Canada, Bonnie Klien, speaks of her experience of being 'assimilated': 'The women who had organized the festival had promised to "accommodate" me, but they make no provisions for my needs. I am expected to fit in and keep up' (cited in Pierson 1993, 196).

In both countries, women from marginalized groups objected to their exclusion. In Australia, disgruntled women from lesbian, working-class, and Aboriginal backgrounds were heard, if not heeded, at the large feminist conferences of the 1970s and 1980s (see Wills 1981, 129). Similarly, in Canada members of these 'out groups' made clear their dissatisfaction with their treatment from inside and outside key women's organizations including NAC (Brown, Jameison, and Kovach 1995). Out groups did not stop at criticizing the mainstream; they also created their own separate organizations. In both countries, groups emerged to represent women from a variety of backgrounds, including those from Aboriginal, lesbian, non-English speaking, disabled, and working-class groups. These groups sometimes undertook political action on their own behalf, sometimes in coalition with other marginalized groups or with the mainstream movement. For instance, women from immigrant and working-class backgrounds formed an alliance to address problems faced by domestic workers in Canada (see Ng 1993, 300). In Australia the Coalition of Active Lesbians (COAL) worked with mainstream groups to organize the Australian non-government organizations' response to the 1995 United Nations Beijing Conference. These organizations also became a base from which marginalized groups challenged the hegemony of the existing power holders within the mainstream movement.

The challenge presented by these out groups in Australia and Canada has been profound. Women of colour have confronted White feminists with their racism, while lesbians have drawn attention to the dominance of heterosexist views within the mainstream. Working-class women have revealed the preoccupation of many feminists with such middle-class concerns as shattering the 'glass ceiling' in the corporate sphere while the wages and condition of those in traditional female occupations have been in decline. Curthoys (1992) suggests that, in Australia, the issue of racism has been especially confrontational. In her view, mainstream feminists have had 'great difficulty in accepting that white women had historically been part of the process of racism and colonialism, wanting to see women as victims of any historical situation' (445). Similar race debates have come to the fore in Canada and have been played out publicly in various forums. These debates have been particularly strong in NAC, as is reflected in its newsletter *ActionNow*.

By the end of the 1980s in both movements the illusion of a universal sisterhood was well and truly broken. In neither case could the mainstream continue to attempt to assimilate the various identities that made up each movement. They have had to do away with universal terms such as 'sisterhood' and adopt what Ang (1995, 3) refers to as a 'politics of *partiality*' (emphasis added). The transition towards this position has been a fraught and difficult process, causing disruption and debate within both movements and unsettling many long-term activists. According to Pierson (1993, 190), in Canada, 'that there is no such thing as "women as women" has been a hard lesson for mainstream feminism to learn.' In the view of Australian feminist stalwart Eva Cox, a politics of difference means that you can 'actually end up with a fragmentation of the issues to the point where you almost become immobilised' (cited in Eisenstein 1996, 121).

In both countries a women's movement has survived, albeit in a more fractured and tentative form than early activists might have envisaged. While the plurality and 'partiality' of both movements may make some feminists uneasy, each now represents a more realistic vision of women in their diversity than was the case in the past.

Ideas

The majoritarian Anglo women's movements in Australia and Canada not only embrace (however tenuously) a diversity of identities within their boundaries, but they also share a tradition of encompassing a range of ideological beliefs, which include 'radical,' 'socialist,' and 'liberal' elements. Interestingly, in both cases, these ideological divisions have been less important than the ability of each movement to embrace an ideological 'middle ground,' especially in relation to engagement with the state. As the following discussion illustrates, in both countries feminist 'ideology-in-practice' has been, if not pro-statist, then at least pragmatic. The two movements also have much in common with regard to ideas about appropriate structures: both are hostile towards hierarchy and both favour consensual structures and practices.

There has been a long history of feminist organizing in both Australia and Canada. Beginning in the nineteenth century, Australian and Canadian feminists actively sought government reform on a range of issues, including the franchise, access to Parliament, property and child custody rights, equal pay, and basic welfare entitlements that recognized their 'special' and different role. The praxis of the early Australian feminist movement was underpinned by a maternalist ideological stance (Lake 1999). Similarly, in Canada maternalism, along with Christian ideas, played an important role in shaping the actions of early feminists (Errington 1993, 73). The women's movements that emerged at the end of the 1960s in some ways continued these traditions in that members looked to the state to advance their claims. However, they were also different in that they rejected the idea that women's claim to equal citizenship should be based on arguments that they would purify or 'humanize' the public realm, or that women were intrinsically different from men.

In Australia and Canada the contemporary women's movements contained both 'radical' and more moderate 'liberal' elements. In Australia the radical arm was to emerge first. The formation of the first Women's Liberation Movement (WLM) groups in 1969 signalled the start of contemporary feminist organizing. With little overlap between the existing and emerging strands of the movement, the new activists remained relatively ignorant of the activities of their foremothers. According to Curthoys (1994), they suffered 'historical amnesia' in relation to the efforts of the established women's movement. In her view, 'they erroneously thought that they were doing something entirely new, speaking out in a way no-one ever had before against a thoroughly unequal and unjust, male-controlled world' (15).

Groups identifying with the WLM formed in Sydney, Melbourne, and other capital cities at the beginning of the 1970s and used the rhetoric of oppression and revolution – a language alien to existing feminist activists. Many members of the WLM found their way into feminist politics as a reaction to how they were being treated within New Left organizations (which were also flourishing at this time). Despite the fact that many women had left these groups because of how they were being treated, New Left thinking nevertheless affected their ideological position. The WLM drew upon the Maoist and Marxist conceptualization of politics characteristic of the New Left: it emphasized revolutionary over reformist strategies, and it adopted a class-based analysis of society. To this it added a feminist analysis of power that emphasized the patriarchal oppression of women (Curthoys 1993, 26).

Initially, the contemporary Australian women's movement took a relatively hostile position vis-à-vis the state. This was not surprising, given the influence of radical and revolutionary ideas within women's liberation organizations. Feminists who adopted a radical perspective argued that engagement with the state would lead to women being co-opted by the patriarchy; therefore, they advocated separatism and consciousness-raising as the keys to women's liberation. Others took a revolutionary position, believing that women's liberation would come about only through the destruction of both patriarchy and capitalism. This, of course, would necessitate the abolition of existing state structures.

In Canada the contemporary movement has included a radical liberationist strand that was uncomfortable about engaging with the patriarchal state (Vickers 1992, 45). Like their Australian counterparts, many of these activists were disillusioned members of the New Left who were looking for ways to address specific women's concerns through grassroots as opposed to government-sponsored activities. This anti-state, radical/socialist strand has also been apparent in Canadian feminist academic political analyses (Sawer 1994).

In both cases these radical views were tempered by more moderate positions. There was always an influential pro-statist element within the Australian women's movement. Those adopting a more positive view of the state were initially found in the Women's Electoral Lobby (WEL). WEL was the brainchild of Melbourne feminist Beatrice Faust, who formed the organization in 1972 as an alternative to the WLM. WEL obviously hit a chord with others in the movement. By the end of 1972 it had branches in every state capital and approximately 1,700 members nationwide. It was, according to Lyndall Ryan (1990, 72), 'without doubt the political bombshell of 1972.' Part of WEL's appeal was that it took a less radical approach than did the WLM, working from the assumption that 'the position of women could be improved from within the system using the methods of change regarded by the system as legitimate' (Wills 1981, 60). Whereas the WLM tended to see the state as integral to women's oppression, WEL was more inclined to emphasize its transformative potential and to see it as part of the solution to women's inequalities.

There was also a strong pro-statist element in the contemporary movement in Canada. This was encouraged, in part, by the broader political culture, which held that the state was a 'benign utility engaged in worthy redistributive efforts and necessary regulatory tasks' (Vickers 1992, 44). It was also directly influenced by the continuity between contemporary feminists and traditional women's groups. Unlike Australian feminists, emerging Canadian feminists drew directly upon the ideas of their foremothers, who saw the state as providing women with a means of protection. This relationship was facilitated by the creation of the Royal Commission on the Status of Women (RCSW), which occurred at a crucial moment in the development of the contemporary women's movement.

In 1967 women belonging to traditional women's organizations, such as the Canadian Federation of University Women, the YWCA, and the Business and Professional Women's Clubs, succeeded in pressuring the Pearson government to agree to establish the RCSW. As the contemporary women's movement was incipient during the debates leading up to the establishment of this commission, it cannot take credit for its establishment. However, it was able to watch the older generation at work and drew heavily upon their pro-statist operational code.

This is not to say that the emerging Canadian women's movement endorsed all traditional feminist values. Different points of view became most apparent after the release of the RCSW report in 1970. The report had 167 recommendations, covering the economy, education, the family, taxation and childcare, poverty, participation in public life, immigration and citizenship, and criminal law. The reaction of feminists to the RCSW report reflected the differences within the movement. Those traditional feminists who had helped instigate the RCSW felt that the report was the first step towards change, and they were keen to get on with pressuring the government to implement its recommendations. Other members of the burgeoning women's movement were less satisfied. For those adopting a more radical women's liberationist perspective, the report's liberal 'equal opportunity' approach was seen to be too limited, and its recommendations were seen as a 'whitewash.' In their view, the report failed to account for 'the root causes of women's oppression,' including the economic system and patriarchy (see Cohen 1993, 6). Some of the more traditional feminists felt that this radical critique was unfair. As they pointed out, the report was never intended to be a 'feminist' document and did not set out to address structural issues.

Despite the fact that many members of the emerging women's movement were critical of the liberal orientation of the RCSW report, it nevertheless had a crucial influence on the development of Canadian feminism. The report became a focus for the activity of the women's movement, with those from traditional organizations working with emerging groups to agitate for government action on issues raised in the report. As Dobrowolsky (2000, 29) states: 'The RCSW was a catalyst for countless individual women and groups across the country with various orientations and mandates.'

It is clear that in both Australia and Canada the contemporary women's movements have included both pro-state and anti-state ideological positions. While the branches of both movements have differed with each other regarding the question of engagement with the state, the degree to which these differences have existed has been overdrawn. The differences that are apparent at the level of theory become much more difficult to define at the level of practice. As Reade (1994, 208) observes in relation to the Australian case: 'WEL and WLM did not consistently operate in opposition to each other, but shared common goals and practices. Both represented different strands of feminist activism and different characteristics, but at any time they could intersect and overlap with one another.'

Similarly, in the Canadian situation it would be incorrect to create an opposition between grassroots and institutionalized feminism, between radical and reformist wings, or between disengaged and mainstream activists, for these various distinctions become meaningless in practice (Dobrowolsky 2000, 29). In Vickers's (1991, 42) view integration, rather than separation, of ideological and practical considerations has been a feature of the Anglo-Canadian women's movement. Like their Australian counterparts, Anglo-feminists worked across ideological lines to embrace a pragmatic position with regard to the state.

Australian feminists share with their Canadian counterparts similar ideas about structures. Both are opposed to hierarchical forms of organization, arguing that they are 'masculine' in character. These ideas have been especially apparent in the WLM strand of the Australian movement. As Summers (1973, 7) explains:

> From its inception Women's Liberation has been anti-organisation in the sense that we have had no elected officers, no formal membership, no formal rules or platform to which people must adhere, and no theories determining the relationship of factions or opposition groups to the movement as a whole. We have justified this stance by pointing out that formal organisation is always oligarchical in that it inevitably produces an elite of leaders who cling to their powerful positions more tenaciously than they adhere to the principles of the organisation they purportedly represent.

Although WEL members adopted more formal organizational structures than did their WLM contemporaries, they too displayed a wariness of these operational modes.

According to Vickers (1992), the ideology of the contemporary Canadian women's movement is a form of radical liberalism. The 'radical' appellation refers to the fact that the movement has been committed to anti-hierarchical methods of organization and has developed critiques of mainstream political institutions. Debates about hierarchy have been played out within the movement since its inception, with many feminists espousing the view that such an organizational form represents a masculine mode of operation that stifles discussion and leads to authoritarian forms of leadership. In its place, feminists, at least rhetorically, have supported a more cooperative and consensual mode of organization – one within which there are no leadership positions, jobs are rotated, and discussion is encouraged.

In summary, the majoritarian wings of the Australian and Canadian women's movement have much in common at the level of ideology. Both include radical elements that were opposed to direct engagement with the state, but they have nevertheless maintained a pro-statist operational code in that they are committed to using the state to bring about gender equality. Moreover, each movement has displayed hostility towards hierarchical organizational forms. In each case, ideology helps to explain the willingness of feminists to develop strategies that engage with the state, and it also goes some way to explaining why the movement has avoided becoming institutionalized. However, ideology alone cannot explain why feminists in the two countries have adopted different strategies or chosen to engage with different institutions.

Examining Differences: Strategies and Structures

The social movement literature makes the point that political activists do not act in a vacuum but, rather, respond to the institutional opportunities and constraints with which they are confronted. This truism holds for the Australian and Anglo-Canadian women's movements, each of which have shaped their strategic choices as well as their internal structures in order to best take advantage of the prevailing political opportunity structure. However, it would be wrong to assume that the POS only operates in a top-down direction. As the following discussion and later chapters illustrate, feminists have been active in shaping the POS. Sometimes they have had little success; at other times, however, they have pushed the POS until cracks emerged. And, where openings did exist, feminists worked to widen them. It follows that POSs are crucial with regard to explaining differences between the Canadian and Australian women's movements.

At the broadest level it can be argued that Australian and Canadian feminists have adopted a similar strategic repertoire in that they have pursued their objectives both from inside and outside political institutions. Inside strategies involve feminists being directly employed within a political institution such as the bureaucracy or Parliament; outside strategies involve feminists remaining autonomous from institutions but seeking to pressure them. The main contrast between Australian and Canadian feminists involves their choices about where to direct their efforts. In Australia feminists have adopted two central strategies: (1) bureaucratic 'entrism,' often referred to as the femocrat strategy (an inside strategy) and (2) lobbying government (an outside strategy). In Canada feminists have focused upon working through the legal and constitutional arms of the state as well as lobbying (outside strategies). The lobbying techniques used by feminists in Canada have been unique, combining traditional approaches to the state with more militant, direct action tactics.

Inside Strategies

In neither Australia nor Canada have feminists enjoyed a great deal of success when engaging directly with the key executive and legislative arms of the state. As is explicated in Chapter 3, in each country various obstacles to feminist goals have existed at all levels of the electoral, party, and legislative process. Electoral rules have favoured male candidates, while parties have, until recently, been reticent to open themselves to feminist demands. Parliamentary procedures and norms have combined with party dominance to block feminist initiatives. However, in both cases the story of frustration with electoral and legislative institutions needs to be qualified. In Australia and Canada women committed to feminist principles have successfully dodged barriers and been able to work both from inside and from outside the state. In Australia Susan Ryan, Joan Kirner, and Carmen Lawrence have worked with external activists and functioned as advocates for women's issues within Parliament. Dawn Black and Grace MacInnes are examples of two women who have done the same in Canada. A second key qualification within the Australian context is the importance of the Australian Labor Party (ALP) to feminist strategies. Although until recently the ALP has been slow to address feminist demands within its own ranks, when in government it has proved to be an important ally for feminists. Most important, it has helped to create opportunities for feminists within another key arm of the state – the bureaucracy. It has been the interaction between the bureaucracy and the (relatively) progressive ALP that has set the groundwork for the Australian 'femocrat' strategy – the central inside strategy of the Australian women's movement.

Inside Strategies in Australia: 'Bureaucratic Entrism'
The 1972 election of the ALP after twenty-three years of conservative rule provided a positive opportunity structure for Australian feminists. Even those from the more radical end of the feminist spectrum, who were suspicious of state intervention, were alert to the possibilities for change under the new government. As Dowse (1983, 210) explains:

> With the advent of a Labor Government, debate within the women's movement over revolution versus reform was short-circuited. Feminists of all persuasions began to believe, or at least act as if they believed, that social reform was a necessary if not sufficient condition of a revolution in the relationship between the sexes.

The Labor government showed a willingness to listen to feminist demands, provided openings for women to enter the bureaucratic arm of the state, and made funds available for women's services. All of this had a dramatic effect on feminist strategies. Even though the theoretical debate about co-option continued, radical and socialist feminists joined with less radical feminists to consider how to best use the reform opportunities presented to them. This did not mean that they shelved their revolutionary goals. As Cox (1990, 44) remembers: 'We might have been dewy eyed in the early days and made extravagant claims as part of the political process, but most of us recognised that the state and bureaucratic intervention could only achieve limited objectives.' Nevertheless, many began to blend radical theory with reformist strategies in order to develop a pragmatic feminist position in relation to the state (see Stone 1974, 104-5; Melbourne WLM 1974, 37).

✓ The femocrat strategy, which involves feminists entering the bureaucracy to work as internal advocates on feminist policy issues, came about shortly after Gough Whitlam's election. The first step towards this strategy was taken when the incoming government appointed a member of a Canberra women's liberation organization, university tutor Elizabeth Reid, to act as women's adviser to Prime Minister Whitlam. In 1974 the government extended the opportunities for feminists to enter the bureaucracy by creating a women's affairs agency in the Department of the Prime Minister and Cabinet (PM&C) and appointing Sara Dowse, another member of the Canberra women's movement, to head the agency. Soon after, many feminists followed Dowse into the bureaucracy and were, according to one former femocract, Lyndall Ryan (1990, 74), 'struck by the possibilities for change in terms of policymaking, bureaucratic structure and the delivery of services.'

The dismissal of the ALP government in November 1975 proved to be a blow to those pursuing this inside strategy. Members of the incoming Fraser Liberal government were generally unsupportive of feminist initiatives developed under the ALP, and constrained the femocrat strategy. Fraser demoted the women's agency from the central department of PM&C to the junior portfolio of home affairs, an act that provoked its head, Sara Dowse, to resign. While femocrats remained within the bureaucracy during the eight years of the Fraser government, their position had more to do with 'holding the line' than 'breaking new ground.' Working with a conservative government, women also saw the gulf widen between 'inside' and 'outside' feminist activists, with much recrimination on both sides over funding cutbacks and negative policy decisions.

Initially, under Fraser, feminists, through their femocrat strategies, continued to target the federal government from inside. Not only did they find the government unresponsive, but they also found it difficult to make progress in many areas because Canberra had put responsibility for some of the women's policy areas (e.g., women's refuges) that had been supported by the Whitlam government back in the hands of the states. Feminists responded to this devolution of power by looking increasingly towards state governments to meet their demands. They found, somewhat unexpectedly, that they could achieve some success, most notably in those states with ALP governments in office. State ALP governments, following the lead of the previous federal government, provided funding for services, created women's agencies (thus enabling the development of a state femocrat strategy), and developed their own women's policy and legislation. In other words, the combination of a progressive political party – the ALP – and federalism provided some Australian feminists with a way to avoid the constraints presented by a conservative federal government, and they adjusted their focus accordingly.

The 1983 return of Labor to the federal government saw feminist attention return to Canberra. To some extent, their expectation that the Hawke and Keating governments would address their concerns was not misplaced. In terms of the femocrat strategy, Hawke returned the Office of the Status of Women (OSW) to the hub of PM&C and supported the development of women's agencies throughout the bureaucracy – agencies that were maintained under Keating.

With the election of the conservative Howard coalition government in 1996, feminists were once again confronted with significant constraints at the federal level. Howard was quick to stem any support to 'special interest groups,' among which feminists were seen to be prominent. He downgraded the role of the OSW and reduced funding for it and other women's agencies, leaving the femocrat strategy in tatters. During the first term of the Howard government most feminists were unable to engage in the 'federalism foxtrot' that had been so useful in the earlier period, when the Liberal Party was in federal office. This was because conservative governments were in power in all the states, with the exception of New South Wales (NSW). However, since the start of Howard's second term in 1998, the pendulum has begun to swing back to ALP at the state level, with elections in Queensland and Tasmania returning Labor governments. The extent to which feminists will be able to make advances at the state level this time around is as yet unknown.

The inside strategies pursued by some feminists in Australia did not meet with the approval of all the members of the movement. Some feminists opposed the femocrat strategy because it advanced the interests of White, middle-class women. Many in the WLM continued to believe that it would lead inevitably to co-optation. One of the WLM's most overt statements of opposition to the entry of feminists into the bureaucracy came from members of the Sydney Mejane collective who, in March 1972, produced a leaflet criticizing the selection procedure for determining the position of Whitlam's women's affairs adviser. The leaflet argued that 'no woman chosen by men to advise upon us will be acceptable to us,' and it criticized the candidates because they had no 'right to act as the single spokeswoman for the rest of us' (Mejane Editorial Collective, cited in Wills 1981, 136).

These critiques were not universal. For instance, while the Mejane criticism of the Australian femocrat cannot be ignored, it is wrong to assume, as do Sawer (1990) and Eisenstein (1996, 20), that this was the WLM's only response to the femocrat strategy. In fact, the action of the Mejane collective attracted widespread criticism from within the Sydney WLM. Some members felt that it was unfair to attack the candidates for the position of women's adviser, while others expressed qualified support for the femocrat initiative in general (for a comprehensive discussion, see Wills 1981, 137-8).[3]

Inside Strategies in Canada

In Canada feminists also attempted to work from within the bureaucracy. Opportunities opened up after the Trudeau government created women's policy agencies within the federal bureaucracy in response to the recommendations of the RCSW. These included the Office of Equal Opportunity in the Public Service Commission, the Office of the Co-ordinator of the Status of Women in the Privy Council Office (later to become the Status of Women Canada Office), and the Canadian Council on the Status of Women. The existing Women's Bureau in the Department of Labour was also upgraded. Initially, a number of feminists were enthusiastic about the creation of these bodies and entered the bureaucracy in an attempt to influence government policy from the inside. However, in the absence of a supportive party like the ALP, and confronted by both normative and structural barriers within the bureaucracy itself, many feminists lost interest in pursuing a femocrat strategy.

Outside Strategies in Australia

Neither Australian nor Canadian feminists have put all their eggs in one strategic basket. Not only have they pursued strategies inside the state, but they have also adopted autonomous outside strategies as well. In Canada, feminists have taken advantage of new openings in the legal and constitutional arena in order to advance their claims, while in both countries feminists have used political lobbying. However, as with inside strategies, the success of outside strategies has varied quite markedly between the two movements.

For those Australian feminists who do not want to enter the bureaucracy, or who are opposed to getting so close to the 'enemy state,' other opportunities exist for pursuing their aims. In particular, these involve lobbying and grassroots organizing. For the less radical WEL – whose first political act was to distribute questionnaires on women's issues to candidates contesting the 1972 election campaign – lobbying has been its raison d'être. Many radical feminists have also been most comfortable when engaging in an arm's-length relationship with the state. Radical feminists have joined with WEL members in lobbying the government with regard to abortion law reform, free contraceptives, equal pay, equal employment opportunity, and childcare centres. Between 1972 and 1975 the Whitlam ALP government removed the luxury tax from contraceptives, reopened the equal pay case in the Australian Industrial and Arbitration Commission, and made some moves towards establishing state-funded childcare. Although, under the Fraser Liberal coalition government, opportunities for feminist lobbying were curtailed, they expanded with the return of the Hawke ALP government. Under Hawke and Keating, the federal government responded to feminist pressure to provide funding for the public provision of childcare – an issue many feminists saw as a litmus test of the government's response to women's issues (L. Ryan 1990, 77). Feminist lobbying also helped to encourage the Hawke and Keating governments to introduce such important legislation as the Sex Discrimination Act, to create a sex commissioner in the Human Rights and Equal Opportunities Commission, and to legislate for equal employment opportunity in the public sector. Although throughout the Hawke/Keating period feminists had to battle with the government's preoccupation with an 'economic rationalist' agenda, which often meant defining their claims within the economic discourse of the time, they faced a relatively positive federal POS.

The see-saw relationship between feminists and the federal government has once again been illustrated under the Howard Liberal coalition government, with feminists confronting a series of constraints to their lobbying strategy. Since 1996 the federal government has reduced funding for most women's organizations that espoused a feminist philosophy, and it has attacked WEL for being a front for the ALP – a claim that the organization strenuously denies (see WEL 1999).

The lobbying strategy pursued by Australian feminists has included asking the government to provide funding to enable them to pursue grassroots activities and to create services. The Whitlam government was the first to respond to these requests, granting feminist organizations funds to establish shelters, rape crisis centres, and health centres. The issue of funding created ructions within the Australian movement, with some members fearing that it would lead them to being used as an unpaid labour force whose purpose was to provide welfare services that should be the responsibility of the state. Others were afraid it would result in the movement developing a 'mendicant attitude to government, trimming demands to accord with those that could be advanced within the bureaucracy' (Eade 1977, 8). Over time, many WLM members came to believe that the advantages of accepting government money outweighed the disadvantages. The radical *Scarlet Woman* editorial collective (1975, 1) summed up the logic of most groups:

> Funding enables us to do work that we wouldn't otherwise be able to do; funding can be important for political reasons ... ; money is available and it is important that we be paid for work which is otherwise voluntary and unpaid; we should exploit government money rather than bleeding our own funds and limited resources; funding has enabled individual women to develop ideas, which at first might be tentative, into projects, and get support for those projects.

Once funding for feminist services became a reality, even the most ardent critics of this strategy began to reassess their position. As Susan Eade, a member of the Canberra Women's Liberation Movement, noted:

> Our involvement in reforms assisted by government funds clearly sig-
> naled modification in our attitudes to working through government
> institutions and to the importance of achieving reform. But we had not
> forgotten the revolution. (Eade 1977, 7; see also *Scarlet Woman* editorial
> collective 1975)

As with the inside strategies, it is apparent that Australian feminist outside strategies have been shaped by the available POS. They have used lobbying tactics to pressure the government to provide such services for women as childcare, to legislate to protect against discrimination, and to provide funding for grassroots organizing. While feminists have by no means achieved all their objectives through these tactics, they have found that they have had a much better chance of success when there is an ALP government in office. Once again, the interaction between institutions – the political party structure, the bureaucracy, and the Parliament – can be seen to be important to shaping the available POS.

**Outside Strategies in Canada: Exploring Legal Avenues
and 'Lobbying with a Difference'**
Canadian feminists, like Australian feminists, have also engaged in exter-
nal political strategies – indeed, probably to a greater extent than have their Australian counterparts. Lobbying has been a key Canadian feminist strategy. However, according to Cohen (1993, 21), Canadian feminists have been engaged in 'lobbying with a difference.' This includes using traditional lobbying techniques (such as meeting politicians and making submissions to government inquiries) 'in a way that causes confrontation, attracts media attention, and gains public notice' (Dobrowolsky 2000, 9). The lobbying approach of the Canadian movement can be seen to have developed along a continuum, beginning with a reliance on pro-statist traditional lobbying tactics during the RCSW period and then moving towards an increasingly anti-statist position. This shift became obvious after the 1984 election of the Mulroney government, and it is reflected in the use of mass mobilizing and militant tactics.

Phase 1: The Pro-Statist Perspective
The RCSW opened up an important positive POS for Canadian feminists and came to directly influence their choice of strategies. Throughout the three years it took to conduct the commission and to produce a report, the federal government became sensitized to some of the issues confronting Canadian women. The commission hearings, which took place throughout

the country and were televised by the Canadian Broadcasting Corporation, played a particularly important role in this regard. After the completion of the hearings, and a year before the RCSW report was handed down, the government introduced an omnibus bill to reform aspects of the Criminal Code that dealt with abortion and contraception – two issues that the commission had found to be of great importance to Canadian women (Bird 1990, 551).

These early responses raised feminist expectations that the government would take quick and decisive action to address the recommendations of the report. When the government proved slow to act, feminists were not deterred. Many of them, having been radicalized by what they had seen and heard throughout the course of the RCSW, began mobilizing to have the government address the issues raised. In 1971 established women activists met with emergent women's liberation and radical feminist organizations in Toronto, where a decision was taken to establish the National Ad Hoc Committee on the Status of Women in Canada. The committee then set about organizing the Strategies for Change Conference. The 1972 conference managed to attract over 500 women representing forty organizations from across the feminist spectrum. It was an event that was to have a lasting influence on the direction of the feminist movement in Canada.

The most important outcome of the conference was the decision to replace the Ad Hoc Committee with a permanent organization, the National Action Committee on the Status of Women. Demonstrating a faith in the existing political process, NAC's stated objective was to lobby the federal government until all the RCSW recommendations were implemented (Black 1993, 168). Not all groups at the conference were happy with this strategy: radical and left-wing elements presented a minority report that emphasized the need for a social structural analysis of women's oppression. For them, lobbying 'diluted the possibilities for radical change' (Cohen 1993, 6). But, when it came to the crunch, radical feminists put their ideological differences aside and joined the rest of the conference in supporting all but one of the report's recommendations. They also agreed to participate in NAC and, by implication, its lobbying strategy.

The lobbying strategy adopted by NAC in the years immediately after the release of the RCSW report appeared to achieve results. After its initial hesitancy, the Trudeau government responded to the pressure of the women's movement and implemented a number of the RCSW recommendations (albeit those with which it was most easy to deal). Given the temper of the times, the government's positive response was not surprising. In the face of a fervent Quebec separatist movement, the government adopted pan-Canadian policies that were aimed at drawing the support of individuals and groups towards the central government (Doern 1983, 251).

To some extent the women's movement was swept up in this vision and was able to make some progress because of it. Between 1972 and 1974 the government made amendments to the Unemployment Insurance Act, the Fair Wages Act, and the Canadian Labour Code in order to give women equal legislative status (CACSW 1974, 1979). Other positive non-legislative changes were also brought about during this time. In 1972 the Secretary of State Department established the Women's Program, which allocated state funding to women's organizations. By 1976, only four years after NAC was formed, its position as the central lobbying organization of the Canadian women's movement was recognized when it secured a government commitment, as well as commitments from other federal party caucuses, to meet with NAC members on an annual basis. The annual lobby became a key event on the movement's calendar for the next decade and a half.

At the beginning of the 1980s, there was a widely shared perception among feminists that lobbying was an effective strategy. According to Findlay (1995, 164), so long as the government continued to initiate reforms relating to women's equality, NAC was able to 'confirm the logic of relying on the state.' By the end of the 1980s lobbying remained a key movement strategy, but feminists had become less sanguine about what could be achieved through it and had begun to couple it with more direct action strategies. What explains this shift in attitude? The primary reason for it relates to a change in the POS concomitant with the election of the Mulroney Progressive Conservative (PC) government. In the face of the government's neoliberal policies, which included cutbacks to welfare and the endorsement of the North American Free Trade Agreement (NAFTA), and its exclusionary approach to constitutional politics, the Anglo-Canadian women's movement found that its lobbying strategy was no longer effective. For feminists, the election of the Mulroney government essentially disrupted the existing positive POS and replaced it with a set of political constraints.

Phase 2: The Shift towards an Anti-Statist Perspective
The election of the Mulroney government saw Anglo-Canadian feminists facing a range of new constraints in the federal arena – the arena within which they had invested their political energy for the previous decade. In response to the new political environment, the feminist movement and its central organization, NAC, underwent a dramatic transformation. As the *Globe and Mail* reported in an article entitled 'Rebicks Departure from the NAC Marks a Shift in the Balance of Power,' 21 April 1993, the Canadian women's movement adopted 'a different face, a more militant style and a bolder strategy.' Although feminists retained a lobbying strategy during the Mulroney period, it became rooted in a very different set of assumptions from those that had prevailed previously. Within this new

environment the view that government could, through rational arguments, be persuaded to undertake measures to ameliorate women's position came to be seen as naive. The shift in position was summed up in
1986 by NAC executive member Marjorie Cohen (cited in NAC 1986, 1, 7):
'NAC should not abandon lobbying but we have to abandon sweet rea-
sonableness. Confrontation must not be avoided; we have to be a thorn in
the side of government, industry and institutions.'

The change in NAC's stance stemmed from several factors. First, Anglo-
feminists were hostile to the neoliberal and neoconservative policies introduced by the PC government. As Brodie and Jenson (1990, 266) explain,
Mulroney oversaw a transformation in the existing order, 'reorienting
public policies to encourage entrepreneurship, investment and risk taking;
rationalizing the management of government resources and programs;
balancing the budget; and reducing both the size and role of government.'
Feminists, who had long emphasized the importance of the welfare state,
were fearful about what these changes would mean for women and the
less well-off members of society. NAC became a vocal critic of cutbacks to
welfare programs. It made a submission to the Forget Commission on
Unemployment Insurance in 1986, defending existing maternity leave
provisions and arguing for the retention of indexed family allowances
(see *Feminist Action,* vol. 1, no. 7, 1986; *Feminist Action,* vol. 2, no. 1, 1986).
It also made statements published in an article entitled 'NAC Disputes

Ottawa Report to UN' in the *Globe and Mail,* 1 February 1990, that were
highly critical of the government's decision to renege on its 1984 election
promise of a universal, national, publicly funded childcare system, arguing that the government backdown would serve only to benefit well-off
parents. In 1990, in an open display of opposition, NAC produced a report
parallel to the one the government prepared for the UN Convention on
the Elimination of All Forms of Discrimination against Women (CEDAW).
In its comments, NAC rejected the official view that the position of Canadian women was improving, arguing instead that cuts to services, the lack
of universal childcare provisions, and changes to unemployment insurance had all had serious negative implications for Canadian women.

Through NAC, feminists also reacted with hostility to other aspects of
the Mulroney agenda. NAC was highly critical of the government's decision to become a member of NAFTA, fearing that this would endanger
women's jobs and lead to the further erosion of the welfare state as Canada
became involved in a race to the bottom with the United States and Mex-
ico. Keen to influence the debate on this issue, NAC became a founding
member of the Pro-Canada Network, a coalition organization with members from labour, church, farm, and peace groups who fundamentally
opposed the neoliberal direction of the PC government. From its inception in 1988 this network not only lobbied but also used direct action (such

as protest marches) to demonstrate against government policies (*Action Now*, vol. 1, no. 8, 1991). During this period, NAC also became involved in other previously out-of-bounds policy areas, including tax reform (particularly the introduction of a goods and services tax) and debates about the national deficit. Increasingly, NAC adopted more radical tactics, refusing to cooperate on government bodies. It staged marches and sit-ins and even took to hissing and booing politicians during meetings (see, for example, Rhinehart 1995, A8; Goar 1989, D4).

A third area of conflict between feminists and the federal government arose in relation to the Constitution. Feminists operating through NAC were loud and conspicuous critics of the Meech Lake Accord and Charlottetown Accord. Their main criticisms related to the elitist process through which these constitutional agreements had been made and the fact that they included provisions to devolve further responsibility to the provinces (see Rebick 1993). Feminists' fear of the latter stemmed from their belief that devolution would create a patchwork of welfare provisions across the country.

NAC's foray into mainstream policy areas and its adoption of more militant tactics cost the organization, and feminists generally, support in the media. Newspaper articles began to appear that suggested that NAC's influence was waning and that questioned its tactics (see, for example, Wente 1995, A2; S. Scott 1994). Perhaps more significantly, it also lost the support of the government, which worked to undermine NAC's legitimacy by referring to it, and treating it, as a 'special interest group.' The government's attitude towards NAC was made obvious in a number of ways. In May 1989 Mulroney supported the minister for the status of women, Barbara McDougall, in breaking a fifteen-year tradition by refusing to meet with NAC representatives at the annual lobby day. The snub followed an earlier blow, which involved the government granting a conservative and anti-feminist organization, REAL Women, funding under the Women's Program while, at the same time, reducing NAC's funding by 50 percent (*Action Now*, vol. 5, no. 2, 1995). When NAC adopted a 'no' position on the Charlottetown Accord, the government denounced the organization as racist, as anti-Quebec, and as one of the 'enemies of Canada' (*This Magazine*, 9 January 1993, cited in Brodie 1995, 32).

NAC protested against its marginalization. At the time of the announcement of the funding cutbacks, NAC president Lynn Kaye stated: 'We view this as a retaliatory measure because we have fought to hold the government to its commitment to end discrimination against women in all its forms' (Kaye 1989, A18). It vehemently rejected the notion that it was only a special interest group, arguing that it had a legitimate claim to get involved in all policy areas because all issues affect women and it took exception to the government's claim that it had become a partisan organization. NAC's position was that it was an independent, non-partisan organization that was opposed to neoliberal policies, not the Progressive Conservative Party per se (see Thobani in Makin 1993). These rejoinders had little impact on the Mulroney government. As one commentator noted: 'The NAC is perceived by senior Tory strategists as an unofficial appendage of the NDP [New Democratic Party]. Even though it claims to speak for all women, it is not heard in a non-partisan voice' (Goar 1989, D4). The election of the Chrétien Liberal government in 1993 did not prevent NAC from continuing to protest against the direction of government policies, thus giving some substance to its non-partisan claims. However, its ongoing criticism also ensured that the organization, and feminists in general, remained marginalized – a very different position from that of the preceding decade.

Anglo-feminist faith in lobbying might have wavered during the 1980s and early 1990s, but women did not give up on engaging with the state from outside. Although they were in a hostile relationship with the government of the day, they persisted with their lobbying strategy – and with some success. Feminists may have lost the economic battle with the government, but they were successful in their efforts to have government shelve legislation restricting access to abortion and reducing childcare support. They also managed to convince the justice minister, Kim Campbell, to legislate to protect rape shield provisions after a negative Supreme Court decision. What these 'successes' show is that, even though, in the main, feminist activists faced a 'constraint structure' in the federal arena, they were still able to make occasional breakthroughs by lobbying. Under such conditions, abandoning the lobbying strategy altogether did not make sense, but they were also prepared to couple this strategy with more direct action. At the same time, feminists were also able to take advantage of openings in other institutional arenas. In a fortuitous turn of events, the Charter of Rights and Freedoms came into effect in 1982, two years before the election of the conservative Mulroney government. Having the charter meant that feminists could advance their claims by shifting their focus from the increasingly hostile federal parliamentary and executive realm to the legal arena.

Litigation

The Trudeau government's entrenchment of the Charter of Rights and Freedoms in the Canadian Constitution created a new, positive POS within which Anglo-feminists could pursue an alternative outside strategy. This opening was one that feminists had themselves helped to influence. Feminist activists had been involved in a long campaign to have the federal government include sex-based protections in the charter. In any event, the charter included two sex equality provisions, Sections 15 and 28, the latter of which was one of the few sections protected from the provincial government override clause. Once the charter was in place, some members of the mainstream women's movement joined with feminists in legal circles to develop a litigation strategy in order to take advantage of the new charter provisions. This involved undertaking 'charterwatching' activities such as conducting a gender audit of existing federal and provincial legislation. It also involved the creation of the Legal Education and Action Fund (LEAF), which was formed to carry out court challenges. The new strategy sat comfortably with the Anglo-movement's underlying pro-statist position. Litigation reflected its belief that changes could be brought about through state structures.

The sex equality clauses of the charter were put in place in 1985, the year after the election of the Mulroney government. Although some feminists were skeptical about engaging with the law and the Constitution, many saw the charter as offering them one way to bypass some of the decisions of the incoming conservative government. Feminists' hope that the charter would provide them with positive outcomes seems to have been borne out in practice. As Sylvia Bashevkin's research points out, during the Mulroney period eighteen judicial decisions were made in relation to 'women's issues,' sixteen of which could be coded as a positive outcome for women and only two that could be coded as negative (see Bashevkin 1998, Appendix A, 255). The positive legal decisions were no coincidence. Through LEAF, feminists played a crucial role as intervenors in many of these cases and had some success in influencing charter jurisprudence. To some extent then, the relationship between Anglo-feminists and the legal arm of the state can be seen as dynamic and interactive. For feminists who faced a hostile government in the federal legislative arena, the positive outcomes from the legal arena have made litigation an obvious alternative to the traditional lobbying strategy.

It would be wrong to claim that the litigation strategy has been embraced by all Anglo-Canadian feminists. While LEAF has been criticized for its White, middle-class perspective, the litigation strategy has been perceived by some as a sellout: litigation merely shifted women's concerns out of one elite male-dominated arena (Parliament) into another (the courts) (see Fudge 1989). Nevertheless, at key moments 'dissidents' have been prepared to support the strategy in order to achieve specific objectives. As Dobrowolsky (2000, 69) points out: 'There was a great deal of ambivalence towards the Charter on the part of leftist feminists ... In the end many joined pro-Charter forces because they realized that these changes were inevitable.'

Feminist Structures in Australia and Canada

It was noted earlier that feminists in Australia and Canada shared similar ideas about structures. In both countries there has been a general hostility towards hierarchical forms of organizing and a preference for flat structures and consensual decision-making processes. Despite these shared ideas, feminists in the two countries have adopted very different forms of organization. While in Australia feminists have resisted all attempts to become institutionalized, in Canada feminists have adopted quite formal structures. The following discussion suggests that these differences are best explained by variations in choice of strategies, which is itself influenced by existing POSs.

Australian Feminist Structures

The ideological position of the women's movement in Australia and its choice of organizational structure are closely aligned. Australian feminists have resisted all pressure to become institutionalized, deflecting efforts both inside and outside the movement to create a peak body. Furthermore, those organizations that do exist have, to a large extent, managed to remain informal and unstructured. Explanations of Australian feminist structures often emphasize the importance of ideological influences. For instance, Sawer and Groves (1994, 441) argue that 'new-wave women's organisations ... were *philosophically* incapable of adopting the kind of centralised, professionalised and differentiated structures which ... are necessary for effective lobbying' (emphasis added). Kaplan (1996, 69) makes a similar point when she argues that feminists resisted institutionalization because they 'felt rather strongly about organised structures that would quickly copy male structures and create inequalities among the members.' Ideology has obviously played some part in this lack of institutionalization, but the practical imperatives underlying feminist strategies, which are themselves an outcome of the prevailing institutional environment, can be seen to have an equally important influence on these structures.

The Australian women's movement has never become as institutionalized as has the Canadian movement. Marian Sawer (1996c, 10) summarizes the Australian women's movement as one that is

> diverse and fragmented and lacked the kind of national presence, which would provide a strong political base for embattled feminists within government. While there was considerable interaction between specialised women's organisations and relevant government agencies, there was no community-based peak body equivalent to, for example, the Australian Council for Social Service.

Instead, 'issue-based coalitions arose out of the women's movement in response to perceived threats or opportunities but they found it difficult to sustain themselves over time.' Not only has there been resistance to the notion of a peak body, but existing key lobby organizations such as WEL have also been reluctant to organize on a national basis.

Hostility towards institutionalization within the contemporary Australian women's movement was evident from the start. Given the WLM's rejection of hierarchy and formal structures, this was not surprising. In a movement where the autonomy of the small group was paramount, any peak organization that attempted to represent the views of the whole movement met strong opposition. According to Wills (1981, 387), the WLM prided itself on the fact that 'whatever line of discussion or activity a group pursued was up to the individual women involved; it had to seek the prior approval of no higher authority for there was none.' The notion of creating a body that could impose authority from above breached all the codes of a movement whose raison d'être was to find ways of overcoming 'structures which stifled individual initiative and spontaneity, and the control of the many by the few' (47).

Influenced by the existing WLM, and by its own radical members, WEL also displayed a high level of skepticism towards hierarchy and central controls – both within its own organization and within the women's movement as a whole (see Asher 1980, 28). From its inception, WEL's structure was state-based, with local autonomous groups acting as the decision-making units. When the issue of a centralized national body was raised at its 1973 conference, it was received with widespread hostility (Summers 1973, 7). A New South Wales conference delegate reflected the general view: 'We are determined to avoid having leaders – and any form of power hierarchy ... [L]ike many other radical feminist organisations, in setting up a structure we want to move on from competitive masculine power politics, involving aggression and backstabbing, to true egalitarianism' (Anon., cited in Summers 1973, 7). The conference agreed not to build WEL into a national body with an overarching structure and separate identity but, rather, to continue as a locally based organization. It created a coordinating committee to disseminate information, but otherwise power to act on local issues remained with local groups; and it was agreed that any campaigns on federal issues first required the support of all the branches across Australia (Asher 1980, 30).

The difficulty WEL experienced in coordinating its political campaigns, particularly at the federal level, led it to rethink its opposition to organizing along national lines. In 1978 the state branches of WEL finally decided to establish WEL Australia as a national body. However, even then, members were tentative about the role of the new body, with one member re-emphasizing the point that WEL remained 'a local coalition of state, territorial and regional groups' (Denoon, cited in Sawer and Groves 1994, 440). Furthermore, as Sawer and Groves note, when a national coordinator was appointed in 1982, lobbying was excluded from her role in order to ensure that power remained with local groups. Recent restructuring debates within WEL demonstrate that there is still strong resistance to central control (WEL 1997).

WEL has never purported to be the voice of the Australian women's movement, nor has it adopted an umbrella structure that shelters different organizations under its auspices. WEL has been one of a number of women's organizations established in order to lobby the government on women's issues. Attempts in the mid-1990s to create a peak body have forced WEL to reconsider its stance on becoming part of an overarching organization. The members of WEL have had a varied response to the proposal, some rejecting it outright, others offering it qualified support. Some have expressed concern that such an organization would: only satisfy the government's desire for a unified position on women's issues; usurp WEL's existing lobbying role; and lead to funding the peak body at the expense of member organizations (see Sexton 1995). Others have argued that, if structured correctly, such a body could enhance feminist access to government and bring about an increase in resources for the movement as a whole (see WEL memo, 31 May 1995).

The first in a spate of attempts to create a peak body occurred in the late 1980s and was instigated by Pam O'Neil, a well-known femocrat and former head of the Sex Discrimination Commission. O'Neil (cited in Neales 1989) advanced a pragmatic defence of her proposal, arguing that women needed a vehicle to 'ensure that their common voice is heard regularly and clearly.' She proposed to develop an organization along the lines of the Australian Council for Social Service (ACOSS). ACOSS was chosen because it was able to link 'a whole lot of diverse organisations which on the face of it would appear to be very diverse ideologically' (O'Neil, cited in Neales 1989). This model appealed to some WEL members and women from the Australian Federation of Business and Professional Women (AFBPW). However, the proposal eventually foundered against a wall of opposition from feminists who deemed it 'elitist' and in conflict with the non-hierarchical principles of the movement (Sawer and Groves 1994, 442).

The closest the Australian movement came to being institutionalized was in 1992, when, at a conference to commemorate the twentieth anniversary of WEL, the Coalition of Participating Organisations of Women (CAPOW!) was formed. The stated functions of this coalition were to lobby government, to prepare submissions, and to provide a unified and powerful voice for women (Sawer and Groves 1994, 443). However, CAPOW! was not established in the same fashion as was ACOSS or other peak organizations. While CAPOW! did act as an umbrella for over sixty women's groups, it was careful not to usurp the autonomy of its member groups. It conceived of itself as a network rather than as a hierarchically structured organization, and it enforced a 'self-denying ordinance' that prevented it from speaking on behalf of any of the organizations involved. These measures demonstrated to groups joining CAPOW! that it upheld the general feminist principles of (1) not imposing majority decisions on the minority and (2) not forcing the movement to speak with one voice. Member groups made it clear that to do otherwise would be to put their support in jeopardy (see Sawer and Groves 1994, 444). CAPOW's prominence was to be short-lived. After acting as coordinator for Australian women's non-government organizations for the 1995 United Nations Beijing Conference, it struggled to maintain its profile. The 1996 election of the Howard Liberal coalition government meant that CAPOW's political and financial support was curtailed, and this spelled the demise of the organization.

The absence of a peak women's organization in Australia is even more interesting in light of government efforts to induce the movement to create such a body. For instance, in the mid-1990s Dr. Carmen Lawrence (the minister for the status of women in the Keating ALP government) and Kathleen Townsend (the then head of the Office of the Status of Women) both indicated their preference and support for such an organization. Lawrence hoped that it would coordinate the information coming to the government, provide the basis for more effective consultation, and enable the movement to speak to the government from a more authoritative position. As a former active member of the women's movement, Lawrence was aware of feminists' fear of being forced to speak in a single voice. However, she claimed that, in a de facto sense, this was already happening because there was no mechanism in place to enable women's organizations to 'thrash out their views' (Lawrence, Interview with author, 1997). While minister for the status of women, Lawrence instigated a feasibility study that would take as its subject the development of a peak body. The final report, which drew heavily on the Canadian NAC model, received a mixed reaction from the feminist community. Members raised the perennial issues of the autonomy of prospective member groups and concerns about hierarchical structures. For Lawrence the timing of the report was unfortunate, as it came just months before the election of the coalition government. Not surprisingly, the incoming government, which was unsympathetic to feminist concerns, shelved the report.

Obviously, there is a correlation between feminist structures and feminist ideology. In recent years this has been reinforced by the pressures to recognize diversity within the movement. As noted earlier, the 'politics of difference' has challenged the very foundations of feminism and has confronted the dominant women in the movement with the limitations of their perspective. The shift away from a discourse of 'sisterhood' to one of 'difference' has had a direct bearing on the structure of the movement. Since the early 1980s the movement has become ever more fractured and dispersed. The large national conferences that had once been a feature of the movement are no longer held; in terms of numbers, WEL has become a shadow of its former self; and few WLM groups still exist. This is not to say that the Australian feminist movement has withered away; rather, it is to say that its activities have become more localized and its claims more tentative.

The politics of difference has no doubt contributed to recent reticence within the movement with regard to building formal structures, but it does not account for its earlier reticence. Nor does it explain why the Australian women's movement has been willing to make compromises with regard to ideological position vis-à-vis the state but has been reluctant to do so vis-à-vis organizational structures. *Gendering Government* suggests that the reason for this is that the structural decisions of feminists have been directly influenced by feminist strategies. The decision of Australian feminists to target the executive arena, to enter the state to work as femocrats (where they achieved important policy reforms), has decreased the need for a highly institutionalized external movement. Femocrats are the first to bemoan the absence of an organized feminist lobby capable of providing external pressure to back up their internal efforts (see O'Neil , cited in Neales 1989). Nevertheless, their presence and relative policy success has meant that there has not been the same imperative for Australian feminists to create an institutionalized body as there has been for Canadian feminists. Had lobbying been the primary strategy of Australian feminists, as it was of Canadian feminists, perhaps there might have been a greater tendency towards institutionalization. Obviously it is impossible to conduct an experiment that involves femocrats being removed from the equation, and we can only speculate about an outcome. However, an institutional analysis provides a more promising path than do existing ideological explanations with regard to exploring variations in the strategies and institutional structures of the Australian and Canadian movements.

Anglo-Canadian Feminist Structures

Although Anglo-Canadian feminists have long argued against hierarchical forms of organization and have supported 'feminist' consensual modes of organizing, they have created, through NAC, a highly institutionalized movement structured along hierarchical lines. Clearly, this structure sits uncomfortably beside feminist ideas about structures. Ideological beliefs do not explain these structural arrangements, so what does? Anglo-Canadian feminists have selected the structural forms that best support their strategies – strategies that are shaped by the prevailing POS.

Since the early 1970s the Canadian women's movement has been highly institutionalized. This has been made most obvious through the maintenance of NAC, which has operated as the central node in the network of the Canadian women's movement, combining under its umbrella structure the various cleavages that make up that movement. NAC has managed to bring 'together, in a fragile coalition, the major ideological elements evident in the English-Canadian Movement' while working to 'maintain some relationship between the French-Canadian and English-Canadian movements' (Vickers 1991, 87). It has also been able to encompass minority groups, especially those from various race and ethnic backgrounds, alongside the Anglophone and (at times) Francophone majoritarian elements of the movement.

NAC's umbrella structure, under which groups rather than individuals operate as its membership base, has given the organization a high degree of stability and, over time, has enabled it to become institutionalized. NAC, as the peak body of the Canadian women's movement, meets each of the criteria for institutionalization set down by interest group theorist A. Paul Pross (1990, 293). First, it has achieved organizational continuity and cohesion, having been in existence since 1972 and, aside from the breakaway of Quebec feminists during the 1980s, has remained relatively cohesive. It has access to its own human and financial resources, employing up to seven permanent staff members from the late 1970s onward; it has had offices in Toronto and Ottawa; and it has a funding base that consists of a combination of membership fees and government funding.[4] NAC has developed an extensive knowledge of relevant sectors of government, working in alliance with women's agencies within the bureaucracy and holding annual meetings with the government of the day as well as with opposition parties. It has had a stable membership base. Twenty-three years after its inception it was able to boast its largest membership base ever, with over 600 women's groups (Manji 1995). Finally, its policy committees develop concrete objectives, the attainment of which requires NAC to bargain with the government (see NAC 1991).

As well as being institutionalized, NAC has operated along formal, hierarchical lines. In a critical appraisal of NAC, president Lorraine Greaves (1991, 104) described the organization as follows:

> By 1986, NAC was a feminist organization without a feminist process. Its executives formed a hierarchy, with the President and a few table officers at the top, Robert's Rules were used routinely in decision-making at the executive and annual meetings, and voting was always the method for resolving conflicts. The importance attributed to the presidential role, while comforting for the public and government, and convenient for the media, was rather a traditional approach for a feminist organization.

The institutionalization of the women's movement through NAC and its hierarchical structure stands in direct contrast to the radical ideological views often espoused within the Anglo-Canadian feminist community. This disjuncture has not been lost on most feminists, especially those in NAC, who have been engaged in long-standing debates about how to rectify it. On one side of this debate have been women with a radical perspective, who support the introduction of non-hierarchical structures, the rotation of organizational positions, and replacing voting with a consensus model of decision making. On the other side are those who accept the importance of these feminist organizational forms but who, for pragmatic reasons, favour more structured models of organization. Within NAC, struggles over radical versus structured organizational forms became most intense between 1986 and 1988 under the presidency of Lorraine Greaves, who was herself at the radical end of the feminist spectrum.

During her presidency, Greaves instigated a review in order to address structural issues. The review produced some radical alternatives to the existing structures, including replacing meetings with social gatherings, replacing the 'bureaucratic' umbrella organization with 'direct action groups,' and replacing the AGM with consciousness-raising exercises (Backhouse 1988). The organizational review report handed down at the 1988 AGM did not reflect these more radical proposals, concentrating instead on broader issues of accountability and representation. However, the debate about appropriate feminist structures and processes within NAC, particularly at the 1988 conference, was very intense (for an account of the conference see *Broadside: A Feminist Review* 1988, 'Editorial,' 9, 8). Although press reports suggested that the organization was 'on the brink of collapse' as a result of these disputes, NAC survived; however, the chasm between feminist thought and practice, on the one hand, and structural concerns, on the other, remained.

Differences over feminist organizational forms have not been the only structural issues confronting NAC. It has also had to attempt to accommodate differences resulting from broader nationalist and regional tensions. NAC has been confronted with the problem of how best to incorporate Francophone feminists – something that it has not always done successfully. For instance, during the constitutional debates of the 1980s, Francophone feminist groups, including their peak body, the Fédération des femmes du Québec (FFQ), withdrew from NAC because they were frustrated with the attitude of Anglo-feminists towards their pro-Quebec constitutional position (Porter, cited in Roberts 1988, 277). While the withdrawal of the FFQ detracted from NAC's ability to claim to speak on behalf of all Canadian feminists, NAC nevertheless maintained its position as the central organization of feminists in the rest of Canada. The issue of regionalism has also created structural tensions within the organization.

For many years feminists from western provinces have complained that NAC is dominated by groups from central Canada, specifically from the Toronto-Ottawa axis (Greaves 1991, 105). The organization began to demonstrate greater sensitivity to these regional voices during the early 1990s, creating positions on the executive for regional representatives and holding its AGM outside Ottawa, starting, in 1993, with Saskatoon.

More recently, NAC has found ways to recognize the number and range of identity groups entering the organization. Women from lesbian, visible minority, immigrant, and disabled groups have forced the organization to challenge its philosophies, including the universalized notions of womanhood and sisterhood that had been the core of feminist activism since the 1970s. NAC has attempted to develop a more nuanced notion of 'woman.' In 1993 Sunera Thobani became the first visible minority woman to be appointed to the NAC presidency. In one of her first press interviews she emphasized the need to accept women's difference: 'I think NAC and women's organizations can recognize that women have different experiences. There is no one universal experience for all women and consequently there's no one universal feminism' (Thobani, cited in McFarland 1993). NAC's decisions in the late 1980s to establish formal caucuses (through which various groups could operate) and to provide positions on the executive for specific identity groups were a response to the growing presence of minority women in the organization and a gradual recognition of differences between women (Rebick 1991, A12). Thobani's appointment paved the way for other woman of colour to assume the NAC presidency. Most recently, Terri Brown, an Aboriginal woman, has taken up the position.

Despite the sometimes bitter and acrimonious debates within NAC over the issues of structure, process, and representation, the organization has been able to hold itself together and remain the key institution of the Anglo-Canadian women's movement. According to a former NAC executive secretary, its resilience in the face of these divisions is a fascinating social phenomenon:

> It's amazing how the organization is riven with internal conflict but can still come to consensus at the AGM. That it can work through issues on the floor and give the organization a mandate for another year. The AGM is fractious but the members also recognize that the easiest way to destroy the women's movement is to work on its splits, so they try to keep it internal. It has a history of working through differences. (interview with author, 1995)

The commitment within the Canadian women's movement to what Vickers (1991) calls 'ongoing dialogue' has clearly played a part in NAC's survival. However, other factors can also be seen to be at work. NAC's choice of strategies – especially its focus on lobbying – has reinforced its need to operate as a strong, cohesive organization. Having chosen a lobbying strategy at the outset, it has been essential that the movement maintain a body capable of undertaking multiple tasks. These include: making policy decisions, quickly mobilizing supporters, coordinating lobbying campaigns, and making deputations to government ministers and agencies. NAC provided all of these functions in its first two decades. The shift to more radical direct action, such as marches and sit-ins, in the past ten years has required the same, if not more, coordination of effort and has, therefore, continued to justify the maintenance of NAC.

While NAC remains the central organization of the Canadian women's movement, other organizations have also emerged (often under the NAC umbrella) to take a prominent role in feminist activities. One organization that has stood out in recent years is the feminist litigation organization known as LEAF. Formed after the entrenchment of the charter in 1982, LEAF was established to run test cases under the equality clauses of the charter. As it turns out, LEAF has played a limited role, operating as an intervenor in, rather than as an instigator of, cases (see Chapter 5). There are a number of interesting parallels between LEAF and NAC. First, LEAF, like NAC, is a formally structured organization. Although not an umbrella organization, it has a similar structure to that of NAC, with a hierarchy and formal rules and procedures. Second, both LEAF and NAC seek to engage directly with the state; however, the former does so at the constitutional and legal level, whereas the latter does so at the Parliamentary level. Finally, the structure of LEAF, like that of NAC, has been shaped primarily by strategic imperatives. In order to use the charter to advance feminist claims, activists needed to create a highly professional formal organization able to identify opportunities to intervene in legal cases.

The Australian and Canadian women's movements have a number of important similarities. They are internally diversified both in terms of the various identities that exist under their banner as well as in terms of the ideological positions they encompass. Further, with regard to strategies, they have both engaged in 'inside' and 'outside' tactics. However, there have been important differences in the nature of these strategies. Australian feminists have opted for an inside bureaucratic strategy as well as outside lobbying. Their Anglo-Canadian counterparts have engaged in lobbying 'with a difference' and have looked towards the legal and constitutional arms of the state. These strategic choices demonstrate that feminists are strategic actors: they look to those areas of the state that are most open to their demands and structure themselves in such a way as to take advantage of them.

The extent to which differences emerge can be explained not only by ideology, but also by the POS open to feminist actors. Shifts in the POS over time have directly influenced feminists' strategic choices. The reason Canadian feminists chose to engage with the legislature and, later, the legal system has to do with the openings produced by the RCSW and the charter and, later, the constraints produced by the Mulroney PC government. Similarly, in Australia, at any given time feminists responded to opportunities arising from the presence or absence of a progressive government.

In terms of being able to exploit the POS, it appears that Anglo-Canadian feminists have made more advances than have Australian feminists. What the above discussion illustrates in relation to Australian feminist strategies is that feminists have had to rely on a progressive political party – the ALP – to operate as an intervening variable to assist them in cracking open political opportunities in other institutions. Thus, in the Australian case, the interaction between institutions is as important in shaping available opportunities as are interactions within the institutions themselves. The reliance on the ALP to provide a positive POS has made Australian feminists vulnerable to the state in a way that their Canadian counterparts are not. When blocked by a conservative political party, Canadian feminists have been able to look to the legal institutional realm as an avenue of reform. Australian feminists have not exploited this alternative route and remain dependent upon the presence of a progressive political party to enable them to make advances in the executive and legislative arenas.

Emphasizing the importance of institutions in shaping feminist choices does not imply that ideology has no role. However, it is wrong to treat ideology as an independent variable, something autonomous from feminist practice. Ideology is not something that stands apart from activists; it is itself informed by feminist engagement with the state. This was obvious in Canada during the period of the RCSW, when skeptical Canadian feminists were encouraged to put aside their hostility towards the state and to engage with it in order to achieve some of the commission's recommendations. Similarly, in the Australian case, it was obvious that once the Whitlam government came to office and opened the door to reform, activists from across the feminist spectrum were prepared to put their radical rhetoric to one side and push for change by working with the state. In both cases, the result of feminist activism was a more pragmatic approach to the state, even though some continued to hold on to revolutionary ideals. Not only did ideology inform practice, practice informed ideology.

A point that will be pursued throughout this book relates to the two-way relationship between feminists and political institutions. It would be incorrect to interpret my argument as one that supports the view that feminist practice in either country has been determined by political institutions; that is, that influence runs only in a top-down direction. Rather, feminist practice and political institutions should be seen as interactive and co-constitutive. Anglo-Canadian feminist influence over the inclusion of equality clauses in the charter and (since its entrenchment) charter interpretation is perhaps the best example of this. More subtle examples are drawn out in the following chapters (e.g., how Australian feminists have been able to create new opportunities once inside the bureaucracy). Shifts in political institutions might encourage feminists to adopt a particular strategy, and then, by engaging with the state, they could help to create further openings.

Political constraints can also influence feminist choices. This is rendered obvious in Chapter 3, which looks at Australian and Canadian feminist engagement with the parliamentary realm. In both countries, feminist actors have faced a combination of structural impediments and entrenched masculine norms that have made it difficult for them to advance their agenda. As a result they have looked elsewhere – in particular, to the bureaucracy and constitutional and legal realms – to advance their aims.

3
The Feminist Electoral Project: Working against the Grain

Majoritarian feminists in Australia and Canada have a long history of engaging with the parliamentary realm. They have been active within political parties, stood as candidates, entered Parliament, and become cabinet ministers. Judging by success at the ballot box, feminists in both countries have made some modest gains over time. Nevertheless, their gains within the parliamentary arena have been slow in coming, and they have also needed to expend a disproportionate amount of energy in order to achieve relatively small rewards. Furthermore, increases in female representation have not necessarily resulted in Parliament becoming a less gendered institution. As a consequence, it is not surprising to find that Anglo-feminist activists in both countries have come to question the value of pursuing an 'electoral project' and that they have been more inclined to look to other political arenas to pursue their aims.

This chapter looks at how Australian and Canadian feminists have engaged with the 'electoral project.' The parliamentary realm encompasses not only the legislature and political executive, but also the party and electoral systems that act as the mediating structures between the legislature and the electorate. The electoral project refers to feminist attempts to use these various institutions to achieve their aims. According to Young (cited in Vickers 1997a, 23), it refers to 'both the presence of women in legislatures as well as the inclusion of women's perspectives, beliefs, interests and diversity in the representational process.' If the success of the feminist electoral project is measured by both the *presence* of women and the *representation* of feminist interests in Parliament, then it can be argued that, in Australia and Canada the project has had limited success. Although there has been some increase in the number of women entering Parliament, political parties and the institution of Parliament remain largely oblivious to feminist concerns.

The thrust of the argument in this chapter, as outlined in Table 3.1, is that the parliamentary arena has presented Australian and Canadian feminists with a primarily closed, rather than an open, political opportunity structure. Despite their efforts to challenge existing impediments within the parliamentary realm, gains have been slow and tenuous. As a result feminists have been dissuaded from focusing too much effort on this arena and, instead, have chosen to engage with other institutions. Young (1996, 237) makes this point in relation to Canada:

> The Canadian [women's] movement's peripheral attention to electoral/ partisan politics can ... be understood as a rational response to elements of the opportunity structure facing the movement. The belief that it is naive to think that the election of women will affect political outcomes

Table 3.1

Political opportunity structures in the electoral, party, and parliamentary arenas

	Australia	Canada
Party system	*Structures* **Negative** Strong alignment Class-based cleavages	*Structures* **Negative** Brokerage system Regionalized system
Electoral system	*Structures* **Negative** Majoritarian (preferential), single member for House of Representatives **Positive** Proportional representation in the Senate	*Structures* **Negative** Majoritarian (FPP), single member for House of Commons **Negative → Positive** Appointed Senate
Parties	*Norms* **Negative** Pre-selection processes that favour masculine status quo	*Norms* **Negative** Pre-selection processes that favour masculine status quo
Parliament	*Structures* **Negative** Executive dominance **Positive** Committee structure	*Structures* **Negative** Executive dominance **Positive** Committee structure
	Norms **Negative** Masculine, aggressive	*Norms* **Negative** Masculine, aggressive

is not simply a reflection of an ideological predisposition away from parties, but is based on a rational assessment of Canadian political structures.

Young's position is equally applicable in the Australian case. The argument does not ignore the fact that there have been significant improvements in the number of women entering Parliament, particularly in the past decade (outlined in Table 3.2 below). The critical distinction is between numerical improvements in women's representation, on the one hand, and the representation of feminist interests, on the other. Whereas there has been an increase in the number of women entering Parliament, this has not translated into an overwhelming improvement in 'women friendly' legislation or into a more feminine parliamentary culture. Indeed, despite the fact that the Mulroney Progressive Conservative government in Canada and the Howard Liberal government in Australia had a record number of women on their benches, during their incumbencies they retreated from addressing women's concerns.

The Party and Electoral Systems

It is impossible to understand the constraints and opportunities facing Australian and Canadian feminists in Parliament without first understanding how they are situated vis-à-vis the political party and electoral systems. For over a century in both countries, parliamentary politics has been dominated by major political parties that have had continuity over time. In each case, the electoral system has been a key factor in shoring up the position of the major parties. While smaller parties in each country have on occasion been able to buck electoral barriers and win seats in Parliament, this has not resolved the problem for feminists. Successful minor parties have either been hostile to a feminist agenda (e.g., the Reform Party and the more recent Canadian Alliance in Canada) or else they have been unable to seriously challenge the control of the major parties, particularly at the federal level (e.g., the Australian Democrats and the Canadian New Democratic Party). The ability of the major parties to monopolize parliamentary power and to alternate as the government of the day has made it necessary for those feminists looking to the parliamentary realm to engage directly with them in order to advance their objectives. However, no matter where these parties sit on the ideological spectrum, they present internal structural and normative barriers that impede the progress of feminist activists. Feminists who have attempted to overcome these barriers by refusing to play the partisan game, by standing as independents, or by creating women-centred parties have not fared any better, being marginalized by the electoral process and within the parliamentary arena.

Party Systems

In Australia the party system goes back to the 1890s, when the Australian Labor Party was created. Emerging out of a decade of industrial unrest, the ALP was created to represent the working 'man's' interests in Parliament. The development of a party of labour provided a strong incentive for capitalist interests to organize into a cohesive party. It proved more difficult to unite these interests. However, in 1944, after various short-lived attempts, the Liberal Party of Australia (LPA) was formed and it has remained a cohesive political force ever since. Upon its formation the LPA found an ally in the existing Country Party (now National Party), which was created in 1920 to represent rural interests. Since the 1940s, when in government these two parties, which share conservative social views, have operated at the federal level and, less consistently, at the state level as a coalition. Throughout the twentieth century the political pendulum in Australia swung between workers' and capital's interests, represented by the Labor and non-Labor parties, respectively.

The underlying class foundations of the Australian party system helped to shape its other characteristics. It contributed to the entrenchment of a two-party system and stable electoral alignments (Bean 1997, 102). Although there is evidence to suggest that, in the past two decades, voting along class lines has declined (due in part to changes in the labour market and improvements in education), this has not resulted in the decline of the two major parties (see Chaples 1997; Papadakis 1993, 6). Both major parties, and especially the ALP, have responded by replacing a class-based electoral strategy with a 'catch-all' approach. Australian voters may be less likely to vote for a party on the basis of their class position, but they have nonetheless tended to remain aligned to one or other of the major political parties rather than any of the alternatives (Bean 1997, 103). Moreover, in recent years there are signs that the Australian electorate is willing to 'protest' against the major parties by casting a vote for an independent candidate or a minor party, such as the Australian Democrats (AD). In the 1998 federal election, Pauline Hanson's One Nation Party – a populist, conservative, anti-immigration, pro-tariff party – attracted close to one million votes (8.4 percent) for lower house candidates (AEC 1999, 71). Having registered a protest vote at one election, these voters tend to come back into the fold of the mainstream parties at the next. This has been demonstrated most clearly by variations in AD support over time and the recent collapse of One Nation's support in the 2001 Federal Election.[1] In the view of electoral analyst Clive Bean (1997, 136):

> despite Australia having experienced many of the underlying changes associated with party turbulence in other countries (such as substantial transformations in patterns of social structure), the dominant political

parties have remained remarkably resilient. The Australian party system continues to be one of the most stable in the world and partisan loyalties remain widespread in the electorate.

Each of these features of the Australian party system – its class-based foundations, the entrenched nature of its two major political parties, and strong partisan loyalties – has presented problems for feminists. The fact that for many years class politics dominated the political agenda made it difficult for feminists (and other non-class actors) to have their concerns taken up by either political party. Issues that were not encompassed within the worker/capitalist dichotomy – such as issues relating to reproduction and childcare – were not taken seriously by the two major parties (see Lake 1999). Even when feminists could legitimately align their interests with one or other of the parties, they were marginalized because their interests often conflicted with those of men. For instance, for many years the ALP was reluctant to support arguments for improved working conditions and equal pay for women because it feared that such measures would interfere with the conditions and pay of the 'primary breadwinner,' who was defined as male (see Lake 1999).

In Canada, for most of the past century control over the federal government has alternated between two major parties, the Liberal Party and the Conservative Party (now known as the Progressive Conservative Party) (albeit frequently operating as minority governments). The Liberal Party has been perceived to be the party of government, while the PC has been seen as the intermediary between the Liberals and third parties. In the mid-1980s Thorburn (1985, 32) summarized the relationship of the two major parties as follows: 'The Conservatives are close enough to the Liberals, ideologically and in the interests they represent, that, should the Liberals become excessively corrupt, susceptible to minority pressures or incompetent, they provide a ready alternative.' The left-leaning New Democratic Party has been the constant third force in Canadian politics over the past thirty years. Like the Australian Democrats, it has offered itself as the 'honest broker' between the two major parties (Brodie and Jenson 1990, 260). While the NDP has played an important role supplying the other parties with new ideas and being a legitimator of dissent (Thorburn 1985, 32), it has never been seen as a viable alternative government at the federal level. The reason for this has largely to do with the first-past-the-post electoral system (i.e., whichever candidate gathers the most votes wins).

Although Canadians share with Australians a party system dominated by two major parties, there are a number of important differences between the two systems. Perhaps the most striking difference is that, in Canada, parties have never been organized along class lines but, rather, have along religious, language, and, especially, regional cleavages (Brodie and Jenson 1990, 249). Moreover, the two major political parties have historically operated as brokerage parties, adopting similar electoral platforms in the hope of capturing the support of the middle ground. The combination of non-class cleavages, together with brokerage politics, has meant that party alignment has been relatively weak in Canada (see Elkins 1992, 69). A longitudinal study undertaken between 1965 and 1991 by Clarke and Kornberg (1993, 301) found that 'many Canadians lacked durable party allegiances, and a sizeable minority did not identify with the same party in federal and provincial politics.' Brodie and Jenson (1990, 260) summarize the effect thus: 'Without the stable anchors of partisan loyalty based on differences among the parties, the Canadian electorate remain[s] volatile, easily swayed by appeals of leadership at one moment and divided by regional or national loyalties the next.'

From the mid-1980s onwards, the brokerage nature of the party system began to weaken as the two major parties adopted quite distinct policy prescriptions to deal with new economic challenges (e.g., large budget deficits) and ongoing political issues (including the Quebec question). This period also saw the rise of new regionally based parties, such as the western-based Reform Party and the Bloc Québécois. The emergence of these parties and the decline of the PC Party as a viable alternative government have dramatically altered the nature of the Canadian party system, which is now better described as a multi-party system. Despite injecting greater variety into debates about policy, the arrival of new parties on the federal scene has not brought about an increased degree of partisanship in Canada;[2] rather, they have served to further entrench the regional fissures within the Canadian party system and have resulted in heightened electoral volatility (see Swayze 1996). This volatility was demonstrated most clearly during the 1993 election, when the Progressive Conservatives were decimated as a political force at the federal level.

To the extent that the Canadian party system operated along brokerage lines, it can be seen to have worked against feminist interests. In Dobrowolsky's (2000, 23) view, some interests and identities, including gender, class, and race, were not addressed through brokerage politics, and 'the aggregation of often feminist interests was clearly not a priority.' Brooks (1996, 347) makes a similar point, arguing that, under a brokerage system: 'Parties in power, or even within sight of being elected to govern, are disinclined to alienate those voters and organized interests who object to such elements of the feminist agenda as the elimination of legal restrictions on abortion, affirmative action in hiring, and a national program of publicly subsidized day care.'

Brokerage politics has meant that 'the women's movement has sought influence by other means' (Brooks 1996, 347), including through lobbying, protests, and, more recently, litigation. Especially since the mid-1980s, Anglo-Canadian feminists, at least those represented by NAC, have found it difficult to exploit the battle between the major parties over the middle ground (NAC having been defined as representing special interests only). Meanwhile, the NDP (the party that is most sympathetic to increasing women's representation) has been unable to achieve electoral success at the federal level because its support is scattered throughout the country rather than concentrated in any particular area.

The regional aspect of the Canadian party system has presented yet another barrier to feminist activists. Just as class dominates political debates in Australia, so regionalism dominates political debates in Canada, making it difficult for those interests that are not regionally based – such as those of feminists – to be given a voice through the party system. The fact that the Canadian party system is asymmetrical – that is, the provincial and national arms of each party are separate, with each having its own membership base – serves to entrench the regional focus of the parties. As Young (1997, 90) notes, while region has had salience as a representational imperative for federal MPs in Canada, gender interests have not. Nor have the more recent developments towards a multi-party system been a boon for feminists. According to Young, under the new multi-party system 'responsiveness to feminism declined.' Since the Chrétien Liberal government came to office in 1993, it has focused on deficit reduction and 'responding to the Reform party's successful calls for fiscal austerity. In this context, there [has been] little potential for feminist activism except in defensive mobilizations' (Young 2000, 178).

Electoral Systems

The efforts of Australian and Canadian feminists to engage with representative institutions have also been hampered by existing electoral systems. Although different systems exist in each country, neither has been conducive to the reform agenda of feminist activists.

For Australian feminists, the problems of the party system have been exacerbated by the majoritarian, preferential voting system used to elect members to the House of Representatives and the lower houses in most of the states. Because the supporters of the two major parties are concentrated in different electorates – which were traditionally divided along the lines of blue- and white-collar workers – the ALP and Liberal/National parties have been assured of many 'safe' seats. These prize seats have not only intensified pre-selection battles within parties – most usually between 'worthy men' – they have also guaranteed long incumbencies, reducing women's chances of being able to contest them (see Lovenduski and Norris 1993). The existence of so many safe seats has also meant that political parties have often been able to take constituents in these areas for granted and, instead, concentrate their efforts on wooing 'swinging' voters in marginal seats. Being able to assume victory in certain seats has meant that parties in Australia have not had much reason to appeal directly to women, who are dispersed throughout the electorate rather than clustered in marginal seats.

This is not to say that women voters have been ignored entirely. For example, in the closely fought 1993 election, the ALP, faced with the prospect of a coalition victory, made a number of commitments in areas such as childcare in the hope of securing the votes of women.[3] Nevertheless, because of the resilience of partisan attachments and the consequent number of safe seats, parties in Australia have not needed to be overly concerned about courting the women's vote.

Feminist groups in Australia have long been aware of the constraints presented by the two-party system and have made some attempts to bypass them by standing as independents or developing their own political parties. In the early twentieth century, suffragist Vida Goldstein attempted, unsuccessfully, to pursue an independent route to Parliament. Other early feminists, such as Edith Cowan, who was the first woman to become a member of an Australian parliament, were prepared to enter the legislature on a party ticket. However, once elected, a few demonstrated a willing-ness to vote against their party in Parliament (Sawer 1996a, iii). Some contemporary women's activists have continued to uphold this anti-party view and have created women-only political parties in order to advance their aims. The rhetoric used by the most recent of these, the Australian Women's Party (formed in 1995), is reminiscent of the views expressed by an earlier generation of non-partisan feminists: '[We need to] by-pass the political machinery that systematically excludes our vital perspectives' (AWP 1996, 21).[4]

A range of impediments that are the result of the Australian electoral system has confronted feminists who have chosen to pursue an independent or minor party route. The single-member majority formula, used federally as well as for most state lower houses since 1919, means that, in order to win, candidates must gain an absolute majority of the votes cast. In cases where a candidate does not win a majority of primary votes, preferences are distributed until this is achieved. The system favours the major political parties because, even if they do not win a majority of first preference votes, they are usually able to influence the flow of minor party preferences to their advantage.[5] Parties that are likely to be pro-feminist in orientation, such as the Democrats, the Greens, or women-only parties, may be able to influence the policy platform of the two major parties by offering them their preferences. But they have been unable to secure the absolute majority of votes needed to break the stranglehold of the major parties and win a seat in the lower house (see Painter 1997a, 181).

The evident problems of entering Parliament through minor parties and as independents has led other contemporary feminists to accept the primacy of the major political parties and, through them, to pursue their electoral aims. Organizations such as the Women's Electoral Lobby, formed in 1972, and Women into Politics (WIP), established in 1992, have enjoined existing political parties to examine their practices and structures so that they are more 'women friendly.' They have also actively encouraged women to participate in electoral politics through mainstream political parties. A number of former WEL members have responded by joining either the Labor or conservative sides of politics and going on to become members of Parliament. For instance, ALP politicians (including former senator Susan Ryan, former Victorian premier Joan Kirner, and Carmen Lawrence), Liberal members Jocelyn Newman, and former NSW minister Virginia Chadwick were all active WEL members before entering Parliament.

Again, those feminists wanting to enter Parliament through the major parties are confronted by a series of electoral barriers. For those wanting to enter the lower house, the barriers are especially acute. The single-member majoritarian system for electing members to the House of Representatives (HoR) works against women candidates because it denies parties the option of having a 'balanced' ticket (either along gender or other lines) (see Lovenduski and Norris 1993). Moreover, because parties have only one chance at winning, they tend to be cautious about choosing candidates who are deemed to be outsiders, a category that continues to include women. This was evidenced in the 1998 federal election, where women represented only 27 percent of all party candidates for the lower house.

The use of a proportional representation (PR) system, based on a multi-member party-list structure, in order to elect members to the Australian Senate has provided feminists with a more positive POS for gaining entry into Parliament. The PR system can be seen to have benefited women and, to some extent, feminist activists in two respects. First, major political parties have shown more willingness to work towards a greater gender balance on their tickets because they can stand multiple candidates (see Gow and Tucker 1996).[6] Second, because the PR system requires candidates to gain a quota rather than an absolute majority of votes, it has been easier for minor parties (such as the Greens and Australian Democrats, who are more inclined to support women candidates and feminist-inspired policies) to gain seats in the Senate.[7] However, it would be wrong to assume that PR, on its own, is an automatic cure-all. As Lovenduski and Norris (1993, 314) warn, it is 'a necessary but not sufficient condition for high levels of female representation.' Most important, PR does not remove the need for political parties to be sensitive to the issue of the under-representation of women.

While feminists acknowledge the advantages of PR, cynics might observe that this electoral system is used only to elect members to the Senate, which, under a Westminster parliamentary system, is not equal in power to the lower chamber. Women wanting to enter Parliament have achieved the best results in the Senate (see Table 3.2), yet the reality is that this is not the house of government. Moreover, senators cannot be elevated to the ultimate position of influence – the prime ministership. PR has offered Australian women a path into federal Parliament, but it has done so in a way that has placed major restrictions on their ability to exercise power. Former democrat leader Cheryl Kernot, in the *Sydney Morning Herald,* 16 October 1997, alluded to this point when she defected to the ALP and signalled her intention to seek a seat in the lower house: 'I have come to the conclusion that the Democrats, at the Federal level are permanently entrenched as a third party ... The reality of the electoral system in this country means that the party will basically be confined to a Senate role.'

A newspaper editorial that appeared in the *Sydney Morning Herald,* 16 October 1997, in relation to Kernot's resignation made a similar argument: 'Despite th[e] high level of voting support, Australia's voting system means the Democrats can only ever hope to play a role in the Senate. While this is an important role, as the Democrats themselves have proved over nearly two decades, it is obviously not sufficient for someone who sees herself as a potential prime minister.'

The existence of compulsory voting for both houses of Parliament is another feature of the Australian electoral system that can be seen to have, at least indirectly, influenced the relationship between feminists and the parliamentary sphere. A number of commentators suggest that compulsory voting has helped to reinforce partisan attachments to one or other of the major political parties (see Aitkin and McAllister, cited in Bean 1997,

Table 3.2

Percentage of women members of lower and upper houses of the Australian and Canadian federal parliaments, 1970-2000

	1970	1980	1990	2000
Australia				
House of Representatives	0	2.4	6.8	22.3
Senate	3.3	10.9	23.7	28.9*
Canada				
House of Commons	0.3	5	14	20.5
Senate	0	0	14	30.5

* This represents a decrease from 32.9 percent in the Senate after the 1996 election.
Sources: Young 1997; Canadian parliamentary Web site <www.parl.gc.ca/>; Australian parliamentary library Web site <www.aph.gov.au/library/handbook/6_part2.PDF>.

103). It has also meant that political parties have not had to work to 'get out the vote' (McAllister 1986, 89). These two effects of compulsory voting have done nothing to encourage Australian political parties to make themselves more open to the demands of feminists.

The Canadian electoral system has important similarities to, and differences from, the Australian system. In both countries a single-member electorate system is used in elections pertaining to the federal House of Commons; however, in Canada, unlike in Australia, a plurality system is used to count the votes. This system, which is based on the simple first-past-the post principle, can exaggerate the winning margin of seats when compared with the winning margin of votes (Painter 1997a, 180). The plurality voting formula has worked to the advantage of those minor parties that have strong regional support, such as the Bloc Québécois and, more recently, the western-based Reform and Canadian Alliance parties, which have benefited from the 'winner-take-all' effect within the regional stronghold. This was illustrated most dramatically in 1993, when the Conservative Party went from forming government to holding two seats, despite the fact that it had collected 16 percent of the national vote (Swayze 1996, 556). At the same time, the Bloc Québécois received 18.1 per cent of the national vote but, because of its concentration in one region, was able to secure 'a solid phalanx of 54 MPs' (Norris 1997, 301). And the Canadian Senate, unlike its Australian counterpart, is appointed rather than elected.

Electoral rules have had a mixed effect on Canadian feminists who want to enter Parliament. From a negative perspective, those feminists wanting to enter the lower house share with their Australian counterparts the problems created by a single-member electorate system. They too have found that, when given one chance, political parties have been loathe to choose women candidates (Vickers 1997b, 139). In 1997 the proportion of women standing as candidates was 24 percent, slightly up from 1993 when women made up 22 percent of the candidates (see <http://www.elections.ca>).

For feminists, one recent unexpected positive effect of the Canadian electoral system relates to electoral volatility. Large and unpredictable swings in the vote have made it possible for female candidates, who are often selected to stand in 'unwinnable ridings,' to be 'swept' into Parliament (Arscott and Trimble 1997, 7, 9). The benefits for feminists of electoral volatility have been especially obvious at the provincial level, particularly where NDP governments have come to office (e.g., Ontario in 1990). As the party most open to feminist demands, the NDP has not only supported women as candidates but also, once elected, has shown support for 'women's issues' in Parliament (Byrne 1997). However, relying on electoral swings is a risky strategy, as women in Canada's provinces have discovered. A trend has emerged in which the fall of a provincial NDP government results in a decrease in the number of women representatives. This was demonstrated clearly in 1995, when a change in government in Ontario saw women MPs reduced from 22 percent to 15 percent; and, in the Yukon Territory, a change of government in 1992 from 25 percent to 18 percent (Arscott and Trimble 1997, 8).

The selection procedures for the Canadian Senate have given feminists further reason to be cautious about an electoral project. Unlike the Australian Senate, which is elected through a multi-member PR system, the Canadian Senate remains an appointed body and, as such, has presented a number of unique barriers to the entry of women. The history of the relationship between the Senate and the Canadian women's movement did not have an auspicious beginning. In 1919, one year after Canadian women had been enfranchised at the federal level, attempts were made to block women's entry into the Senate on the ground that they were not 'persons' under the Canadian Constitution – a claim that was upheld by the Canadian Supreme Court. Women's organizations mobilized around this issue, and, after more than a decade of agitation, the ruling was overturned in 1929 by the British Privy Council (for an account of this campaign see Errington 1993, 80). Since this time women have been appointed to the Senate, but gender parity has not been achieved. Since 1930 only 35 women have been appointed to the Senate, and by 1993 just 15 of the 104 senators were women (*Canadian Parliamentary Review* [Winter] 1993-4). Until very recently the rate of women's appointment to the Senate has remained slow, despite criticism from the Royal Commission on the Status of Women (1970) and from the Royal Commission on Electoral Reform and Party Financing (1991). Feminist lobbying for the introduction of a system of PR, if not a guaranteed 50 percent of Senate positions, has gone unheeded (NAC 1992, 'The Women's Agenda').

There is a range of reasons that explain why women have traditionally found it so difficult to gain entry to the Senate. First, as Landes (1987, 168) notes, 'the main criterion for Senate appointment is based on custom and convention: the upper house is selected on the basis of patronage or party service.' Both Liberal and Conservative governments have been guilty of using the Senate for these political purposes. Prior to increases in remuneration for HoC members, the Senate, which offered much better salaries than did the HoC, was, according to Landes, 'utilised as a retirement pension for loyal MPs' (169). Prime ministers have also been known to open up safe HoC seats by transferring a member to the Senate. Given that women have found it difficult to exercise influence and authority within political parties and the Parliament, their opportunities for being selected to the Senate have been greatly diminished.

Another factor working against women gaining entry into the Senate pertains to tenure. Instead of having a fixed term, senators are subject only to a mandatory retirement age of seventy-five. Although the Canadian Senate might be a weak chamber relative to the HoC, the combination of incumbency, good remuneration, and the relatively light workload means that Senate positions are highly sought-after. The general rule of the stronger the competition, the less likely that out groups will be elected (or in this case, selected), has, until recently, certainly held with regard to the Canadian Senate. In recent years there have been signs that the government is becoming more sensitive to achieving a gender balance in the Senate. During his first two terms as prime minister, Jean Chrétien chose more women than men to fill Senate vacancies, raising the total number of female senators to thirty-one (see <www.liberal.ca/commissions/nwlc/english/election.html>). These improvements may well be a sign that women are becoming less marginalized in Canadian politics. However, whether improved female representation will make the Senate a useful site for feminist activism remains to be seen.

Political Parties: Confronting Constraints and Making Opportunities

Australian and Canadian feminists have faced obstacles not only at the level of party and electoral systems, but also within the parties themselves. Although members of both movements have engaged with major political parties in an attempt to make them more 'women friendly,' these organizations continue to provide major impediments to a feminist electoral strategy. Some of the barriers confronting feminists within political parties are structural (e.g., pre-selection processes that have prevented women from being chosen to stand in safe, or winnable, seats). Other impediments are normatively based (e.g., entrenched gender values and the operation of male patronage). Generally, structural and normative constraints have operated in concert to prevent feminists from succeeding within the major parties.

Australian Labour Party

Since the 1970s the ALP has been the more progressive of the two major political parties in Australia. This has largely been due to the efforts of Gough Whitlam, who challenged the traditional labourist position of the ALP and advocated social democratic ideals and 'positive equality,' including the improvement of access to education and services for all (Eisenstein 1996, 17). This new direction within the ALP was attractive to many members of the emerging women's movement who supported Whitlam's vision and who were encouraged by his moves to support equal pay and open the path for the entry of feminists into the bureaucracy. Since 1983, under Hawke (and, to a lesser extent, during the Keating period), there was a return to labourist rhetoric and policies – indicated most clearly by the industrial accord between the ALP and trade unions – which was reminiscent of the pre-Whitlam period. This more traditional approach to politics was tempered by an ongoing commitment to broad equality goals, which were compatible with those of feminist activists. Some feminists were attracted by Labor's position on issues relating to women and entered the party in order to pursue these objectives. As discussed in later chapters, especially in relation to the bureaucracy and to federalism, an alliance between feminists and the ALP has proved to be very important in terms of creating a positive POS for feminists in other institutions. Feminists, however, have found it much more difficult to achieve success within the party itself. Despite endorsing affirmative action policies, the party has shown a reluctance to support women as candidates, MPs, or cabinet ministers.

One of the major structural barriers to feminist entry into Parliament through the ALP can be linked to the party's pre-selection process. Although these processes vary between the states, each uses some measure of branch participation as well as participation from trade unions and factional and head offices. Being a minority – women make up only 37 percent of ALP branch members – has meant that women have traditionally been overlooked in pre-selection battles.[8] Former ALP senator Margaret Reynolds (1996, 46) remembers the difficulty of being a woman in the male-dominated pre-selection process: 'I got up there and looked out at a sea of male faces, most of them reading the Sunday newspapers. There were a few of my women and men supporters at the back, but there was just this solid block of men. Even before I started I thought "What am I doing? I haven't got a hope here. It's all been decided." It was my first attempt and I did not expect to win, but I did expect to be listened to.'

In attempting to win pre-selection, female candidates have also had to confront male-dominated party factions, which play an important role in shaping these contests. As former ALP minister Susan Ryan argues: 'One of the major obstacles to gaining women's support for the Labor Party has been its traditional structure: machines, steering committees, complicated trade union connections. These antiquated, unrepresentative, male dominated hierarchies with their mysterious and indirect ways of getting the numbers for pre-selections and the election of Party officers deter many women who are otherwise attracted to Labor policies' (cited in Curtin and Sawer 1995, 152).

State and national executives also have the ability to intervene in the ALP pre-selection process, arbitrating any disputes. Especially in lower house contests, this head office input has been used to advance the cause of favoured men rather than to improve women's positions. There have been a number of instances of such favouritism in recent years, including in the safe Victorian federal seat of Batman (1995) and in the safe New

South Wales federal seat of Blaxland (1996). In both cases the respective ALP state office overlooked well-qualified women who had strong support at the branch level in order to appoint male candidates.

Feminists active in the ALP have long been aware of the problems related to pre-selection and have pressured the party to take ameliorative action. In 1981 they successfully lobbied to have women appointed to one-third of all administrative positions within the party, hoping that this might be reflected in candidate selection outcomes. A decade later, when it became obvious that these initial affirmative action measures had not had the intended effect, feminists agitated for the introduction of quotas to guarantee women a minimum of 35 percent of the winnable parliamentary seats at the federal and state levels by 2002. In 1994, after much internal pressure, including that from high-profile women such as incumbent Victorian and West Australian premiers Joan Kirner and Carmen Lawrence, respectively, the party agreed to the measure. In 1995, in response to the slow pace of change within the party, Joan Kirner established an Australian version of the American-inspired Emily's List (an acronym for Early Money Is Like Yeast). The list raises money to support women with a commitment to feminist principles to run for ALP seats.

Since introducing quotas, the party has shown a willingness to support women in winnable positions on the Senate ticket, with the result that in 1999 women held 32 percent of ALP Senate positions. The relative success of women in this chamber can be explained by two factors. First, and most obvious, they do not have to jump branch hurdles, which impede the entry of women to lower house seats. Second, head office has been willing to intervene to place women into winnable positions on Senate tickets. This has no doubt been encouraged by the 'balancing factor' of the PR electoral system, which allows the party to place 'favoured sons' as well as the occasional 'outstanding daughter' in a winnable position on the party ticket. However, in lower house seats, the combined influence of male-dominated branches, factions, and head office intervention in favour of male candidates for single-member seats (e.g., in the cases of Blaxland and Batman) all remain as obstacles to feminists wanting to enter Parliament through ALP (Altman 2000, 6). As Sawer (1997b) points out:

> In 1994 there was much rejoicing among feminists when the ALP intro-
> duced a quota whereby women would constitute 35 per cent of all its
> parliamentary parties by 2002. However, there has been as much trouble
> as ever over single-member seats, particularly in NSW and Queensland,
> and where the quota is being honoured, those chosen are those with the
> seal of approval from one of the party's factions, those who have demon-
> strated their loyalty to a male-controlled faction.

According to former ALP senator Susan Ryan (1999, 193), the quota 'is bitterly resented by many men in the party.' One of the most frequently heard criticisms of the use of affirmative action measures has been that it interferes with merit. The problem with this argument, as Reynolds points out, '[is] that "merit" is in the eye of the beholder.' In effect, 'traditionally Australian mateship has perpetuated the assumption that men will be more likely to have the appropriate mix of qualities to suit them for parliamentary life' (Reynolds 1996, 37). The introduction of the quota has led to improvements in the number of women contesting elections and entering the HoR.[9] After the 1998 election the number of female ALP members in the House of Representatives (MHR) reached its highest level ever, standing at 24 percent. The ALP met the 30 percent quota in time for the 2002 deadline, when it returned twenty women members (of a total of sixty-five) after the 2001 election. The influence of this crucial threshold of women is yet to be tested.

Australian Liberal and National Parties

The parties on the conservative side of politics in Australia have also been important as a site for women, and some feminists, wanting to enter Parliament. As mentioned earlier, former WEL members have gone on to a political career in the Liberal Party, although over time some of these former activists (e.g., the minister for the status of women in the Howard government, Jocelyn Newman) have come to disavow feminist objectives (see Cadzow 2000). Dame Beryl Beaurepaire, who held the post of the convenor of the National Women's Advisory Council during the Fraser government, was well known for her commitment to equal opportunity for women and for making good use of her access to the prime minister in order to advance those views. Kerry Chikarovski, who in 1998 became the first female leader of the Liberal Party in New South Wales, has also defined herself as a feminist. And, during her time as minister for the status of women in NSW, she advanced a liberal feminist agenda (see Chappell 1995). Current Liberal senators Marise Payne and Helen Coonan are also known for their support of liberal feminist values. Despite the presence of feminists in the ranks of the conservative parties, however, in recent years, amongst both male and female members of these parties, there has been little tolerance for feminist principles. In government, the conservative parties have demonstrated an unwillingness to support state-funded childcare, affirmative action policies, and state regulation of wages in order to achieve equal pay outcomes.

Women wanting to enter Parliament through the LPA have also faced barriers at the pre-selection stage. Until recently, Liberal Party branches had the ability to determine who would receive party endorsement. As with the ALP, the result was that women were overlooked as candidates as the party sought parliamentary recruits who replicated its existing members: between 1901 and 1990 only five Liberal women sat in the HoR. Changes to the LPA's pre-selection process, which allows state executive representation on pre-selection panels, have been implemented in order to help counteract the influence of patronage (see McDiven 1996, 97-8). However, even with these structural changes, women who are pre-selected for the Liberal Party still tend to be placed in marginal or unsafe seats.[10]

For women wanting to gain pre-selection in the National Party, the hurdles have been particularly high. Like the LPA candidates, the National Party candidates have been traditionally drawn from a small pool of well-connected men. The local branch pre-selection process adopted by the party has served only to entrench this practice, making it impossible for head office to intervene (should it ever be so inclined) to break the operation of male patronage.[11] Add to this the fact that it is the most socially conservative and, in the view of one of its own members, the most patriarchal of all existing parties (personal communication, Jennifer Gardiner, NSW National Party, MLC, April 1997), it is not surprising that it was only in 1996 that the first female National Party member was elected to the HoR.

While rejecting the notion of quotas, on the basis that it interferes with the operation of 'merit,' feminists within the Liberal and National parties have encouraged these organizations to adopt some measures to encourage the greater participation of women.[12] In the 1980s the Victorian Liberal Feminist Network was established to advance feminist ideas in the Liberal Party. In 1993 the Liberal Women's Forum was created to encourage more women to join the Liberal Party, arguing that the 'imbalance [in terms of men and women's representation] should not be allowed to continue' (Women's Liberal Forum 2000 <http://www.nsw.liberal.org>). Since its formation, this forum has played an educative role, conducting seminars to inform women about the Liberal Party and the nature of Parliament, convening workshops on public speaking, and running mock pre-selections. In 1995 the forum was successful in getting incoming leader John Howard to place a woman candidate in each state in a winnable position on the party's Senate ticket (Kingston 1996).

While the forum has increased awareness within the Liberal Party of women's unequal representation within Parliament, it has not been a 'feminist' initiative; rather, as Brennan (1997, 282) notes, it has operated 'simply as a network designed to encourage and support women seeking entry into parliament ... the Liberal Women's forums of the 1990s are not identified with any policy positions; they are simply intended to promote the careers of individual women.' The fact that the Howard government has had the largest number of women members in the history of the federal Parliament but has had the least impressive record of any government since the 1970s in terms of supporting feminist organizations, women's services, childcare provisions, and international women's rights agreements (see below) suggests that feminists still have a long way to go in terms of having their objectives embraced by the conservative side of politics.

Australian Democrats

Arguably, the party most amenable to women in terms of gaining entry into Parliament and support for feminist principles has been the Australian Democrats (ADs). It is the party that can lay claim to the best record on women – not only in terms of their position within the organization, but also as candidates and as a percentage of the party's elected representatives. Since its inception in 1977, three out of five national Australian Democrat presidents and three of its six federal party leaders have been women. After the 1996 election, five of the seven Democrat senators (71 percent of its representatives) were women. Aside from the minor green parties, the Democrats have fielded the most female candidates for the HoR (1990, 27 percent of total AD candidates; 1993, 25 percent; 1996, 35 percent). One possible explanation for these figures is that the party's pre-selection process operates on the basis of a ballot of all eligible members – a process that acts as an 'antidote to behind-the-scenes number-crunching and powerbroking' such as occurs within the traditional political parties (Sawer 1997c, 238). These results can also be attributed, in part, to the fact that, as a new party, it did not inherit an entrenched masculine culture. As former national president Heather Southcott noted: '[We] didn't have to get into an existing system dominated by men. We had the opportunity to start things on an equal basis' (cited in Sawer 1997c, 238).

Not only has the AD helped women gain positions of power within the party, but it has also – at least since 1986 when Janine Haines, a committed feminist, was elected leader – tolerated feminist viewpoints. The 'strong feminist element' in the party has not sat comfortably with all members, with one former senator citing this as the reason for his resignation from Parliament (see Haines 1992, 149). When the ADs are able to hold the balance of power in the Senate – which has been the case since mid-1999 – they are able to wield influence on issues dealing with feminist concerns. The ability of former AD leader Meg Lees to negotiate with the Howard government to remove the incoming goods and services tax (GST) on essential food items is a case in point (see Lees 1999). The ADs have also been involved in an unsuccessful campaign to push the government to remove the GST on tampons, breast pumps, and feeding pads – issues around which the feminist community has rallied. However, the rub for feminists in all this is that, due to the single-member majority voting system used to elect members to the HoR, the ADs have mostly been relegated to the role of 'keeping the bastards honest' from a base in the Senate rather than being able to offer a viable alternative government.

Canadian feminists have responded to the barriers in the party and electoral systems in a way similar to that of their Australian counterparts: they have pursued a mixture of independent and partisan strategies. As with Australian suffragists, those in Canada 'rejected the evils of partyism in favour of an independent, virtually suprapolitical stance' (Bashevkin 1993, 6). However, this did not keep them from entering into strategic alliances with political parties in order to 'get their foot in the door' of Parliament. For instance, the first woman parliamentarian in Canada, Nellie McClung, who had long expressed anti-party sentiments, was elected to the Alberta legislature in 1917 as a Liberal candidate; however, once inside, she proceeded to vote with her conscience. Contemporary Canadian feminists have been involved in creating alternative organizations, including separate political parties, such as the Feminist Party of Canada, which existed between 1979 and 1983, and other women's organizations that aim to encourage women's entry into politics. The now defunct Women for Political Action was formed in 1972 to provide training for potential women candidates and to pressure parties to change their practices. In 1984 an elite group of thirty women formed the Committee for '94, with the aim of achieving gender parity in the House of Commons within ten years (Young 1996, 235-6).

The key national umbrella women's organization, NAC, has also worked to encourage women's entry into Parliament. Its policy in relation to women's representation has been to lobby parties and government to change the structures that disadvantage women, and it has pledged itself to encourage women's participation in electoral politics through providing training and funding (NAC 1992, 'The Women's Agenda,' 14). However, as Young (1996, 237) notes, NAC's commitment to women's participation in these institutions has, in recent years, become more rhetorical than actual, reflecting a shift from a 'multi-party' to an 'anti- party' stance. In Dobrowolsky's (2000, 23) view, the parties' common emphasis on a neo-liberal agenda has helped to influence this change, providing 'a sharper target for feminists as compared to the parties' ill-defined brokerage positions of the past.'

While Canadian feminists have been attracted to independent strategies, they too have been confronted with the reality of a political system that is dominated by partisan politics. Their response to this reality mirrors that of their Australian counterparts to the extent that those Canadian feminists wanting to enter Parliament have had to become active within political parties. And, like Australian feminists, one of the biggest hurdles that they have had to overcome has been gaining party pre-selection in winnable ridings. In Canada the barriers to winning party endorsement have tended to be more consistent across parties than in Australia; this is due to the fact that all parties have employed similar local-level pre-selection arrangements. The locally based selection process can be seen to have worked against women candidates in two respects: (1) it has tended to favour candidates who reflect the status quo (i.e., those who are White, male, and middle class) if not actually openly discriminating against women candidates (Brodie 1994a, 79; Erickson 1993, 83); and (2) it has made it difficult for the central party apparatus to intervene to encourage positive action in relation to women candidates.[13]

Like their Australian counterparts, Canadian feminists have not sat back and accepted these as inevitable problems but have worked hard within political parties to make them more gender sensitive. They have found that those parties most sympathetic to their claims – the NDP and the Liberal Party – have been the most open to reform from within. As Bashevkin (1993, 25) notes: 'Within both parties, feminist activists made impressive gains by the mid-1970s, as task forces and new woman's rights organizations were established (the NDP Participation of Women Committee and the Women's Liberal Commission were created in 1969 and 1973 respectively) and as more women became visibly influential, particularly as holders of major party and public office.'

After the initial flurry of reform in the early 1970s, feminists were able to hold their ground before making further inroads into party structures and practices in the early 1980s.

New Democratic Party

The NDP has the most impressive record of all parties with regard to undertaking reforms to improve women's position both within the party and as candidates. In 1981 it introduced an affirmative action strategy to encourage more women to stand as candidates, and in 1983 it adopted measures to achieve gender parity on the two governing bodies of the national party. These measures appear to have had some positive results, with the number of female NDP candidates reaching 40 percent in the 1993 federal election and the party electing two successive women federal party leaders since 1989. The downside of the NDP for Canadian feminists is that, although it is the party most sympathetic to feminist issues (see Young 2000), and although it has stood the most number of women candidates,[14] it is unlikely to gain representation at the federal level. This is largely because of the regional bias that is built into the party and electoral systems. As noted earlier, when the NDP has been successful at the provincial level it has been a boon to the feminist electoral project. As Byrne's (1997) research shows, under the Bob Rae NDP government in Ontario, women, many of whom espoused feminist principles, secured 42 percent of the Cabinet positions and used them to advance a feminist agenda. Under the Rae government, feminist ministers were successful in influencing improvements in childcare, parental leave, employment equity, funding for anti-violence against women initiatives, and access to abortion. Nevertheless, in a common pattern, the positive opportunities open to feminists diminished quickly once the Mike Harris PC government came to office.

The arrival on the federal scene of new regionally based parties, including the Bloc Québécois, Reform, and, more recently, the Canadian Alliance, has served to further marginalize the NDP at the national level. In Young's (2000, 178) view, in recent years the anti-feminist Reform Party (now the Canadian Alliance Party) has replaced the NDP as the dynamic element of the Canadian party system. This shift has had a serious deleterious effect on women wanting to be elected at the federal level. It has meant that, since 1993, the issue of the election of women has dropped off the political agenda and that the upward rate of change in women's candidacy in a number of the parties has slowed. In fact, the number of women candidates fell from 408 in 1997 to 373 in 2000.

Canadian Liberal Party

The Canadian Liberal Party has been less supportive of affirmative action than has its NDP counterpart. Although during the 1980s the internal National Women's Liberal Commission (NWLC) recommended that the party introduce a quota system so that women would be assured of constituting 50 percent of its candidates, it has resisted these measures (Young 2000, 164). Nevertheless, during the 1970s and 1980s it responded to feminist pressure by adopting measures that guaranteed women positions on the national executive. It has also been active in recruiting women to winnable ridings and providing them with campaign funding (Young 1997, 88). More recently, the leadership of the Liberal Party has been involved in 'parachuting' prominent Liberal women into safe ridings, a strategy that has come in for some criticism from party members. These measures have had a positive influence in terms of the number of Liberal women in Parliament. The Liberal Party can now boast the best record on women members of the House of Commons (seventy-two since it was created in 1867), with its closest rival, the PC Party, a long way behind (thirty-seven since 1867) (see <http://www.parl.gc.ca>).

Progressive Conservative Party

Aside from the neoconservative Canadian Alliance and the earlier Reform Party, which have totally rejected arguments for the need for separate representation of women, the PC Party has been the least supportive of using interventionist measures to address the party position of women. Its key response has been to adopt measures to 'encourage' women to become involved as PC candidates. For a time, it also reserved some positions on the national executive for the internal Women's Federation and established a 'talent bank' of suitable women for appointment to political office as well as a campaign fund to support women candidates (Vickers 1997a, 36). However, in recent years the PC Party has reversed some of these decisions. In line with the stance taken by the Reform Party, the PC Party has removed all affirmative action strategies, disbanding the PC women's association and removing all requirements for a gender balance at national meetings (Young 2000, 182).

In summary, both Australian and Canadian feminists have been active within political parties in that they have attempted to make them more open to a feminist electoral project. In both countries feminists have had some success in encouraging parties to undertake reforms that make it easier for women to be pre-selected as candidates for Parliament. But these improvements have been slow to emerge, with structural and normative barriers proving difficult to shift. In Canada, since the emergence of the Reform Party and Canadian Alliance, it has become particularly obvious that these improvements are also highly tenuous and that advances can be quickly undone. Moreover, for those feminists seeking to use an electoral project to achieve their objectives, access to a parliamentary seat is only half the battle. They must also contend with barriers within Parliament itself.

Parliament: Normative and Structural Barriers

Historically, women have been poorly represented in Parliament at both the federal and state/provincial levels in Australia and Canada. In 1990, almost a century after the emergence of the suffrage movement and over two decades after the emergence of the contemporary women's movement, women occupied fewer than 7 percent of the seats in the Australian HoR and made up only 14 percent of the members of the Canadian House of Commons. Moreover, women had fared little better at the provincial and state levels. It has only been since 1990 that the percentage of women entering the federal and state/provincial parliaments in Australia and Canada has increased in any significant measure (see Table 3.2).[15] These improvements can be seen, in part, to be the result of the push by feminists to have political parties introduce affirmative action measures and to select women candidates to stand for election. For the past two decades in Canada, and since 1996 in Australia, these increases can also be seen as a matter of 'luck' insofar as they have been the result of unexpected electoral swings that brought into Parliament women who were standing in what were thought to be unwinnable seats.[16] Although women's presence in the Australian and Canadian parliaments is now greater than at any time in history, even with these increases the number of women representatives is unimpressive by international standards. In 2000 Australia was ranked twenty-second and Canada twenty-eighth out of 116 in an International Parliamentary Union survey of women in national parliaments (see <http://www.ipu.org>). Moreover, in both federal lower house chambers, and in most provinces and states, women representatives remain well below the critical threshold of 30 percent – the threshold at which it is thought that women could 'make a difference.'

There is no question that, purely in terms of simple justice, the improvement in women's representation in Parliament is important. However, as my concern is with feminist strategies, other considerations also need to be taken into account: primarily, to what extent do the women who are elected to Parliament uphold and advance feminist values? As numerous commentators on women's representation have pointed out, there is nothing to guarantee that an increase in the nominal *presence* of women in Parliament will improve the substantive *representation* of women's interests as they are defined by feminists (for a discussion see Gotell and Brodie 1991, 66-7; A. Phillips 1991; Arscott 1995b; Vickers 1997a). The validity of this argument was borne out in Canada after the election of the Mulroney PC government. Although the 1984 election saw an unprecedented twenty-seven women elected to the House of Commons and an increase in the number of women in Cabinet from two to six, the government's neoconservative policy agenda meant that this numerical increase was not translated into improved representation of 'women's interests.' In the view of most Anglo-feminists, Mulroney's agenda, which resulted in major cutbacks to women's services and welfare provisions, proved to be 'fundamentally incompatible' with their demands (Gotell and Brodie 1991, 63-4). Indeed, as Bashevkin (1998, 190) argues, during the Mulroney period women in the PC Party were some of the most vocal critics of the actions of feminists and were especially critical of NAC. The 1993 appointment of Canada's first woman prime minister, Kim Campbell, further highlighted the important difference between numerical and substantive representation. Although Campbell had gained some respect from the feminist community in her earlier role as attorney general (when she moved to protect existing provisions for protecting rape victims in court), as prime minister she showed little sympathy for feminist groups and their causes (Bashevkin 1998, 193). As NAC (1993) argued at the time of Campbell's appointment, having a woman prime minister was not enough: what was needed was a woman prime minister who was committed to women's issues.

Since the 1996 election of the conservative Howard coalition government, Australian feminists have come to experience first-hand the limitations of relying on numerical improvements to enhance the representation of issues of concern to women. Despite having more women than ever on its benches, the government has dismantled many feminist-inspired initiatives. In areas such as childcare, affirmative action, and remedies for sex discrimination, government support has either been withdrawn or has been under threat, while the Office of the Status of Women and women's programs have suffered significant budget cuts (see Brennan 1997; Kingston 1997; Sawer 1997a). The record of conservative governments in Australia and Canada has once again reinforced the fact that there is a fundamental difference between increasing the number of women representatives and improving the representation of women.

But what of those feminists who do make it inside the doors of Parliament? What are the obstacles and opportunities confronting them in their efforts to pursue an equality agenda? In both countries feminists have confronted a range of barriers, some of which have a normative base and some of which have a structural base. In both cases, strong masculine norms have operated to frustrate the efforts of feminists within Parliament. These normative barriers have been reinforced by structural barriers, including partisanship, regionalism, and strong political executives.

Parliamentary Gender Norms

The dominance of masculine norms within the parliamentary realm in Australia and Canada has obstructed a feminist electoral project in a number of ways. The claim that both parliaments reflect masculine norms should not be taken to infer either that all men act in this way or that women are incapable of acting in a 'masculine' manner. The point is that, historically, the parliamentary culture has had a masculine flavour in that it is an adversarial arena within which loud, aggressive, and combative behaviour is the norm. Members of both sexes have responded to this culture, to a greater or lesser extent, by tailoring their behaviour to fit in with those norms that have been deemed 'appropriate' (March and Olsen 1989). Women, like men, do not have a universal code of behaviour. It is therefore unrealistic to expect that merely increasing the number of women in Parliament will result in substantive changes in either the policy choices or behaviour of parliamentarians. Increasing the numerical representation of women is a prerequisite for changing the masculine nature of Parliament, but it is not sufficient to guarantee this outcome.

Female politicians find that they are caught in a double bind within the parliamentary arena. Prevailing masculine norms valorize certain qualities (e.g., being tough, unemotional, and combative); however, when women act in ways that reflect these qualities, they are often ridiculed or patronized. One explanation for this reaction by male politicians is that 'a woman who enters a legislature as a member is an anomaly, a deviant in the sense that she is defying traditional limits on acceptable feminine behaviour' (Langevin, cited in Bashevkin 1993, 86). Derisive terms, ranging from 'slut' to 'sweetheart,' have been used by male members of both sides of politics in Australia and Canada to attack women who attempt to play the political game by using masculine tactics. On the other hand, if women members adopt traditional 'feminine' behavioural traits within Parliament – such as acting in a more passive, consultative, or emotional manner – they are often perceived as weak and not equipped for the demands of office (see Lawrence 1994, 3). Australian Liberal MP Kathy Sullivan (1994, 31) explains the double bind facing women in Parliament: 'The biggest mistake you can make is to be a pseudo man because the men hate that. They want to have their cake and eat it too. Many of the men want women to be feminine but they do not want them to talk like women or think like women.'

Reports given by women politicians in Australia and Canada concerning the operation of masculine norms within the two parliaments are remarkably similar (for Canada, see Young 1997, 92; Bashevskin 1993, 86; for Australia see Haines 1992, 149-50; Mitchell 1996). The behaviour of members on the floor of the house, especially during question time, provides an unambiguous example of the operation of masculinity within both parliamentary arenas. The loud, bullying, posturing tactics used by politicians can be seen to reflect a highly masculinized culture that alienates many women members. Australian ALP politician Wendy Fatin (cited in Mitchell 1996, 227) has described her experience of this culture in the following terms:

The biggest gap in my capacity, was my inability to perform well in the Chamber. I performed appallingly because I had never taught myself how to deal with that arena. I had never been screamed at by men before ... I had never lived in an environment of screaming and shouting or sneering. It was so alien to me.

Marion Boyd (cited in Lawrence 1994, 3), a Canadian politician, expresses similar sentiments:

Besides verbal attacks and the manipulation of tone, other forms of behaviour are harder to quantify. This behaviour comprises a range of efforts to humiliate and intimidate members, usually women (it's not reserved for women I hasten to add) as they fulfil their electoral roles in the House. Non-verbal tactics including significantly increasing volume – that is, more heckling, coughing and hissing when a women rises to speak, introducing a wall of sound before she has even started her words, blowing kisses across the floor of the house and mocking the high pitched voices of female members.

For women parliamentarians walking the line between being perceived either as too masculine or as too feminine constitutes a fine balancing act that exacts high costs from those who fail. As Australian ALP member Carmen Lawrence (1994, 3-4) has argued:

> If you are not able to hold your own in that company, you will fail. You will not become a minister, you will not become Leader of the Opposition, you will not become a senior front bencher. And one of the difficult things for women in parliament is the fact that they have, if you like, a disposition because of their upbringing, not because of their great virtue, I hasten to add, to be more polite, to be less critical, to be less rowdy, not to engage in interjections.

Lawrence goes on to argue that 'it is a case of the institution demanding certain responses and the failure to provide them meaning that you will no longer be part of the institution.' It is not only the masculine mode of behaviour within Parliament that is a hurdle for the feminist electoral project, but also the way the institution deals with 'women's issues.' Feminist politicians in both Australia and Canada have found that their attempts to use Parliament as a vehicle for reform have been undermined by the prevailing culture. One of the main challenges for these women has been to get their male colleagues to take their concerns in areas such as childcare, domestic violence, and sexual assault seriously. Reactions of male politicians in both parliaments to such issues range from genuine misunderstanding to blatant disrespect. For instance, in Canada in 1982 the male members in the House of Commons greeted a report on wife-battering with jeers and laughter (Levan 1996, 328). In Australia, Senator Susan Ryan (1994) experienced much hostility and personal abuse from other parliamentary members when steering through reforms in the area of sex discrimination and affirmative action. In both Australia and Canada issues relating to abortion and women's right to choose remain highly contentious, with parties on all sides unwilling to enforce a partisan position on the issue. Women's movement activists in both countries have been frustrated in using insider and outsider strategies in relation to Parliament. Consequently, they have looked to other political institutions (i.e., the bureaucracy and the courts in Australia, and the Charter of Rights and Freedoms in Canada) to give them control over reproductive rights.

There is nothing to indicate that the normative hurdles faced by feminists in relation to Parliament cannot be overcome. Because norms are not static it is possible for them to be changed to make the parliamentary arena more conducive to a feminist electoral project. There are some signs of a shift occurring. As a result of pressure from female politicians, changes have been introduced to the operation of Parliament. These have involved changing sitting hours as well as curbing blatant forms of sexist behaviour (for a discussion of changes in the Canadian Parliaments, see Burt and Lorenzin 1997, 211; for Australia see Broughton and Zetlin 1996, 60). However, the point to be emphasized here is that nominal gender representation does not necessarily lead to substantive gender representation. It is not just the number of women but, rather, their feminist orientation that makes the difference.

Structural Barriers

Within Australia and Canada structural features of Parliament have worked to reinforce the normative obstacles faced by feminists. The two most important of these, partisanship and regionalism, have operated to a greater or lesser degree in each country as impediments to a feminist electoral project. Partisanship has been a particularly powerful force in the Australian Parliament, making it difficult for feminist politicians, regardless of upon which side of the political divide they sit, to get their issues onto the political agenda. In Australia feminists have found it particularly hard to act as 'representatives of women' on the floor of Parliament or to work across party lines to come to a common position on issues relating to women. Of course, there have been occasions when this has occurred. For example, in the early 1980s women senators worked across party lines to bring on an adjournment debate on the UN Convention on the Elimination of All Forms of Discrimination against Women (see Sullivan 1994, 25). In the early 1990s, women parliamentarians in the NSW legislative council staged a mass walkout during a debate on the criminalization of abortion (see Morgan 1993, 28). However, these examples are exceptions to the rule. As Broughton and Zetlin (1996) argue, in general it appears that faction, party, and constituency – rather than gender – continue to be the primary factors determining the voting behaviour of women MPs within the Australian Parliaments.

Within the Canadian context, women legislators have had a greater capacity to work across party lines in order to advance certain women's issues. In 1990 women from different parties united to form the Association of Women Parliamentarians (AWP). The AWP was not established to deal with policy issues per se; rather, it served as a network that enabled female MPs to discuss such common issues as electoral reform. Canadian women MPs have also shown a greater willingness than their Australian contemporaries to cross the floor to vote on issues directly related to women. In recent years women parliamentarians have joined together to vote on issues such as abortion and the rights of Aboriginal women under the charter. According to former Senator Lorna Marsden (1993, 45) informal caucusing is also a common occurrence: 'I think there is a women's caucus. It is not organized and does not meet at Thursday lunch, for example, but when there is interest, people do caucus. It is a network as opposed to a caucus, but it works across party lines; it works between the House and the Senate. It exists. There is an information flow.'

If Canadian female parliamentarians have been able to work across party lines, they have also had to contend with another important cleavage within the Canadian Parliament – regionalism. In Canada, regional political issues have long been a central concern, no matter which party is in power. Regionalism has been the subject dominating House of Commons debates; it helps determine who is appointed to the Senate and, as discussed below, to decide who is appointed to Cabinet. Canadian governments' preoccupation with regionalism has made it difficult for women MPs, and the women's movement in general, to raise issues related to women within the parliamentary arena. An exception to this occurs when women's issues and regional issues coincide (e.g., during the charter debates). Overall, as Young (1997, 91) notes, regionalism has operated as one of the main constraints on the feminist electoral project in Canada.

One important difference between the Australian and Canadian political systems is the existence in Canada of the Charter of Rights and Freedoms. Although the charter reaffirms parliamentary sovereignty and the Westminster system,[17] in practice the role of Parliament has diminished since the charter came into effect in 1982. There is debate about the extent to which the charter has led to the 'judicialization of politics' and about whether this enhances or reduces democracy in Canada (see Cairns 1995b for the former view; see Mandel 1994 for the latter). Nevertheless, it is generally agreed that there has been a fundamental shift of power away from the parliamentary arena towards the courts, 'encourag[ing] citizens and groups to achieve their interests through the courts and the legal process' (Simeon 1994, 33). As discussed in Chapter 5, this shift has functioned to discourage feminists from focusing on the legislature and to encourage them to pursue gender issues such as equality, abortion, pornography, and sexual assault within the legal and constitutional arena.

Another set of constraints confronting Australian and Canadian feminists in relation to Parliament relates to the domination of the Cabinet over the legislature. This is a phenomenon common to most Westminster systems. Over time, as legislative decisions have become more complex and political parties have become more powerful, there has been a gradual shift in power away from the legislature towards the executive. With the ability to decide the legislative agenda, Cabinet has come to dominate the legislature. As a result, it has become more important than ever that not only the legislature, but also the Cabinet, represents a range of interests – including gender. In practice, in both Australia and Canada women in general, and feminists in particular, have been excluded from the executive. And for those few who have gained entry into this inner sanctum, it has been difficult to raise gender equity issues.

In Australia, between 1975 and 1996, there was only one woman in the federal Cabinet at any one time, except for the period between 1989 and 1990, when there were no women at all. After the 1996 election two women were appointed to Cabinet, but this increase came nowhere near to reflecting the extent of the increase in female members on the government benches (from eleven to twenty-five). A major stumbling block for women's entry into the Australian Cabinet is party dominance of both state and federal parliaments. The practice employed by the ALP – caucus election of Cabinet members – has meant that factionalism has been central to the selection procedure (Simms 1996, 29). Under such a system, 'merit' and other concerns, such as the need to strike a balance along regional or gender lines, have been at best secondary considerations. Just as they have in pre-selection, backroom deals to determine factional nominations for Cabinet posts have worked to exclude women from ministerial positions in ALP governments. Under Liberal/National coalition governments Cabinet selection procedures are left to the prime minister's or premier's discretion. Yet it can be argued that women have not fared any better under these arrangements. Female Liberal and National Party backbenchers must contend with different problems, including those of patronage (see Jaensch 1994, 121). For women who, traditionally, have not been influential in either parliamentary party, this system clearly works to their disadvantage. Furthermore, in establishing the Cabinet, coalition governments have also been preoccupied with balancing urban and rural interests (121), which has had the effect of pushing other interests, including those related to gender, further into the background.

Even where there have been improvements in the number of women in the Australian Cabinet, there has been no guarantee that they will represent feminist concerns. Those who do, do so at their own risk. The inclination of many ALP women towards feminist principles has meant that under Labor governments there has been a greater chance that female Cabinet members will act as advocates for women's issues. This was certainly the case with the first female ALP Cabinet member, Senator Susan Ryan, who, despite widespread community opposition, pushed to have Cabinet support the introduction of sex discrimination legislation (Ryan 1999). But advancing this agenda had its costs. As Ryan explains: 'If I had not been "distracted" as my colleagues saw it, by these campaigns for women, and had avoided the constant fuss and resentments they provoked, I might have had a longer and calmer voyage through parliament. But I wasn't there to get the long-service medal' (283).

Under coalition governments, the presence of women in Cabinet has not resulted in a higher profile for feminist concerns within the political executive. Indeed, in some respects, such as in the case of Jocelyn Newman, the opposite could be said to be the case. Acting as minister for the Status of Women, Newman has supported such measures as reducing funding commitments to feminist organizations (including WEL) and for public childcare, at the same time as she has advocated support for an anti-feminist lone father's lobby organization (Cadzow 2000).

In Canada, the barriers women face in relation to Cabinet have been slightly different from those faced by Australian women. Although, as in Australia, prospective women ministers are frustrated by a lack of party support, they also have an added impediment: in Canada, federal Cabinet selection is determined first and foremost on the basis of 'the geographic diversity and cultural duality' of the country (Smith 1990, 366). As Smith argues: 'It is misleading to depict the Cabinet as no more than a collection of sectional "veto groups"... but it is equally erroneous to ignore the durable effect of a federalized Cabinet on policy formation. Canada is still a country of sharply divided regions, with geographic and cultural boundaries that enclose distinctive ways of life, and the Cabinet continues, as it always has, to reflect this fact' (Smith 1990, 373).

In recent years, successive Canadian federal governments have tended to be more willing to select women for Cabinet posts than have successive Australian governments. Until 1984 no more than three women had been appointed at any one time to federal Cabinet. However, Mulroney maintained six women in his Cabinet, and, during the second term of the Chrétien government, nine women were in the executive. Improvements are also obvious at the provincial level, especially where NDP governments have been in office. For example, in British Columbia, under the Harcourt NDP government, women held 33 percent of the government positions and 31 percent of the Cabinet positions. When the NDP held office in Saskatchewan between 1991 and 1995, women made up 20 percent of the NDP caucus and 17 percent of Cabinet. In the Rae NDP government in Ontario, eleven of the twenty-six members of Cabinet were women. By contrast, in 1995 under the Alberta PC government, only 5.4 percent of the Cabinet was female.

However, just as in the Australian case, the number of women in Canadian cabinets has not necessarily led to feminist-inspired legislation. Again it is apparent that this has more to do with the party in office than with the number of women in the executive. As has already been noted, under the PC Mulroney government, female Cabinet members did little to support a feminist agenda, while some, including Minister for Women Barbara MacDougall, demonstrated outright hostility towards feminist issues and activists. In the provinces we find that NDP governments have tended to be supportive of women's issues. For instance, in 1991 the NDP government in British Columbia created the first Canadian free-standing ministry of women's equality and provided it with a substantial budget (Erickson 1997, 123; for Ontario, see Byrne 1997). While the presence of

NDP governments has given feminists a boost in the provinces, due to the barriers created by the Canadian electoral system it has not been able to open up the same opportunities at the federal level.

External Engagement with Parliament

Obstacles at the party, electoral, and parliamentary levels have combined to make it difficult for feminists to pursue an 'inside' electoral strategy. Nevertheless, members of the women's movement in both countries have lobbied Parliament from outside in an attempt to have politicians introduce legislation favourable to women. In both cases, alliances have been made between feminists inside and outside Parliament in attempts to influence the legislative agenda. Parliamentary committees have provided an important forum within which these links may be made.

In Australia, WEL and other women's organizations have frequently given evidence to parliamentary committees on mainstream issues that have an impact on women, including matrimonial property law, industrial relations, and tariff protection, to name a few. Feminist organizations have also been instrumental in pressuring for, and participating in, committees that deal directly with women's issues. The most obvious example is the inquiry undertaken in Australia between 1989 and 1992 by the House of Representatives Standing Committee on Legal and Constitutional Affairs into equal opportunity and equal status for women. Seventy-three women's groups presented submissions to the committee. The *Half Way to Equal Report* (1992) produced by the committee was ground-breaking in that it was the first sustained investigation into women's issues undertaken by the Australian Parliament. It was followed in 1994 by the Senate Standing Committee on Legal and Constitutional Affairs inquiry into gender bias and the judiciary. In recent years, the Joint Standing Committee on Electoral Matters has also undertaken an investigation into the reasons for the under-representation of women in Parliament. The efficacy of these inquiries, at least as far as feminists are concerned, is, however, questionable. As Sawer (1997b) points out: 'None of these inquiries or reports told us anything we didn't know.'

Canadian feminists have also lobbied the legislature from outside with regard to issues of concern to women. NAC and other women's groups have been active in giving evidence to parliamentary committees in a range of areas, including the charter, unemployment, free trade, the Court Challenges Program (which provides funding for organizations involved in court challenges under the charter), electoral reform, and gun control. Women's groups have also played a role in pressuring the legislature to create subcommittees to investigate issues directly related to women, including the issue of equality rights (which resulted in the Royal Commission on Equality in Employment, also known as the Abella Commission) (see *Feminist Action* vol. 3, 1985). Another significant parliamentary inquiry involved the Canadian Panel on Violence against Women, which was created in 1990 as a direct result of feminist pressure after the antifeminist-inspired Montreal Massacre (see Levan 1996, 335-51).

There is one arena related to the parliamentary sphere within which Canadian feminists have been particularly successful, especially when compared with their Australian counterparts – the arena concerning royal commissions. Royal commissions, which are a unique feature of Westminster systems, have been used for a variety of political purposes. In both Australia and Canada, governments have used such bodies as a way of 'shelving' difficult policy problems (see Simeon, cited in Jenson 1994, 62, fn. 5; Prasser 1994, 8). However, in Canada royal commissions have also been seen as 'core institutions of representation' and have become major 'supporters and funders of research' (Jenson 1994, 41, 59). This has meant that feminists, as well as other social actors, have faced a relatively favourable POS in relation to this institution and have conducted themselves accordingly.[18] Not only have feminists successfully lobbied to have Parliament establish commissions to address policy issues specifically concerning women, but individual feminist 'experts' have been instrumental in shaping the research agenda and/or tenor of royal commission reports (see Begin 1992; Arscott 1995b, 71).[19]

The Canadian Royal Commission on the Status of Women was pivotal in providing a forum for the representation of women's interests, while its forty research papers, as well as its final report, provided the burgeoning women's movement with the background material from which it could formulate its future objectives. During the 1980s feminists were given the chance to pursue specific women's interests through a number of other royal commissions. In 1987 NAC joined with the Canadian Commission on New Reproductive Technologies to push for the creation of a Royal Commission on New Reproductive Technologies (RCNRT) (see *Feminist Action* vol. 2, no. 7, 1987). The lobbying efforts of the coalition proved to be successful, and in 1989 the RCNRT was established.

Feminists have also been actively involved in other commissions that have dealt with more general policy issues. Both the 1985 MacDonald Commission (on Economic Union and Development Prospects for Canada) and the 1991 Royal Commission on Electoral Reform and Party Financing (RCERPF) received detailed submissions from women's groups such as NAC (see *Feminist Action* vol. 1, no. 2, 1985; *Action Now* vol. 2, no. 4, 1992). As a result of feminist pressure, the latter also undertook extensive research into the issue of women's representation (for two excellent discussions of the RCERPF, see Jenson 1994; Arscott 1995b).

Success in lobbying a government to establish a royal commission, or to participate in its hearings, does not ensure feminist policy outcomes.

Members of the Canadian women's movement became cognizant of this during their dealings with the RCNRT. Although feminists had fought for the creation of this inquiry, once it was established they adopted a highly critical position on it. Their criticism related to the commission's seemingly flawed methodology and unrepresentative nature. With the backing of an extensive range of women's groups, NAC withdrew its support for the inquiry during the course of the proceedings and rejected the recommendations of the report (see *Action Now* vol. 2, no. 3, 1992; vol. 2, no. 6, 1992). NAC was also disappointed with the RCERPF report because it rejected NAC's suggestion of adopting a PR electoral system (Arscott 1995b, 58).

Parliamentary committees in both countries, and royal commissions in Canada, have obviously provided an avenue for feminist input into legislation and policies. However, as power has accrued to the political and administrative executive, it has become obvious to many social activists in both countries that the main game, in terms of influencing policy, lies elsewhere. Matthews and Warhurst (1993, 89) make this point in relation to Australia: 'As a result of its eclipse by the executive, Parliament is used mainly as second resort when efforts to influence ministers or the bureaucracy have failed. Intensive lobbying against a bill generally indicates that the hostile pressure groups have been unsuccessful in their representations to the relevant minister.' Pross (1990, 289) suggests that the same process has occurred in Canada: 'The political executive and senior administrators have worked out the basic form of public policy. Consequently, lobbyists and others wanting to influence public policy have done so by approaching and persuading civil servants and cabinet Ministers rather than parliamentarians.'

As Chapter 4 illustrates, majoritarian feminist activists in Australia and Canada have long been aware of the importance of the bureaucracy with regard to achieving their objectives. For those operating in Australia, the POS within the bureaucracy has been much more favourable than has that within the parliamentary realm; and, not surprisingly, feminists have been more inclined to engage with this institution both as 'femocrat' insiders and as lobbyists. Parliament may have been a closed structure as far as feminists are concerned, but this is by no means the end of the story. Feminists have looked to other, more open and favourable, institutions to achieve their objectives.

4

The Femocrat Strategy: Challenging Bureaucratic Norms and Structures

Faced with a number of hurdles in the parliamentary realm, majoritarian feminists in Australia and Canada have looked to other institutions to pursue their aims. Not surprisingly, they have been drawn towards those institutions that will provide them with the best chances of achieving their equality goals. For feminists in Australia, this has meant looking towards the federal and state bureaucracies, where they have been able to exploit opportunities to their own ends. Once inside, feminists have not only been able to take advantage of existing openings, but they have also been able to create new ones. Anglo-Canadian feminists have also attempted to engage with bureaucratic structures at the federal and provincial levels but with less success. Although feminists have made some inroads in certain provinces, overall they have met with constraints in the bureaucratic arena that have stymied a 'femocrat' strategy. Confronted with a variety of barriers at the bureaucratic level, and a more favourable political opportunity structure within the legal and constitutional realms, Anglo-Canadian feminists have understandably directed more attention towards the latter.

In assessing the political opportunities and constraints faced by Australian and Canadian feminists in the bureaucratic arena, the focus here is not the entry into the bureaucracy of women per se but, rather, the engagement of majoritarian feminist activists with this arena. To be precise, the focus is on what has come to be known as state feminism (see Stetson and Mazur 1995), which I refer to as the 'femocrat strategy.' The term femocrat is an Australian neologism and has been applied in a number of senses. It has been used pejoratively by conservatives, who see these women as representing a select band of 'special interests' in the bureaucracy. Other feminists have also used it as a term of derision and abuse, seeing those within the bureaucracy as selling out the women's movement and profiting from women's disadvantage (Summers 1986, 60). However, some femocrats have appropriated the phrase to define themselves and have imbued the term with a more positive meaning. According to

Eisenstein (1996), the sense in which the term is used by femocrats reflects their praxis. In its 'original' usage, it referred to: 'A feminist woman who had entered the public service bureaucracy to advance the cause of women and whose responsibilities were defined in this manner by male bureaucrats or politicians who appointed her' (68). Due to the movement of femocrats out of designated 'women's policy' positions into the mainstream of the bureaucracy, the term has undergone a redefinition and has come to be understood by its practitioners as 'a powerful woman within government administration, with an ideological and political commitment to feminism' (ibid.). The sense in which the term 'femocrat project' is used in the following discussion draws upon this definition, referring to the entry of feminists into all areas of the bureaucracy in an effort to influence public policy making through a feminist perspective.

When evaluating the results of the femocrat strategy, the critical measure is the extent to which feminist activists have been influential within the bureaucracy. Following Malloy's (1999, 268) work on advocacy structures in the Ontario civil service, 'influence' is understood to relate to 'the power to develop policy, compel co-ordination, and ensure implementation.' The particular concern is with the extent to which feminists have been able to act autonomously with regard to applying a gender analysis to public policy making. Autonomy here refers to the extent to which femocrats have been able to operate independently of the women's movement when the need arises. Autonomy is a Janus-faced value. In its positive guise, it enables femocrats to act swiftly to take advantage of opportunities inside the bureaucratic institutions which, because of their opaqueness, may not be apparent to those outside. Without some degree of autonomy, femocrats would find that a window of reform had closed before they had had time to act. In its negative guise, autonomy diminishes the degree of accountability that femocrats have to the broader feminist community. The following discussion considers the extent to which femocrats have been able to walk this fine line between taking advantage of openings while still being accessible and answerable to the concerns of those lobbying from outside.

A second measure of femocrat success has been the extent to which they have been able to achieve an entrenched position within the bureaucracy. This refers to their location within the bureaucracy – whether at the centre or the periphery – and the permanency of their position. There is some debate within the feminist literature about the pros and cons of the location of femocrat positions. There are heavy arguments favouring a strong central position, such as in the Department of Cabinet or Privy Council, that is close to the locus of power. Others argue that this is a precarious location, easily abolished by incoming governments hostile to a femocrat project, and so favour a devolved approach where femocrat officers are situated within line agencies across the service. Although more diffuse, this model enables femocrats to cover the detail of policy. Most ideal is a model that straddles both the centre and the periphery, allowing for greater security, access to power, and a depth of knowledge about specific policy issues.

Judging the project by these two measures, Australian feminists have achieved a greater degree of success than have their Canadian counterparts. In Australia femocrats have exercised a significant degree of influence, bringing a gender perspective to bear on public policy making in a range of areas. In order to achieve this degree of influence, they have at times needed to operate autonomously. While this autonomy has sometimes created tensions with other feminist activists, it has also meant that femocrats have made inroads in policy areas not articulated by the broader movement. Although Canadian feminists have been able to achieve some degree of institutionalization at the federal level and in some provinces, they have tended to be located on the periphery and have lacked central influence. Moreover, they have struggled to assert a feminist policy perspective, especially in mainstream economic policy areas.

Femocrat Strategy in Australia and Canada: Policy Machinery and Outcomes

Australian and Canadian feminists have had very different experiences with regard to engaging with the bureaucracy. Both in terms of their institutional position and their policy influence – two key indicators of success – Australian feminists have achieved more than have their Canadian counterparts. Before analyzing the POS that has helped to shape these outcomes, it is important to outline the nature of their differences.

Australian Women's Policy Machinery

The Australian femocrat strategy began soon after the election of the Whitlam Labor government in 1972. Although, as noted earlier, there was some disquiet within the feminist community about entering the state, many were keen to take advantage of the opening presented by the election of a seemingly progressive government.[1] It was not surprising then that, when the prime minister advertised in 1973 for an adviser on women's affairs, over 400 women, many of who were prominent feminists, applied for the position (L. Ryan 1990, 74). The successful candidate, Elizabeth Reid, a university tutor and member of the Women's Liberation Movement in Canberra, saw the position as 'a reasonably genuine invitation to really try and get some ... things done' (Eisenstein 1996, 20). That most of the other sixteen shortlisted, but unsuccessful, applicants entered 'women's policy' areas of the bureaucracy soon afterwards suggests that they shared Reid's sentiments. In the following decade several hundred feminists were to enter the bureaucracy at the state and federal levels to work as femocrats.

The appointment of Elizabeth Reid to the position of Whitlam's adviser on women marked the beginning of Australian feminists' direct engagement with policy making. However, Reid was not in the public service proper but, rather, was a member of the prime minister's staff. It was not until 1974 that feminists actually entered the public service, when Sara Dowse, another Canberra feminist activist, was appointed to head the Women's Affairs Section in the Prime Minister and Cabinet Department. From the start, femocrats were keen to have a women's coordinating agency located within a central department such as PM&C rather than to have to create a separate department that they feared would become 'a waste-paper basket for women's problems' (Sawer 1996b, 5). With access to Cabinet documents and close contact with the prime minister, the Women's Affairs Section became the centre of the women's policy machinery.

In November 1975 the Liberal/National coalition government under Malcolm Fraser replaced the Whitlam Labor government. Despite concern that the femocrat strategy would be jeopardized by the change of government, initially this proved not to be the case. Between 1975 and 1977 femocrats were provided with an opportunity to establish an extensive network of women's agencies, thus further entrenching their position within the public service. The Women's Affairs Branch (WAB) was retained within PM&C, in line with Fraser's objective of making his department the supreme policy-making body (Sawer 1990, 33). With the central position of the branch secured, Sara Dowse set about developing what Sawer (1990, 30) defined as a 'wheel' model, which was to become the hallmark for women's policy machinery in Australia. Under the wheel model 'functional experts examine[d] policy at its point of origin for its impact on women, backed up by a strong co-ordinating body with access to all cabinet submissions.' Working with this model, the government established ten new women's units across a range of departments and statutory authorities, each of which reported back to the WAB in the PM&C. It also created an inter-departmental working group to help coordinate the development of women's policies. In 1978 an independent National Women's Advisory Council (NWAC) was established to provide government with a mechanism for consulting with women in the community.

During the second term of the Fraser government, femocrats found themselves in an increasingly tenuous position. After the government was returned to office in 1977, it transferred the central women's agency to the junior ministry of Department of Home Affairs and Environment and appointed a minister who turned out to be hostile to the objectives of the agency. Dowse resigned in protest. Without access to Cabinet submissions and a central location, the WAB found it very difficult to maintain its role as coordinator in the wheel of women's agencies. The branch had a very low profile during this period. Lyndall Ryan (1990, 81), a former femocrat, saw this as a double edged position: '[It was a] boon because feminist bureaucrats could do things without attracting attention from the Right – or giving credit to the Fraser government; and a curse because no-one knew what the femocrats were doing.' In 1981 the Review of Commonwealth Functions abolished most of the 'spokes' of the women's policy machinery (i.e., the women's units in a range of departments). By 1983 the wheel of women's machinery was essentially moribund.

With the election of the Hawke Labor government in 1983, federal women's policy-making machinery was given a boost, with most of the spokes being re-established, and it was to remain in a relatively strong position throughout the next thirteen years of ALP government. Prior to coming to office, the ALP demonstrated an understanding of the importance of having a centrally located unit, arguing that, with its return to PM&C: 'The [Status of Women] Office's access to essential government information would be restored, and it would be possible to brief Cabinet on the likely impact on women of all proposals before it. Most importantly, the Prime Minister would confer status and authority on a function that inevitably involves sensitive consultations with other Ministers and their Departments' (ALP 1983, cited in Summers 1986, 63).

On election, the ALP acted on this understanding by reinstating the hub of women's policy machinery, now entitled the Office of the Status of Women (OSW), in PM&C and enhancing the position of women's machinery in line departments. Throughout the Hawke and Keating ministries the women's policy machinery consisted of the OSW in PM&C; women's units and 'desk officers' within departments; an Equal Employment Opportunity Bureau in the Public Service Board; and, until 1993, a National Women's Consultancy Council. At the same time, femocrats began to move out of specifically designated women's agencies into mainstream policy areas, extending their influence throughout the bureaucracy.

From its central position in PM&C, the OSW has found it easy to attract the attention of the prime minister of the day as well as to enjoy the clout that comes with being in a central position in its relations with other departments. As a head of the OSW during the Hawke/Keating period noted: 'We are able to use our position in the prime minister's department in our dealing with other agencies to ensure that we get their compliance' (interview with author, 1995). The Office of the Status of Women's institutional position has, at various times, been further enhanced by strong support from feminist ministers within the Cabinet. The 1983 appointment of Senator Susan Ryan to the position of minister assisting the prime minister on the status of women helped to draw Cabinet attention to feminist policy initiatives. There was an absence of strong Cabinet support during the late 1980s, when women's affairs was relegated to junior ministers, but it was regained under Keating when high-profile Cabinet minister and former WA premier Carmen Lawrence was appointed to the position of minister for women's affairs. The appointment of Lawrence, who was well known for her commitment to feminist issues and who was a former WEL member, was seen by femocrats as a crucial development. In the view of a senior femocrat at the time: 'Having a minister for women's affairs in Cabinet has been very important. The fact that the minister has been Carmen Lawrence, who is intelligent, interested, and a good advocate in Cabinet for women's issues, has been especially important' (interview with author, 1995).

Feminists were not only making inroads within the federal bureaucracy throughout the 1970s and 1980s, but they were also making inroads within the states. Between 1976 and 1990 each state and territory responded to feminist agitation to create women's policy machinery, with most adopting the hubs-and-spokes model that had been implemented at the Commonwealth level. As with the Commonwealth, state ALP governments demonstrated a willingness to appoint women active in the feminist community to head these agencies. In the states, key feminist appointments have included Carmel Niland, Helen L'Orange, and Robyn Henderson (NSW); Mary Draper (Vic); Carmel O'Loughlin (SA); and Liz Little (Tasmania).

Since the election of the conservative Howard government in March 1996, the OSW has been maintained within PM&C. However, budget cuts of 38 percent have meant that the office has had to reduce its staff from forty-eight to thirty-one and reduce its functions (Harford 1996, A5). At the same time, many of the spokes of the women's policy machinery have been abolished or downgraded. The Women's Statistics Unit, co-funded by the OSW, has been disbanded. According to Margo Kingston of the *Sydney Morning Herald,* 8 March 1997 (p. 40), the adoption of a mainstreaming strategy has also seen the OSW hand over some of its functions, such as its central register of women for government board appointments, to line departments. Prominent feminists were negative towards the 1996 appointment of former political journalist Pru Goward to head the OSW. Although some felt that her high profile would draw attention to the work of the OSW (see Wright 1997, 13), others, such as WEL founder Beatrice Faust (cited in Hawes 1997) criticized her appointment because of her weak links with the women's movement and her lack of bureaucratic experience. Goward resigned her position in October 1999, and the government took over six months to announce a replacement. Former femocrat Anne Summers (cited in Cadzow 2000, 23) laments the decline of the OSW under Howard, stating that, although the coalition government 'decided not to abolish it ... they might as well have for all the good it does.'

Canadian Women's Policy Machinery

The creation of women's policy machinery at the federal level in Canada differed from the Australian experience in terms of its personnel as well as in terms of its institutional position. The impetus for the creation of the machinery was also unique. The 1971 decision of the Trudeau government to establish the first designated women's policy agency – the Office of the Co-ordinator for the Status of Women in the Privy Council Office[2] – came not so much from the women's movement as from the government itself. The government was conscious of the need to be seen to be addressing the 1970 Report on the Royal Commission on the Status of Women (Heitlinger 1993, 81). This rationale also underpinned the establishment of other agencies at the federal level. Between 1971 and 1974 the government created the Office of Equal Opportunity in the Public Service Commission and the Canadian Advisory Council on the Status of Women (CACSW), and it also appointed advisers in the Departments of Justice, Health and Welfare, Secretary of State, and Employment and Immigration.

Unlike in Australia, in Canada feminists did not rush to join the bureaucracy. Although the first coordinator of the Status of Women, Freda Paltiel, encouraged input from the women's movement during the development of these initial agencies (Morris 1982, 296), other feminists were not encouraged to enter the civil service itself. According to O'Neil and Sutherland (1997, 207), this set the pattern for future years. Rather than working within the state, the movement entered into a 'strategic alliance,' where it would work from outside with key public servants to bring about incremental change. The movement helped to set the terms of this relationship. While Canadian feminists were supportive of the development of women's policy machinery, they did not show a strong interest in being directly involved in the structures that were being created within the state. In contrast to the Australian femocrats, they did not debate the form this machinery should take (see Arscott, Rankin, and Vickers n.d.). According to one of the first Canadian femocrats, Sue Findlay (1995, 83), these bodies 'were not considered noteworthy by the women's groups that had just spent a number of years defining the need for government action to improve the status of women in Canada.' In 1972, when the government first established women's policy mechanisms, most members of the movement stayed outside and concentrated on lobbying the government to fund the 1972 Strategy for Change Conference. From the outset then, members of the movement demonstrated a preference for effecting change by working from outside rather than inside the bureaucracy.

In direct contrast to Australia, Canadian women's policy machinery (with the exception, for a time, of the Women's Program, which is discussed below) came to be staffed by career civil servants rather than by femocrats. As a former Canadian femocrat states: 'Civil servants in women's policy agencies ... have seldom been drawn directly from activists in the women's movement. Rather, they were career civil servants who happened to be women and happened to be sufficiently committed to women's rights that they were prepared to accept the job of femocrat' (Geller-Schwartz 1995, 57).

Findlay (1987, 38) has described the first appointments to women's agencies as 'public servants, generally unprepared to challenge the existing procedures and priorities, particularly from a feminist perspective.' The initial appointments to the position of coordinator for the status of women fit this mould. While the first coordinator, Freda Paltiel (1990, 4), was a career public servant who was a self-defined feminist, many of her successors avoided the feminist appellation. Martha Hynna, Paltiel's replacement, was a lawyer and civil servant who did not label herself a feminist (Morris 1982, 335), while another head of the agency, Loranger, had no experience with women's issues and, according to one report, considered the job 'simply as another step in her eleven year career as a public servant' (344). The 1976 appointment of Maureen O'Neil, a bureaucrat who had been active in the Ottawa women's movement, broke the pattern for a short time. However, after her appointment, the practice of appointing career public servants continued. And the pattern of staffing of women's policy machinery with career public servants rather than feminists has been reproduced at the provincial level (see Malloy 1999, 274-5; Rankin and Vickers 1998).

Initially, the Women's Program, established in 1974 within the federal Department of Secretary of State in order to fund women's groups to develop projects to advance the status of women, was an exception to the norm. The head of the program, and the staff appointed to work in the agency, fit the femocrat archetype much more closely than did their peers in other federal women's agencies. The staff and modus operandi of the Women's Program were both overtly feminist. According to Sue Findlay (1987, 40), the first director of the program: 'All [personnel] were defined as feminists and were largely drawn from feminist groups ... A feminist perspective clearly determined the Program's development, and was reflected in project definition, staff recruitment, and the Program's organization and management.'

In her capacity as director, Sue Findlay strongly influenced the orientation of the agency. She had come to the position with a background in the New Left Movement and the burgeoning Canadian feminist movement of the 1960s, and she was firmly committed to advancing the interests of grassroots feminist organizations by using the resources of the administrative state. Her commitment was informed by a belief that it was possible to take advantage of particular political moments 'to liberate the resources of the state for the purposes of reform' (1995, 94).

Nineteen seventy-five, International Women's Year (IWY), proved to be the high-water mark for the Women's Program. The government had initially wanted to devote IWY resources to the promotion of its own priorities on women's issues but bowed to pressure from the Women's Program, the CACSW, and women's groups to allocate some of the money to the program. It provided half of the five-million-dollar budget to the Women's Program to fund seminars and cultural programs, and to provide grants to women's groups and individual women to develop their own projects (Geller-Schwartz 1995, 46). The decision to allocate the funds in this way was seen by women both inside and outside the bureaucracy as a win for femocrats, confirming the view held by some that the state could sometimes be used to advance women's interests.

The sense of victory was short-lived. As Geller-Schwartz explains:

> As soon as International Women's Year was over, the central agencies resolved to bring the 'wild-eyed' feminists under control. This was done by imposing, in the name of efficiency and accountability, a bureaucratic procedure for allocating grants so burdensome that the staff in the Women's Program felt they no longer had time to work with the women's movement. The feminist perspective in the bureaucracy had lost its material base. (46)

In terms of its orientation, the Women's Program was unable to maintain its 'radical intent,' instead shifting its focus away from direct consultation with grassroots feminist organizations towards funding national and status of women's groups who fit more neatly within the government's equal opportunity agenda (Findlay 1995, 229). During the last twenty years, strict guidelines have ensured that funding has been provided only to those organizations that conform to government priorities, while organizations dealing with contentious issues, including lesbianism and abortion, have been ruled ineligible to apply.

Since the 1970s there has been an effort to cultivate expertise in gender analysis within women's agencies in the Canadian federal civil service, and many women working in these areas have been politicized by their experiences (Karman 1996). However, the overtly feminist strategy adopted during the early years of the Women's Program has not continued. According to two senior bureaucrats in the SWC, in recent years most appointees to positions in women's agencies in Ottawa have had an interest in, and knowledge of, feminism, but it has not been usual for them to be outwardly feminist or to use this term to define themselves (interviews with author, Ottawa, 4 October 1995; 27 November 1995). This pattern appears to be replicated at the provincial level. At least in Ontario and British Columbia, two provinces with established women's policy machinery, staff tend to be seconded from other agencies regardless of their background in 'women's policy' or their commitment to feminist principles (see Malloy 1999, 274; Teghtsoonian 2000). Quebec appears to be an exception to the rule in this regard. Appointments to the Quebec Conseil du statut de la femme have been likely to come from feminist backgrounds and have tended to be well regarded by the Quebec feminist community (Rankin and Vickers 1998).

Another obvious difference between the Australian and Canadian femocrat experience relates to the location of women's policy machinery within the bureaucracy. Unlike in Australia, where the Office of the Status of Women has, for all but a brief period, been situated within the central coordinating department of PM&C, in Canada the femocrats have had a less central, and weaker, institutional base. Initially, the women's policy machinery was established within the Privy Council Office (PCO) – the significance of which was not lost on its founder, Freda Paltiel (1997, 29): 'The strategic position [within the PCO] of the co-ordinator [for status of women] was a crucial factor, enabling the integration of a gender perspective into all policy issues.' However, in 1976 the Office of the Co-ordinator for the Status of Women was removed from the central coordination agency to become a separate department (the Status of Women Canada [SWC]) – a move that made it difficult for the office to gain access to crucial Cabinet minutes.

Operating as a stand-alone department, the SWC was expected to act as the central coordinating agency within a system of women's policy machinery that spanned the Canadian civil service. Since 1976, under the direction of Minister Marc Lalonde, other agencies were expected to 'integrate' women's policy issues into their agenda. Under the Lalonde model, each department was to establish an internal branch to provide input on women's issues in policy and program development. The push towards integration was reinforced in 1978 through the policy document *Towards Equality*, which provided the SWC with a plan through which it could reinforce the integration model and encourage departments to look at the implications of the government's policy on women. Although the SWC deemed the integration model a success (SWC 1993, cited in Geller-Schwartz 1995, 47), many other commentators were less enthusiastic. According to Findlay (1987, 44), the directives from the SWC were often vague, making it difficult for public servants in other agencies to give them substance. Former femocrat Geller-Schwartz (1995, 57) argued that 'repeated efforts to structure government to formally integrate women's interests were met with a wall of bureaucratic indifference, if not hostility.' Others felt that the integration strategy could never be successfully implemented because of the SWC's difficulty in carrying out its coordinating function. Operating as an independent agency, the SWC was unable to form the close links with other departments that would enable it to carry out either a coordinating or an advisory role (Burt 1990, 198, 208). According to Findlay (1987, 44), its peripheral position meant that the SWC has not had access to either 'formal authority or informal power.'

The weak institutional position of the SWC had further implications. Unlike the Australian OSW, which has been able to use its central location to secure the attention of the prime minister while relying on women's offices in line departments to influence other senior ministers, the SWC has found it difficult to gain a profile within the Canadian Cabinet. It has had to rely on the power and credibility of the minister responsible for the portfolio to draw the attention of the prime minister and Cabinet to the work of the agency (O'Neil and Sutherland 1997, 211). When senior Cabinet ministers have had responsibility for Status of Women issues, they have been able to use their position on key Cabinet committees to advance the position of the SWC, especially in relation to funding matters. However, there is nothing to guarantee that this portfolio responsibility will be given to a senior Cabinet member. Although the 1987 Neilsen review of government organization recommended that the minister responsible for the Status of Women be permanently represented on the key Priorities and Planning Committee in Cabinet, no action has been taken to implement this recommendation. At those times when ministers have not been members of the inner Cabinet (as was the case in 1994, with Sheila Finestone), they have had to seek leave to either join Cabinet in order to discuss an issue related to women or they have had to gain access to Cabinet submissions that might have had some bearing on such issues (O'Neil and Sutherland 1997, 219).

The Women's Program, which, alongside the SWC, has been a key feature of the women's machinery at the federal level, has had a relatively weak institutional position. Having survived the attack on it after IWY, the program remained in the Department of Secretary of State (SOS) but was forced to compete for attention and resources from other identity programs, especially those for indigenous and language communities. In 1993 the SOS was split in two and the Women's Program became part of the Department of Human Resources Development. Here the program 'sat in limbo for two years,' unable to fit neatly within the overriding economic focus of the department (Senior Policy Officer of Women's Program, interview with author, 1995). In 1995, in a move that consolidated the two most important federal women's agencies, the program became part of the SWC. The merger was beneficial for the SWC because, through the Women's Program, it was brought into contact with women's organizations with which, previously, it had had no relationship. However, the benefits for the Women's Program were not so direct. Although it now had access to SWC expertise and a minister who had responsibility for women's affairs, it was situated in a more marginalized department – one that had less clout in Cabinet (O'Neil and Sutherland 1997, 219).

The other main arm of Canada's women's machinery has been the Canadian Advisory Council on the Status of Women (CACSW), which existed between 1973 and 1995. The CACSW, also created in response to an RCSW recommendation, was established as a stand-alone government-funded organization with a mandate to advise the federal government on issues of interest and concern to women in Canada. Throughout its charter, the CACSW was noted for its 'excellent research' (Geller-Schwartz 1995, 45). However, its ability to perform its advocacy role was constantly questioned. The problem, according to many outside feminists, stemmed from the fact that the council was appointed by, and reported to, the government of the day rather than to Parliament (as the RCSW had recommended), thus casting a shadow over its independence. There was also a perception that overt feminists were not seen as acceptable members of the CACSW. As Morris (1982, 355) notes: 'Those identified as too single-minded in their commitment to an ideological position or cause have little hope of appointment in the council.' The decision to disband the council in 1995 was met with only mild protests from feminists, whose biggest concern was the loss of its research capacity (NAC 1995, *A Very Political Budget*). This reaction suggests that the women's movement did not see the CACSW as an effective advocate at the federal level.

At the provincial level, women's policy machinery has also been placed at the periphery. A variety of models have existed across the country, reflecting different provincial political environments (Rankin and Vickers 1998). Most combine some form of coordinating bureaucratic agency – such as the Women's Directorate in Ontario, the Ministry of Women's Equality in British Columbia, the Women's Bureau in Alberta, the Women's Policy Office in Newfoundland – with women's sections in such line departments as labour, health, and family. Each province also supports a status of women council that advises the provincial government on women's issues. Aside from Quebec, where the feminist-inspired Conseil du statut de la femme has developed extensive services for women regardless of the party in office (Arscott, Rankin, and Vickers n.d., 31), other provincial machinery tends to be relatively weak. Even the free-standing Ministry for Women's Equality in British Columbia 'lacks the interdepartmental clout or legitimacy' to achieve compliance with gender-based policy analysis tools (see Teghtsoonian 2000, 7; Malloy 1999, 283).

In summary, the institutional position of femocrats in Canada has been very different from their position in Australia. Whereas in Australia feminists have been able to create a core agency within the PM&C and use their institutional position to influence policy developments in a manner that benefited women, in Canada feminists have been less successful. In Burt's (1990, 201) view, officials who work in these agencies remain 'embedded in a subordinate position within the state.' O'Neil and Sutherland (1997, 216) summarize the situation as follows:

> The simple fact is that Canadian governments have never created an in-house capacity to deliver policy on women. There is no organisation below the Minister Responsible – only a certain amount of goodwill. A proliferation of small and weak agencies at the margins of policy-making and of central administration will undo in confusion ... what they can contribute in dedication.

Australian Femocrats and Policy Outcomes

There are important differences between Australian and Canadian femocrat strategies in terms of their ability to influence policy outcomes. Australian femocrats can be ranked higher than their Canadian counterparts on this score. The influence of the former has been assisted at times by their ability to operate separately from the wider women's movement. However, it is important to note that Australian femocrat policy advances have been most obvious when the ALP has been in office.

The first twenty years of Australian feminist intervention in the federal bureaucracy yielded some significant policy outcomes. Femocrats instigated or influenced the development of feminist policies in a range of areas. Commonwealth-funded childcare places increased from none in 1969 to 246,000 in 1994. Women's refuges grew from eleven in 1974 to 317 in 1994, and in 1996 Australia was estimated to have more women's health centres per capita than any other country (Eisenstein 1996, 50). In 1988 the Hawke government released the National Agenda for Women (NAFW). This was the first in a series of five-year plans to address the specific needs of women in areas such as education and training, housing, and health care. A strategy to combat domestic violence was a feature of the first plan, with $1.6 million committed over three years for the creation of a Commonwealth task force (*OSW News Brief*, May 1988). Since 1996 the Commonwealth has maintained its commitment to fight domestic violence, spending twenty-five million dollars over three and a half years on the federal/state government Partnerships against Domestic Violence Program. A women's budget statement, to measure government spending on women's issues across portfolios, was devised and used to maintain government commitments to women. The Child Care Cash Rebate, introduced in 1994, recognized childcare as a legitimate work-related expense for the first time. In 1990 femocrats at the federal level also secured government funding for women's organizations under the Australian National Agenda for Women grants program. Funding for these women's groups peaked in 1993 at one million dollars (Crowley 1993, 11).

The reform of superannuation benefits has also been an important issue on the femocrat agenda.

Femocrats have had significant input into federal legislation in the areas of sex discrimination (1984), Equal Employment Opportunity for public service employees (1984 and 1987), and affirmative action (1986, 1992, and 1993). The influence of femocrats has also extended to the international sphere. They helped to secure the government's signature on the UN Convention on the Elimination of All Forms of Discrimination against Women (CEDAW) and the International Labour Organisation Convention 156, which deals with workers with family responsibilities. In 1992 femocrats participated in drafting the UN Declaration on the Elimination of Violence against Women and presented a report to the Committee of CEDAW on policies and programs to improve the status of women (*OSWomen*, September and December 1992).

One of the most significant achievements of the femocracy involved expanding the purview of government to encompass areas that had not previously been seen to be the subject of public policy. For instance, in the mid-1980s, under the direction of Sue Brooks (1984, 31), the OSW worked on 'extending [its] influence into the mainstream of economic policy determination ... and [t]o challenge the underlying assumptions and often limited data on which traditional economists often make their policy recommendations.' The pioneering work of Meredith Edwards, which discredited assumptions about income sharing within families upon which social security policies were made, is an example of the femocracy's foray into mainstream economic policy making (see Sawer 1990, 58). Through their work, femocrats also demonstrated the structured nature of discrimination against women and gave definition to issues such as domestic violence, sex discrimination, and the gender gap in wages. Faced with the evidence presented by femocrats, governments were no longer able to dismiss these problems as 'private' concerns but, rather, were forced to see them as systemic problems that required a policy response.

One of the interesting aspects of the Australian femocrat project is how femocrats have been able to take advantage of existing opportunities and create new ones. Part of the femocrats' success has been due to their central institutionalized position, which has enabled them to become alert to certain issues, or opportunities for reform, in advance of outside women's groups. Moreover, they have had the wherewithal to pursue these issues without external pressure from feminist groups. A number of examples stand out. Franzway, Court, and Connell (1989, 59-60) have commented on the way femocrats agitated strongly for childcare 'during a period when other feminists tended to overlook it.' One head of the OSW noted that, during her period, a window of opportunity existed for making changes in the areas of superannuation reform and maternity leave. The OSW was able set in train reforms even though, at the time, there was no pressure from the external feminist activists to do so. According to this femocrat, the OSW made use of the opening provided by the Keating government and managed to gain the government's commitment to remove discriminatory provisions in superannuation legislation and to make moves to introduce a maternity leave payment for working women outside the public sector (interview with author, 1995).

Such autonomy has also been apparent at the state level. According to a director of the Office of the Status of Women in South Australia (SA), femocrats in that state have been able to bring about changes in the state government's position on abortion, including the development of Australia's only free-standing abortion clinic, with very little input from external women's groups. In an interview with the author in 1997, this senior femocrat explained that 'it was a very delicate process and we were afraid if women's groups started lobbying the government on this issue, we might lose the battle. We worked closely with the minister on this issue and managed to get a positive outcome without the issue going to Parliament.'

The autonomy of Australian femocrats has not always sat easily with the broader women's movement. Indeed, many feminists outside the bureaucracy have claimed that those inside have been unaccountable and out of touch with the needs of women in the community. Femocrats have been criticized for failing to make inroads into certain policy areas and for compromising in others. One of the most relentless complaints has been about their limited ability to affect the lot of working women. While femocrats had some influence over Affirmative Action and Equal Employment Opportunity (EEO) legislation, both initiatives were criticized for being too weak and, in the case of the latter, for serving the interests of those women who were already advantaged in the workforce (see Poiner and Wills 1991). Feminists have also been highly critical of the inability of femocrats to shift the government's position on enterprise bargaining – a position that they allege will have seriously detrimental effects on women workers (Wills 1995, 128; Jamieson 1995). While childcare for working women improved significantly between 1974 and 1994, feminists in the community pointed out that it still did not meet the demand (Brennan 1994, 211). Government has also refused to entertain the idea of introducing a paid maternity scheme for women outside the public sector.

Canadian Femocrats and Policy Outcomes
The weak position of women's policy machinery has had ramifications for the capacity of Canadian femocrats to influence the development of women's policy. Unlike its Australian counterpart, the Canadian femocracy appears to have influenced the direction of policy but has been unable to act autonomously at crucial moments. In Canada, women's

agencies have been unable to gain federal government commitment to key policy areas such as state-funded childcare, and they have not demonstrated the same ability to analyze mainstream policy from a gender perspective as have their Australian counterparts. Where women's agencies have shown initiative, their efforts have often been criticized by members of the external women's movement who have perceived them as pursuing the government's agenda.

In Canada, the development of women's policy began in earnest after the release of the RCSW report, which became the blueprint for government action (Paltiel 1997, 27). Although the Trudeau government was slow to take action on the report and unwilling to implement all of its recommendations, it did address some key concerns. Between 1971 and 1975 it introduced maternity leave provisions to the Canadian Labour Code (something Australian women have not yet achieved), removed overt gender discrimination in a range of legislation, and began funding women's organizations through the Women's Program. These changes were influenced by the work of Paltiel and of the Interdepartmental Committee (IDC) on the Status of Women, which she headed. In turn, the committee depended on the RCSW to justify its arguments for reform (O'Neil and Sutherland 1997).

During the mid- to late 1970s, the SWC and the CACSW were closely involved in the drafting of the Human Rights Act, which established the principle of equal pay for equal work in the federal public service and created the Human Rights Commission (HRC). While these developments were greeted favourably by the women's movement at the time, in the long term both measures proved to be relatively ineffective with regard to addressing discrimination against women (Morris 1982). Since the mid-1970s, much of the work of the SWC has focused on the development of general policy statements aimed at meeting UN commitments. These statements, including *Towards Equality*, *Dimensions of Equality*, and *Federal Plan for Gender Equality*, have been criticized by external feminists for being mere 'window dressing,' for addressing only those areas that are acceptable to mainstream government departments, and for putting no pressure on federal finances (Geller-Schwartz 1995, 48; Burt 1993, 225; Findlay 1987, 46). The inability of femocrats to stem cuts to the funding of women's groups through the Women's Program – reduced from $13 million in the late 1980s to $8.6 million in 1994 (SWC 1995b) – also raised the ire of outside women's groups (see, for example, *Feminist Action* vol. 1, no. 4, 1986; vol. 2, no. 7, 1987; *Action Now* vol. 2, no. 4, 1992; vol. 3, no. 1, 1993; *Montreal Gazette*, 20 November 1993, A13).

Other reports to come out of women's policy agencies have also met with negative responses from the women's movement. In 1987 NAC claimed that the CACSW report into domestic violence, *Battered But Not Beaten*, presented a distorted picture of domestic violence (*Feminist Action* vol. 2, no. 6, 1987). In 1988 CACSW's *Immigrant Women in Canada: A Policy Perspective* was roundly criticized by NAC, which argued that the report used unreliable statistics, did not identify the differences between immigrant women, or adequately outline the structural forces that operate as discriminatory barriers (*Feminist Action* vol. 3, no. 3, 1988). Women's agencies have also come in for attack for their inability to influence mainstream policy areas. The lack of any gender analysis of tax reform during the mid-1980s was one issue of contention (*Feminist Action* vol. 2, no. 5, 1987). Free trade has been another example. Whereas the Anglo-feminist community in general and NAC in particular were opposed to Canada joining NAFTA (*Feminist Action* vol. 1, no. 2, 1985), the SWC lauded its potential benefits for women. Adopting the government's rhetoric, the SWC argued: 'Trade is a major engine of growth for Canada's economy, and every woman and man in the country gains from it. This is why the free trade agreement-in-principle is so important to our future' (*Perspectives* vol. 1, no. 1, 1987, p. 1; see also *Perspectives* vol. 1, no. 2, 1988). Feminists also reproached women's agencies for not providing a thorough analysis of the impact of changes to the Canadian Assistance Plan (CAP), the federal government's social welfare funding mechanism (*Action Now* vol. 5, no. 4, 1995).

Similar criticisms have been directed towards women's policy agencies at the provincial level. As Malloy (1999, 278) notes, feminists have voiced their concern over how the Ontario Women's Directorate has downplayed, or deliberately ignored, issues 'such as childcare, same-sex rights, anti-racism efforts, private sector employment equity, and particularly economic issues such as the effect on women of trade agreements, the overall tax policies and social spending cuts.' In British Columbia, the Ministry for Women's Equity has been criticized for moving away from its initial feminist approach to policy analysis and towards a less radical perspective, which emphasizes equity rather than gender power relations (Teghtsoonian 2000).

Facing criticism from outside activists is something Canadian femocrats have shared with their Australian counterparts. They have been further handicapped in that, in contrast to Australian femocrats, policy makers in Canadian women's agencies have found it difficult to bring a feminist perspective to bear on key policy areas and have not been able to exercise the same degree of autonomy. One outstanding example of this relates to femocrats' inability to convince government to develop a universal, national, state-funded childcare system (Findlay 1987, 46). In her 1990 study of this policy area, Burt (1990, 204-8) found that the SWC had been unable to provide any leadership on the issue and had left the running to 'a plurality of women's groups and day care associations.' Senior SWC officer Zeynap Karman has also hinted at the difficulty femocrats have had in instigating gender-sensitive policy in particular areas. In a 1996 speech to the UN, Karman (1996, 7-12) noted, in relation to three key areas (women's unpaid work, child support, and pension reform), that it was members of the external women's movement rather than internal femocrats who first identified the issue and called for government action. In each case, the role of the SWC was limited to educating rather than taking the initiative on these issues. It saw its role as 'sensitizing other policy makers to the importance of considering unpaid work in their policy development'; suggesting 'directions for change' in relation to child support; and, 'disseminating the available information on gender and providing analyses for use of the various players' involved in pension reform (8-13).

There is evidence to suggest that Canadian femocrats have been able to achieve positive policy outcomes in a limited range of specifically designated 'status of women' areas. According to Heitlinger (1993, 91), they have helped to secure funding for 'wife battering, child sexual abuse and other forms of family violence.' They have put the issues of economic equality and the integration of work and family on the agenda of First Ministers Conferences. Like their Australian counterparts, Canadian femocrats have also been influential in the international arena, taking a leading role in the United Nations Development Fund for Women (UNIFEM) and the CEDAW. And they were responsible for initiating the resolution leading to the UN Declaration on the Elimination of Violence against Women (SWC 1995a, 63, 71). Canadian femocrats have been active within the OECD on issues relating to women and the economy, and they have developed policy guidelines on women and development for the Canadian International Development Agency (CIDA) (SWC 1995a, 63-4).

To the extent that Canadian femocrats have been able to influence the policy agenda, much of their impetus can be seen to have come from outside the bureaucracy. While this is, in one sense, a positive outcome, demonstrating a degree of communication between those inside and outside this arena, it also has its drawbacks. Without some degree of autonomy, Canadian femocrats have not been able to operate as swiftly as their Australian counterparts in taking advantage of openings. When a commitment is made to policy reform, Canadian femocrats have tended to play a supportive, educative role rather than framing the direction of policy reform themselves. They have also found it more difficult to influence mainstream policy issues.

Political Opportunities and Constraints in the Australian and Canadian Bureaucracies

Although the federal bureaucracies of Australia and Canada have their foundation in a Westminster tradition, each operates quite differently and, as a result, provides feminists in the two polities with vastly different POSs. Differences in the POS exist at three levels: bureaucratic culture and norms, bureaucratic structures, and variations in the interplay between the bureaucracy and the political party system. In Australia, weak neutrality norms have combined with the presence of ALP governments to provide a relatively positive POS for feminists in the bureaucracy. By contrast, in Canada, strong neutrality norms, decentralized structures, and the absence of a supportive party, at least at the federal level, have made it difficult for majoritarian feminists to pursue their aims by following this route.

Bureaucratic Norms: Gender Dimensions and the Role of Neutrality
An important factor to emerge from this comparison of the experiences of Australian and Canadian feminists within the bureaucracy is the significance of bureaucratic norms in shaping the available POS. In both cases these norms, which have underlying gender dimensions, have influenced the extent to which the bureaucracy has been open or closed to feminist demands. The following discussion focuses on one of the most important of these – neutrality. The degree to which each bureaucracy has upheld this norm has been highly significant to the success of the femocrat project in each country. (See also Table 4.1.)

Bureaucratic Norms in Australia
On taking up the opportunity to enter the administrative arm of the state during the Whitlam era, Australian femocrats were confronted by a bureaucracy that was both nominally and substantively gendered. Women were under-represented in the public service as a result of an affirmative action policy favouring returned servicemen – a policy that remained in place until 1959 – and a 'marriage bar' that meant that, upon marriage, women who had made it into the service were forced to resign.[3] The bar was abolished in 1966. Equally problematic for women wanting to use the bureaucracy to advance a feminist agenda was its underlying substantive gender norms. The model public servant – rational, calculating, detached, and objective – was definitively masculine. The hierarchical nature of the bureaucracy was perceived by feminists to be an expression of masculine power and was regarded as antithetical to the cooperative, consensual organizational forms said to be preferred by feminist activists (see Lynch 1984, 42-3).

The Career Service that was still firmly in place when femocrats entered the Australian public service in the early 1970s also reflected hidden gender aspects. Under the Career Service model, promotion still rested on seniority and an unbroken, full-time work history – something that many women did not have. Furthermore, it served to reinforce women's domestic role because it was predicated on the assumption that career public servants had the support of a full-time homemaker (see Burton 1991, 3).

Other normative aspects of the Australian bureaucracy also reflected underlying gender dimensions. The egalitarian ideals that came to be the backbone of the Australian bureaucratic culture served to protect the position of the 'common man' within the service and to exclude groups that fell outside this definition – including women (Caiden 1990, 35). Up until the 1970s the Australian bureaucracy was characterized by a conservative bureaucratic elite that was keen to maintain the status quo. According to Caiden, it amounted to a system of 'institutionalised racism, sexism and prejudices against non-whites, Catholics and Jews' (39).

Interestingly, one traditional normative aspect of a Westminster style bureaucracy – neutrality – was not so strongly enforced within the Australian context. According to Kernaghan (1985), the concept of bureaucratic neutrality as it is applied in Westminster systems has six aspects. Included within this definition is an understanding that public servants do not engage in partisan political activities; do not express their personal views on government policies or administration; and execute policy decisions loyally, irrespective of the party in power, and regardless of their personal opinions. Although in recent years Australian bureaucrats have followed the Westminster traditions of non-partisanship, of remaining above the political fray, public servants have been allowed to represent particular points of view within the bureaucracy. This tolerance of internal advocates opened up an important POS for Australian feminists wanting to engage with the bureaucratic institutional arena.

Since the time of European settlement in Australia, there has been a tradition of certain social actors, especially producer groups such as trade unions, manufacturers, and farmers, looking towards the state to meet their demands. These groups – defined by Miller (1964) as syndicates[4] – not only attempted to influence government policy through external lobbying, but also sought to engage directly with the bureaucracy by having the state create agencies through which they could advance their claims. Government responded by creating the Industrial Conciliation and Arbitration Commission as well as marketing and tariff protection boards. Miller defined these bodies as 'organs of syndical satisfaction, which put the force of the state to work for the settlement of grievances, without overtly involving the government, in the sense of the ministry of the day,' (128). It is important to note here that these bodies not only served the demands of the syndicates, but they also enabled government to gain some control over these strong social forces and, to some extent, 'canalize their demands' (136). The overall effect of the creation of these organs was to entrench the view that, in Australia, the administrative arm of the state existed for utilitarian purposes (see Goodsell 1990, 346-7).

The tradition of sectional interests looking towards the administrative arm of the state, and government providing them with agencies through which they could advance their claims, had a profound influence on Australian feminists. Most important, it has encouraged them to look to this arena in an attempt to satisfy their demands (Sawer 1991). It was a conscious strategy on their part. As one former senior femocrat has stated: 'In a society which believes firmly in centralized wage fixation principles, and the role of the state ... it is not at all surprising that Australian feminists have seen it as important to use state apparatus as one way of achieving feminist objectives ... Were our society differently ordered then Australian feminists might be using other ... machinery' (Marie Coleman, cited in Eisenstein 1996, 81).

The pattern of feminist engagement with the bureaucracy did not replicate precisely that of the aforementioned syndicates. For instance, feminists did not attempt to gain a separate statutory agency but, rather, entered the public service proper to work as 'inside agitators.' This meant that the government of the day has been able to become overtly involved in their actions (e.g., by altering the structure and position of women's agencies). Nevertheless, the intention of the movement was similar to that of these other social actors. As Eisenstein (1996, 81) notes, it 'developed a concept of women as a sectional interest, with a claim for state protection.' There were original elements to the feminist strategy as well: it combined the traditional demand for a position within the bureaucracy 'with a modern, feminist-inspired ideology that directly challenged the patriarchal status quo' (Eisenstein 1996, 82). According to Eisenstein, the femocrat strategy was a form of 'feminist judo' – an attempt by feminists to use the capitalist patriarchal state against itself (81).

The tolerance for advocates of sectional interests within the Australian public sector has presented majoritarian feminists with a positive POS within the bureaucracy. It has legitimized their use of bureaucratic structures to pursue the interests of their 'syndicate' – ostensibly Australian women. Although governments may have regarded women's units with more suspicion than they did other 'client-driven' agencies, an acceptance of internal advocates has permitted femocrats to advance their claims, and to take public positions on issues, to an extent not tolerated under the traditional neutral public servant model. A former OSW head believes that the acceptance of 'inside agitators' within the Australian bureaucracy has been advantageous for women's agencies, including the OSW. In her view, 'the OSW behaves differently in the bureaucracy and is expected to do so. It has a history of advocacy and because its constituency is half the population it can sometimes pull rank with other departments' (interview with author, 1995).

Certain traditional bureaucratic norms initially presented hurdles to a femocrat project; nevertheless, the tolerance of advocates within the bureaucracy provided an important opening for those pursuing this strategy.

In time, some of the other traditional norms were also challenged, and in some cases eroded, as a result of bureaucratic reforms. As discussed below, bureaucratic reforms, at least during the Whitlam period, were one of the positive spinoffs of the interaction between a progressive political party (the ALP) and the bureaucracy – a spinoff from which femocrats were able to prosper.

Bureaucratic Norms in Canada
Anglo-feminists wanting to use the Canadian bureaucracy for their own ends faced similar normative barriers to their Australian counterparts. On entering the bureaucracy, women met with a highly masculine culture that, until the end of the 1950s, had been reinforced through the preferential hiring of returned soldiers as well as restrictions on married women within the service. At the beginning of the 1970s, when feminists first looked to these institutions, a military subculture was evident within the public service, with the consequence that it was 'paternalistic, hierarchical and unsympathetic to women's advancement' (CACSW 1988, 16). In addition to these normative attributes, the bureaucracy continued to hold firmly to the ideal of neutrality. Compared to Canberra, Ottawa has followed more closely the pattern of 'the Whitehall model and the Weberian ideal,' emphasizing the characteristics of 'anonymity, non-partisan neutrality, [and] a permanent career path' (Bourgault and Carroll 1997, 92). As Bourgault and Carroll state: 'The Whitehall model, as it has developed in Canada, seems to be one of the least affected by political partisanship than any of the Anglo-American countries' and this is a feature which is considered to be 'among the most important qualities of the ... public service of the future' (95, 100).

The continuing potency of neutrality as a core bureaucratic value in Canada has presented a major obstacle to the femocrat project. The idea of neutrality – that 'administrators can rise above their own beliefs and the political fray to fix their sights on the public interest, broadly conceived' – is, like other traditional bureaucratic values (such as merit), profoundly gendered (Stivers 1993, 38). The notion of neutrality suggests that there is a set of universal norms that can be used to look at the world. However, when considered in detail, these norms reflect underlying gender assumptions. For instance, the importance of individuals being able to detach themselves from situations and act with 'dispassionate objectivity' reflects an emphasis on traditional masculine traits (40). Meanwhile, values such as emotion, sensibility, and passion – that is, emotions that have been identified as 'feminine' – are regarded as excessive and laden with bias.

By upholding neutrality as a central bureaucratic norm, Ottawa is asserting a claim to impartiality. However, from a gender perspective, this neutral public servant model has operated to maintain entrenched gender values. Women have found it difficult to gain access to the senior ranks of the civil service because they have been seen as threatening to the status quo (CACSW 1988, 26). According to a study of women in the Canadian public service, when women began entering the service in large numbers they were 'screened for risk,' and only those who could fit within the existing model – which effectively meant older women without children – were promoted to senior positions (CACSW 1988, 25-36). Neutrality has also meant that, within the bureaucracy, there has been little tolerance of advocates in general, and feminists in particular, because of the specific nature of their claims; that is, to unsettle existing gender norms.

The prejudice against internal 'feminist agitators' in Ottawa has been noted by former Canadian femocrats. They talk of initiatives being stonewalled and trivialized, treated with indifference and impatience by senior managers, or met with a 'wilful misunderstanding' (Findlay 1987, 39; CACSW 1988, 26; Geller-Schwartz 1995, 57). According to Geller-Schwartz:

> Civil Servants are supposed to be the anonymous, efficient, unbiased administrators of the machinery of state ... Even if the male-dominated bureaucracy had been prepared to recognize that certain policies (other than the obvious issues such as maternity leave) could have a differential impact on women, the idea that civil servants should adopt the role of internal lobbyists for women as a definable group was an anathema. (49)

The recollections of Sue Findlay, who was the first head of the Women's Program, reinforce this point. As noted above, Findlay and the other officers in the Women's Program came closest to the Australian femocrat model, being drawn directly from the external women's movement, with their feminism recognized as a credential for their job. Findlay (1995, 217, 231) discusses the resistance of senior male managers in the public service to feminist projects and argues that they made an effort to block connections between internal feminists and grassroots organizations, thereby hoping to disrupt the radical intent of the programs. Findlay also outlines the hostility directed towards her because of her feminism. This was demonstrated most clearly when, after a reorganization of the department in which the program was based, Findlay was required to reapply for her job and then found to be unsuitable for the position. The reasons given for her rejection were telling. The rating board found that: 'Her crusading may, on occasion, colour her judgement and objectivity and antagonize managers without her realizing it – thus limiting her effectiveness in this job' (cited in Findlay 1995, 214). In any case, Findlay appealed the decision and was reinstated. Nevertheless, the experience illustrated the extent of resistance to feminist advocates, who were perceived as challenging the neutral public servant model. This resistance has been enduring. In a 1995 interview with the author, a senior officer in the Women's Program noted the difficulty women's agencies had in being heard within the bureaucracy. 'It's tougher for us because our position is seen to be imbued with a feminist ideology and does not fit within the traditional neutral mould.'

Strong neutrality norms have also been evident within some Canadian provinces and have had a similar constraining effect on femocrats working at the subnational level. In Ontario, for example, the Women's Directorate's 'chief concern was maintaining institutional (bureaucratic) conformity [as opposed to playing an advocacy role] to secure sufficient political and resource support to achieve feminist policy objectives' (Malloy 1999, 279). When feminist advocates drawn directly from the women's movement entered the directorate under the NDP government in the early 1990s, it became marginalized. As Malloy explains: 'No longer a "safe" organization that conformed to the institutional environment of the bureaucracy, the OWD was avoided and bypassed by most economic ministries' (281). Although the Anglo-women's movement is the focus here, it is interesting to note that, in Quebec, feminists have had more success using the bureaucracy to advance their claims regardless of the party in office (Arscott, Rankin, and Vickers n.d.). One possible explanation for this difference is that, as a result of its unique cultural heritage, the bureaucracy in Quebec has a different normative base. Writing on French Canada and the 'bureaucratic phenomenon,' Herman Bakvis (1978, 101-24) tentatively suggests that French-Canadians have a different approach to bureaucracy than do their Anglo counterparts. Although Bakvis did not test whether neutrality norms operated in a different way in Quebec than in the rest of Canada, his work does suggest that this is a path worth exploring within the Quebec context.

In Canada, a period of bureaucratic reform in the 1970s and 1980s led to a greater commitment to developing a more representative civil service. During this period the Trudeau federal government introduced affirmative action programs to advance the representation of Francophones, Aboriginal groups, and women in the bureaucracy. Of all of these programs, the attempt to increase the bilingual character of the public service was given the most emphasis and has achieved the most success, at least in numerical terms. Acting on the recommendations of the Royal Commission on Bilingualism and Biculturalism (commonly referred to as the B&B Commission), Ottawa worked throughout the 1970s to make the public service bilingual. The effort saw the number of French-speaking public servants increase from 18.2 percent in 1972 to 38 percent in 1996, a level of representation that is higher than their proportion within the Canadian population (see Brooks 1998, 224-5).

From one perspective, Ottawa's decision to make the bureaucracy more representative through affirmative action programs might be seen as providing a POS for Anglo-feminists. It might be presumed that feminists could 'ride on the coattails of bilingualism' in order to make use of the reform environment to enter the bureaucracy and to advance their claims on behalf of women. It is the case that, through affirmative action strategies, women were able to increase their numerical representation in Ottawa, including at senior levels. In 1982 women comprised 4 percent of senior executives; by 1993, this figure had increased to 17 percent. However, these numerical improvements were not translated into any serious challenge to the status quo in terms of neutrality norms. There are a number of factors that might explain this. First, as Kernaghan (1985, 17) notes, the purpose of affirmative action strategies was not to emphasize group characteristics but individual abilities. In other words, although these programs led to the entry of members of different identity groups into the bureaucracy, they did not lead to a greater degree of tolerance for them as advocates of their group; rather, there remains an ongoing expectation that, once inside, a civil servant's 'activities should not jeopardize the tradition of the Public Service as a politically neutral institution' (Canada, Treasury Board, 1993 cited in Kernaghan 1997, 109). According to Kernaghan (1985, 20): 'Bureaucrats are obliged to accommodate whatever representative inclination they may have to the values deemed most important by their political superiors. Neither government policy nor practice usually permits a bureaucrat's active sense of representativeness to override considerations of accountability, efficiency, effectiveness and neutrality.'

Second, to the extent that representation was an important aim of the government, women's concerns were never given the same priority as were other issues, especially the representation of language minorities. According to the CACSW, under the Trudeau government women's concerns did not have the same impact as did those of other under-represented groups. In the CACSW's view, this was because women were not united around a common goal, as were Francophones and Aboriginal groups, and because women were less likely to vote as a block (CACSW 1988, 23). Former femocrat Maureen O'Neil also noted that, within the bureaucracy, women's issues were given lower priority than were those of other identity groups. In her view, this was not an attempt to 'keep women powerless'; rather, 'other social groups, such as Indians are regarded in a more "charitable" light by the government who harbor some predispositions of "guilt." Women as a group are not seen in the same way' (O'Neil, cited in Morris 1982, 504).

Another senior women's affairs bureaucrat agrees that there has been a preoccupation with the Quebec question and, to a lesser extent, with Aboriginal issues. This has meant 'that it has been a constant struggle for women and black issues to attract attention' (interview with author,

1995). In sum, improvements in numerical representation of previously excluded groups, including Francophones and women, have done little to unsettle neutrality as a core bureaucratic value within the Canadian federal public service. Moreover, feminists have found that they have had to compete with other identity groups to put women's issues on the agenda. Rather than these other identity issues opening a path for the expression of feminist concerns, more often than not gender concerns have been sidelined by the more pressing and politically sensitive race and culture identity issues.

Canadian Bureaucratic Structures

In Canada, structural barriers have operated alongside normative barriers to hamper the femocrat project. Of most importance has been the degree of decentralization within the bureaucracy. The push for decentralization within the Canadian public service began in 1962, after the release of the Glassco Commission Report. The commission's proposals, summed up by the term 'let the managers manage,' transferred to line departments some central agency functions, including control over awarding contracts, classification of positions, and the reallocation of funds within programs (Veilleux and Savoie 1988, 534). While there was a swing back to centralized control after Glassco (Aucoin 1988, 154), later administrative reform programs, including the Lambert Commission in 1978 and the Increased Ministerial Authority and Accountability (IMAA) program in 1986, attempted to stem the tide by giving managers 'more latitude and more direct responsibility to manage the resources entrusted to them' (Mulroney, cited in Veilleux and Savoie 1988, 535).

Femocrats in Ottawa were directly affected by the decentralized structure of the public service. The decisions taken in 1976 to transfer the Office of the Co-ordinator of the Status of Women out of the Privy Council Office in order to create the SWC and to introduce an integration model for women's policy were both the result of the drive for greater decentralization. As discussed above, these moves frustrated the work of femocrats: the SWC was left without the institutional stature to carry out its coordinating role, while femocrats in line departments lacked the support and resources to ensure that departmental policies were 'gender sensitive.' As Arscott, Rankin, and Vickers (n.d., 18) note, 'there is evidence to suggest that this complex set of status-of-women machinery left women's inputs fragmented and unfocused.' Heitlinger (1993, 85) summarizes the problem posed by decentralization as follows:

> As a rule, federal departments do not want to share information about their respective policy agendas with any other department, let alone with the 'Missionary' Status of Women Canada. The differential impact

of policies and programmes on women is generally poorly understood by 'mainstream' bureaucrats lacking a feminist perspective, and is often confused with personnel policies of equal employment opportunities for women employees of the federal government. Deputy ministers in particular devote very little time to the evaluation of the impact of their policies and programmes on women.

Findlay (1995, 143-4) agrees that decentralization has been detrimental for the development of women's policy in Canada. In her view,

> departmental managers appear to be driven by commitments to autonomy and competition rather than co-operation and co-ordination. The practice of 'letting the managers manage' places real limits on political commitments to reforms. Because managers are for the most part men, this practice is particularly effective in limiting the implementation of commitments to women's equality.

Interaction between the Bureaucracy and Party Systems

One of the central arguments of this book is that the POS is shaped not only by the engagement of social actors with institutions, but also by the interplay between various political institutions in any given polity. The interaction between Australian feminists, the bureaucracy, and the ALP is a good illustration of this point. Although, as noted in relation to the parliamentary realm, the ALP has not been a particularly useful institution as far as a feminist electoral project is concerned, the relationship between the party and the bureaucratic realm has been much more fruitful. The election of Labor governments at the federal level in 1972 and between 1983 and 1996, and since the mid-1970s at the state level, helped to create openings for feminists wanting to engage with the bureaucracy. Yeatman (1990, 89) emphasizes this point:

> The significance of the party in power for the development and tenor of the femocracy cannot be underestimated. It is unlikely that Australian femocracy would have been developed to the extent it has without the crucial coincidence of a reforming federal Labor government and a dynamic women's movement in the period 1972-75, and without the renewal of this connection with the Hawke Labor government in 1983.

The alliance that developed between the ALP and the femocracy was not without its costs: in return for a position within the bureaucracy, femocrats were expected to help 'sell' the government's policies to women in the wider community. However, without the influence of the ALP on the public service, it is unlikely that the women's movement would have had the same opportunity to use bureaucratic structures to advance its objectives.

The significance of the ALP for feminists wanting to engage with the bureaucracy became apparent under the Whitlam government. In its effort to modernize and broaden its constituency base, the government was keen to gain the support of the burgeoning women's movement and, as a result, was prepared to respond to at least some of its demands. These included the development of women's policy and women's policy units – measures that fit neatly within the notion of 'positive equality' that the Whitlam government used to support its reform agenda. As Whitlam (1975) told the delegates at the International Women's Year Conference

Table 4.1

Political opportunity structures in the bureaucracy

	Australia	Canada
Bureaucratic norms	*Norms* **Positive** Weak neutrality norms/tolerance for bureaucratic advocacy	*Norms* **Negative** Strong neutrality norms/ intolerance for bureaucratic advocacy apart from language and cultural minorities
Bureaucratic structures	*Structures* **Positive** Centralized women's policy machinery	*Structures* **Negative** Decentralized policy machinery, including women's policy machinery
Intervening political party system	*Structures* **Positive** ALP (federally and in states) **Negative** Coalition (federally and in states)	*Structures* **Positive** NDP (BC, Ontario) **Neutral/Positive** Liberal (federal) **Negative** Progressive Conservatives
Bureaucratic reforms	*Norms* **Positive** Equal employment opportunity **Negative/Neutral** New managerialism	*Norms* **Positive** Equal employment opportunity **Negative/Neutral** New managerialism

in 1975, 'the aim of these [women's] policies and programs has been to give women the pre-conditions necessary for them to be able to freely choose the lives they want to lead.' As noted earlier, with the election of the Whitlam government, members of the women's movement were given the encouragement and the means to enter the bureaucracy in order to advance their goals.

Other aspects of the agenda of the Whitlam government further bolstered the femocrat project. One of the most important decisions of the government as far as femocrats were concerned came in 1974 with the establishment of the Royal Commission on Australian Government Administration (RCAGA). The commission, which was headed by the highly respected public servant H.C. Coombs, was unlike any previous public service review both in terms of its process and its subject matter. Not only did it review the traditional administrative reform concerns of efficiency and responsibility, but it also expanded its field of vision to address issues such as welfare administration, equal opportunity, alternatives to hierarchy, regionalization, and the employment of minorities and women (Beilharz, Considine, and Watts 1992, 111). The RCAGA was groundbreaking in that it saw important administrative issues as social questions. As Beilharz, Considine, and Watts argue: 'Coombs identified ways in which the public service had given greater power to people who were already privileged, and argued for changes in the composition of the bureaucracy to redress this' (ibid.).

The RCAGA was unable to complete its report before the dismissal of the Whitlam government, and many of its recommendations were never implemented (Matthews 1978, 270-1). However, some of the proposals that were adopted were important in challenging the traditional gender aspects of the bureaucracy and, at least indirectly, the femocrat project. The cessation of special protection for ex-servicemen and non-graduates, and the creation of an office of equality of opportunity helped to redress the nominal gender imbalance in the public service (Self 1978, 319). The move from seniority- to merit-based promotion and the introduction of lateral recruitment enabled women to gain entry to senior bureaucratic positions without needing to work their way up through the gender-biased career service. The commission led to the introduction of EEO programs and machinery that encouraged more women and feminists to enter the senior ranks of the public service.[5] Furthermore, femocrats were able to take advantage of changes in the bureaucratic cultural milieu encouraged by the RCAGA. As Eisenstein (1996, 33) argues: 'The ideal type of the Australian bureaucrat was being transformed. The gray-suited, conforming civil servant of the past ... was being joined by a cohort of reformers, committed to change and appointed on this basis. Femocrats fitted well into this new role: they were "stirrers," reformers, and people with an agenda for change.'

As it reported in 1976, two years after the first femocrats became entrenched within the federal bureaucracy, it cannot be reasonably claimed that the Coombs Commission provided the impetus for the femocrat strategy. However, its recommendations for a more responsive, sensitive, and representative bureaucracy, with a less hierarchical structure, helped to undermine existing gender norms and contributed to a climate within the public service that was more responsive to femocrat claims than had earlier been the case.

After the dismissal of the Whitlam government in 1975, one of the few bright spots on the horizon for femocrats was the growth of women's policy machinery in the states. The development of the femocracy at this level during the 1970s and 1980s occurred under the direction of ALP governments. The reasons for their support of the femocracy were no different from those that had motivated the Whitlam government at the federal level. During this period, state ALP branches were also undergoing a process of modernization and, through the creation of women's agencies, were keen to demonstrate to voters that they had a commitment to women's issues.[6] Following the lead of the federal ALP, some state governments chose to undertake their own bureaucratic reform program. For instance, in 1977 ALP premier Neville Wran appointed former Whitlam adviser Peter Wilenski to head a review of NSW government administration. Like the Coombs report, the review supported the idea of a bureaucracy that reflected more closely the race and gender complexion of society. It dealt in detail with the issue of discrimination against women in the public service and recommended the introduction of affirmative action programs to bring about equal opportunity in the public service (see Review of New South Wales Government Administration 1977, Part E).

The reinstatement of women's machinery within PM&C under Hawke in 1983 meant that femocrats regained the opportunity to achieve some influence over the Commonwealth policy agenda. Both the Hawke and Keating governments learned from Whitlam the importance of attracting broad-based electoral support, and they were keen to target women voters (Curtin 1997, 8). Maintaining women's policy machinery and developing women's policies were part of their strategy for achieving this objective. Hawke's five-year National Agenda for Women can be seen in this light. Keating maintained this agenda and, aware of his negative image with women, also appointed the high-profile feminist and former head of OSW, Anne Summers, to devise and promote a set of policies to attract the women's vote. Initiatives to come out of this partnership included the childcare allowance, the childcare rebate, increased funding for childcare places, anti-domestic violence policies, and a program for improving women's health.

Between 1972 and 1975, and 1983 and 1996, the concern of federal

ALP governments to attract support from a wide range of interests, including the women's movement, worked to the advantage of the femocracy. Under Labor, the potential power of the women's vote gave femocrats a great deal of leverage and became one of their most powerful weapons. They made use of the electoral cycle to shore up their own position as well as to win important government commitments in a range of areas, including funding for refuges, health care centres, and, most obviously, childcare. Anne Summers is unambiguous in her acknowledgment of the utility of elections: 'As a femocrat I learned to love elections because that is when you really have a good chance to get what you want' (cited in Eisenstein 1996, 210).

It would be wrong to assume that the alliance between the ALP and femocrats has been secure or trouble-free. During the thirteen years of ALP government since 1983, femocrats had to confront a number of hurdles. For a start, the electoral cycle provided infrequent opportunities for femocrats to assert their influence. Outside of these times, they could sometimes find it difficult to gain the ear of the government. More profoundly, it appears that, in order to be effective, femocrats found it necessary to mould their demands to fit the ALP's political agenda. As Eisenstein claims, 'the alliance with Labor came with a price tag. In effect, the femocrat ideology and that of the Labor party were made to dovetail sufficiently for Labor to win power using the votes of women. But this meant limits and compromises on what femocrats were able to push for' (174).

The introduction of a series of public sector reforms under the rubric of 'new public management' during the Hawke and Keating governments also tested the alliance between femocrats and the ALP. The assumption underlying the new public management introduced by the ALP federally, and later by state governments of both political persuasions, was that the bureaucracy was unresponsive and wasteful. According to Bryson (1987, 260), their desire was to 'hone the bureaucracy into a well-tuned instrument to put into effect government policy, and perhaps more centrally, to curb expenditure.' The techniques considered appropriate for this task were drawn from private-sector management practices. They included an 'output' rather than a 'process' focus; the identification of clients; the setting of departmental goals and performance indicators; and program budgeting. The Career Service was replaced with a Senior Executive Service, members of which were appointed for their generic management skills rather than their specialist knowledge (Beilharz, Considine, and Watts 1992, 120).

The introduction of corporate management practices to federal and state bureaucracies brought mixed results for femocrats. On the one hand, they benefited from the reforms in a number of respects. The extension of EEO programs and the creation of the Senior Executive Service meant that femocrats, and women in general, were able to improve their positions in the top echelons of the public service (for a full analysis of improvements in promotion and appointment rates for women in senior APS positions, see Sherry 1994, 85-8). The creation of EEO units provided a new opening for 'specialist feminist' positions, establishing an enclave for femocrats within the bureaucracy. The increased requirements for planning and, in some cases, devolution of responsibility, were supported by some femocrats, who saw these practices as opening the possibility for greater input into decision making (Neary, cited in Eisenstein 1996, 188). The discourse of managerialism has also been seen by some feminists as increasing their scope for placing claims on the state. During her time in the NSW bureaucracy, former femocrat Clare Burton (1996, 187) reflected:

> As an outside critic of the process, I could see that it was mobilizing a value system and a view of the world that looked on the face of it to be undermining some of the values and issues we were concerned with. But as a practitioner, I am finding that it is a jumble of ideas, they're constantly being negotiated and contested and argued about and compromised and so on ... So it's a very contradictory sort of situation really. Which one must use to advantage.

At the same time, the reforms created problems for femocrats. Working in policy areas where the outcomes are not always easily quantifiable, they had difficulty demonstrating the efficacy of their actions. Moreover, according to Sawer (1996c, 3) 'femocrats had to shift from social justice discourse to market discourse (stressing human resource and efficiency arguments for gender equity) in order to be "heard."' The belief that generic management skills were appropriate for any policy area contributed to the devaluation of the 'specialist' skills of femocrats outside the area of EEO. The creation of the Senior Executive Service, structured along private-sector lines, brought with it the expectation of long work hours without adequate appreciation of family responsibilities (Bryson 1987, 267).

Within an environment where 'small government' was the objective, femocrats had little scope for expanding their field of influence; instead, they were left struggling to protect the gains they had made in such areas as the universal, state supported childcare system. As a result of these changes, women's policy came to be more narrowly defined, pertaining to those few areas (such as childcare and domestic violence) where it was possible to identify an undisputed 'special' need for women. Nevertheless, as a number of commentators have been at pains to point out, having femocrats in place under the ALP, even if only to uphold existing gains, was preferable to having no one at all to represent 'women's interests' within the bureaucracy (see Franzway 1986; Eisenstein 1996, 197).

The saliency of this argument becomes most apparent when the Liberal Party is in office and the position of femocrats has been at its most tenuous, both in terms of their institutional position and their influence on policy. The current Howard government has pursued the new public management path with vigour, reducing the role of government even further through contracting out government services. As noted earlier, it has also shown little sympathy for feminist aims or support for women's policy machinery. It may be the case that, under ALP governments, femocrats have been reduced to bringing about 'least worst outcomes,' but this is preferable to being completely marginalized, as has tended to occur under coalition governments.

In Canada, at least at the federal level, feminists have not enjoyed the benefit of an alliance with a progressive political party. As a result, they have found it difficult to overcome existing normative and structural constraints in order to use the civil service to their advantage. As with the parliamentary realm, the NDP has operated at the provincial level to offer feminists some opportunities for entering the bureaucracy. This occurred in the early 1990s in Ontario under the Rae NDP government, which recruited women directly from the feminist movement, and in British Columbia under the Harcourt government, which created the Ministry for Women's Equality (see Malloy 1999; Teghtsoonian 2000). However, because of electoral barriers, it has not been possible for the NDP to win government at the federal level. The response of those parties that have secured government at the federal level has swung between disinterest under the Trudeau Liberals (Young 2000, 150), who were more focused on improving the representation of Francophone and Aboriginal issues, to outright hostility under the Mulroney PCs. It was under the Mulroney government that federal ministers denounced feminist initiatives and supported funding through the women's program for the neoconservative, anti-feminist organization REAL women. Similarly, in provinces with PC governments (e.g., Alberta), women's machinery exists but lacks a feminist perspective. Indeed, in 1996 the president of the Alberta Advisory Council for Women, Margaret Leahey, refused to support affirmative action and declined to define herself as a feminist (Arscott, Rankin, and Vickers n.d., 37). As these examples demonstrate, party support does make a difference with regard to what opportunities are open to feminists in the bureaucracy. But this support has been harder to find in Canada than it has in Australia as the NDP, the party most sympathetic to feminists' claims, is able to achieve office only in some provinces and never at the federal level.

Engaging from 'Outside' the Bureaucracy

For Australian feminists, a positive POS within the bureaucracy has encouraged members of the women's movement to work as insiders within this institution. But feminists outside the bureaucracy, including those who have reservations about the femocrat strategy, have also looked to this arena in order to advance their claims. As Sawer and Groves (1994, 455) discovered in their research into networks within the Australian women's movement, the OSW was named, more than any other organization, as an advocacy partner of Australian women's groups. Observing the differences between the Australian and Canadian women's movements, Sawer (1994, 54) makes the following point: 'Australian women's organisations have interacted as much with state agencies they have helped to create and sustain as directly with each other. There seems to be much more of a sense of ownership of these patches of territory, and awareness of the role of "femocrats" as internal advocates for feminist causes.'

Eisenstein (1996, 200) has also noted the tendency of Australian feminists to centre their lobbying effort on bureaucrats rather than politicians. This is despite the fact that many women's groups remain critical of the work of femocrats. As Sara Dowse (1984, 139) notes: 'What has intrigued me ... throughout my life as a feminist activist is the fact that, despite my philosophical abhorrence of the modern capitalist state, when I want something done I look just to that arena. My expectations are low, but my directions are clear. And despite the claims to the contrary, so do most of my feminist sisters, even the most radical among them.'

In Australia, the femocracy has helped to shape the strategies of the women's movement in a positive sense; that is, opportunities at the bureaucratic level have led the movement to focus much of its energy on this arena. In Canada the situation is reversed. Internal bureaucratic barriers, especially the decentalized structures and the intolerance of internal advocates, have made it difficult for feminists to gain a firm foothold within the Canadian civil service. Although women's policy machinery has been established, compared to Australia it has been weak in terms of its feminist credentials and its institutional position. These problems have made it difficult for women's agencies to bring about policy reforms that are seen to be acceptable to the external women's movement.

This has had the effect of encouraging Anglo-feminists to work from outside the bureaucracy rather than to enter it to work as inside agitators. In many ways, the emphasis on lobbying from without has been more effective. As seen earlier, external feminists have often been the ones to instigate reforms, pushing women's agencies to take up these issues. Clearly though, it has been important for members of the external women's movement to have women's agencies inside the bureaucracy to process its demands. To the extent that Canadian femocrats can claim success, it has been because of the leverage they have achieved through this partnership with the external movement (see Heitlinger 1993, 91; Findlay 1987, 48). As Geller-Schwartz (1995, 50) argues: 'Bureaucrats and politicians respond to pressure from non-government interest groups, while resisting internal lobbyists. Femocrats have worked directly, indirectly and even surreptitiously, using external organizations to further their own institutions' policy goals.'

However, the point is that these agencies, even with the support of a well-organized external movement, have not been able to exercise the level of autonomy that would encourage more feminists to enter the bureaucracy to push for reforms.

Australian and Canadian feminist activists have had markedly different experiences with the bureaucratic sphere. Australian feminists have found it to be a relatively open institution, especially when the ALP has been on office. However, the alliance with the ALP is not the sole reason for the success of the femocrat strategy. Normative differences between Canada and Australia, particularly relatively weak neutrality norms in the Australian bureaucracy, have been very important. Without an alliance with a progressive political party and without the ongoing strength of neutrality norms and a decentralized bureaucracy, Canadian feminists have found it hard to get ahead in the institutional arena. This has led them to look for opportunities in other spheres. The entrenchment of the Charter of Rights and Freedoms has made the constitutional and legal institutions obvious feminist focal points.

5
Feminists and the Constitutional and Legal Realms: Creating New Spaces

Anglo-Canadian feminists may well have found it difficult to make progress through a bureaucratic route, but they have been more fortunate with constitutional and legal routes. With the entrenchment of the Charter of Rights and Freedoms in 1982, they have faced a much more positive political opportunity structure in these institutions and have, at times, successfully exploited them for their own purposes. Moreover, in doing so, these activists have helped to create new openings, thus demonstrating the two-way interactive relationship between social actors and political institutions. In contrast, Australian feminists have found it very difficult to use these institutions for their own purposes. Without access to a bill of rights and with the existence of a range of structural and normative barriers within the legal system, they have been reluctant to focus their attention on this area.

The literature on women and politics often ignores the constitutional and legal realms in favour of discussions about feminist engagement with Parliament and the bureaucracy.[1] Focusing on the constitutional and legal system acknowledges that these institutions operate as key variables, shaping not only the action of government but also the relationship between the government and society and between social actors themselves. The rule of law not only affects how governments act and think, 'it also determines the limits of what we imagine our options to be' (Krygier 1997). Fudge (1987, 546) makes a similar point:

It is important to recognize that the courts and litigation strategies are no less arenas of political debate and instruments of political mobilization than legislatures and traditional lobbying. No matter how distinctive the courts' institutional form or rhetoric of decision-making, judicial institutions make political decisions – decisions which are directly related to the distribution of power and the maintenance of, or encroachment upon, existing social relations.

The focus of this chapter is on the constitutional and legal systems; specifically, it is on their provisions for the protection of individual rights. It considers not only the constitution of each country, but also the legal and executive machinery that has been developed to enforce its protections. In Chapter 6, I assess the influence of the federal aspects of the Australian and Canadian constitutions on feminists.

As with the parliamentary and bureaucratic realms, the Australian and Canadian (outside Quebec) constitutional and legal realms share a number of similarities. Both have a common law tradition and a written constitution with unwritten constitutional conventions. The two legal systems also share a number of common nominal and substantive gender characteristics. In both Australia and Canada, women have traditionally been excluded from the legal realm as jurors, advocates, and judges. The law has also treated women differently than it has treated men; it has upheld the public/private distinction, assuming that women belong in the private (domestic) sphere and men in the public sphere. Further, in both countries the law has, to a greater or lesser degree, maintained a 'male standard' that is applied to all individuals. There are also some important differences between the two systems that have made it possible for feminists in Canada to help unsettle some of these gender features and to use these institutions to advance their aims. These are outlined in Table 5.1. In Canada, positive POSs include a nascent rights-based culture, constitutionally protected sex equality rights, and structural features of the legal system that enhance access to the courts. By contrast, Australian feminists have confronted a much less favourable POS in this area. Without a political culture concerned with individual rights, with no rights instrument, and with structural impediments within the court system, they have been unable to challenge existing gender norms; instead, they have attempted to bring about reforms in the area of statute law and through quasi-legal institutions. In many ways, this is a precarious strategy, and it leaves them exposed, especially at times when a conservative government is in office.

The Gendered Nature of the Law

Variations in the success of Canadian and Australian feminists with regard to the legal and constitutional arena have turned, in part, on the extent to which they have been able to challenge the gendered nature of the law. The later discussion details the reasons why Canadian feminists have been more successful than their Australian contemporaries at unsettling existing norms. This section outlines what is meant by gender norms in the legal sphere. In doing so, it draws on the work of feminist legal scholars who, over the past two decades, have begun to unravel the multiple ways in which legal structures in liberal democracies are gendered. What they have shown is how laws themselves, as well as the legal institutions in which they develop, are imbued with masculine assumptions and biases about the 'correct' roles of men and women in society. The reason for this bias concerns more than the fact that there are more men than women in

Table 5.1

Political opportunity structures in constitutional and legal institutions

	Australia	Canada
Legal principles	*Norms* **Negative** Continuing use of male standard Uphold public/ private distinction	*Norms* **Notionally positive** Challenge male standard through a substantive definition of equality (although not secured)
Rights protection	*Structures* **Negative** No constitutional rights instrument **Positive** Quasi-legal institutions, including the Industrial Commission and HREOC	*Structures* **Notionally Positive** Constitutionally entrenched Charter of Rights and Freedoms with sex equality clauses
	Norms **Negative** Weak rights culture	*Norms* **Positive** Emerging rights culture
Funding for court challenges	*Structures* **Negative** No court challenges funding Limited access to Legal Aid	*Structures* **Positive** Federally funded Court Challenges Program
Access to courts	*Structures* **Negative** Limited standing and *amicus curiae* provisions	*Structures* **Positive** Extensive standing and *amicus curiae* provisions
Feminist judges	*Norms* **Negative** No outwardly feminist judges	*Norms* **Positive** Presence on the Supreme Court bench of a number of judges sympathetic to feminist claims

law-making positions within the legislature and judiciary, although this is undeniably part of the explanation. More profoundly, the reason for this bias concerns the extent to which certain expectations and stereotypes about men and women have become embedded within the law and have been perpetuated over time. Feminist legal scholars have highlighted two important ways in which the law is gendered: first, it universalizes men's experience and applies a male standard to the subjects of the law; second, it upholds and maintains the public/private distinction.

Gendering the 'Neutral Subject'

Feminist jurisprudence has enhanced how the law is understood by eluci-dating the gender characteristics of the so-called abstract individual upon which the liberal legal systems of Australia and Canada are based. While the law claims to approach individuals in a neutral way, it actually uses a male standard to judge their behaviour. Moreover, although claiming to adopt a position of 'point-of-viewlessness,' the law actually imposes a point of view that is imbued with masculine norms. As Canadian profes-sor of law, Kathleen Mahoney (cited in Department for Women 1996, 13), argues:

> To begin with, one must realise that every decision-maker who walks into a court room to hear a case is armed not only with the relevant legal texts, but with a set of gender and race-based values, experiences and assumptions that are thoroughly embedded, some of which adversely impact and discriminate against women. To the extent that judges labour under certain biased attitudes, myths and misconceptions about women and men, the law can be said to be characterised by gender bias.

The masculine nature of the law is evident at a number of levels. One of the most obvious of these is the application of a male standard, or the use of the male comparator, across the legal spectrum. Traditionally, the law has treated women not on the basis of whether they are equal individ-uals but, rather, on the basis of whether their actions and experiences are the *same as* or *different from* those of men. MacKinnon (1989, 220-1, cited in Neave 1994, 260) expresses this clearly: 'Under the sameness rubric, women are measured according to correspondence with men, their equal-ity judged by proximity to his measure. Under the difference rubric, women are measured according to their lack of correspondence with men, their womankind judged by the their distance from his measure. Gender neutrality is the male standard.'

By treating women as though they were the same as or different from men, the law upholds men's experiences as the norm and is unable to deal with women's unique experiences and characteristics. The application of a sameness approach to the law may have enabled women to gain access to basic rights such as suffrage and equal pay, but it has not helped to ameliorate many of the social and economic disadvantages women have historically suffered. Nor can a sameness approach deal with women's biological differences. This has been most obvious in the way the law has dealt with pregnancy. For instance, in its ruling in the *Bliss* case, the Supreme Court of Canada argued that discrimination on the basis of pregnancy is not discrimination on the basis of sex.[2] The court's decision was based on the following 'logic': because not all women become pregnant, discrimination against those who are pregnant cannot be said to be based on sex.[3] As Brodsky and Day (1989, 15) note, by adopting this view the court overlooked the fundamental fact that 'only women become pregnant and that laws that discriminate against those who are pregnant discriminate against women.'

The Legal System and the Public/Private Distinction

Another significant contribution of feminist jurisprudence has been to outline how the legal system, by making presumptions about the 'proper' role of men and women, has historically upheld the public/private distinction. Men have been regarded as belonging to the world of the public sphere and work, as well as being masters of the home, while women have been identified with the private sphere, having responsibility for the home and family. The law in Australia and Canada has also traditionally upheld the liberal notion that the state should not intervene in the private realm, leaving those who exclusively inhabit it – historically, women and children – without protection against patriarchal authority. The idea that men and women 'naturally' inhabit different spheres has been reflected in the law in a myriad number of ways. These include sanctioning different pay rates for men and women, a reluctance to become involved in 'domestic' disputes (including violence in the home), a resistance to the notion of rape in marriage, and setting different criteria for men and women with regard to child custody and divorce (for a detailed discussion of the implications of the public/private dichotomy, see Pateman 1989; see also Scutt 1990, 204).

Over the past two decades feminist legal scholars and practitioners have made some progress in challenging legal assumptions about the 'natural' position of men and women in society. On occasion they have successfully intervened to bring about greater parity in pay rates and increased protection for victims of domestic violence, and they have convinced judges to accept the fact that husbands can rape wives because, contrary to historical opinion, upon marriage a woman does not consent 'irrevocably to sexual intercourse with her husband' (Scutt 1990, 474).

One of the problems confronting women in their dealings with the legal system is that their experiences of discrimination, whether in the home or in the workplace, are usually not shared by judges or other members of the legal establishment.[4] The opinions and life experiences of judges matter because, as Graycar (1995, 269-71) clearly documents in her discussion of the gendered nature of judgments, judges often appeal to notions of 'common sense' and their own personal experience in making judgments. Because this common sense is often based on a very narrow conception of the world, assumptions and misconceptions about women's experiences are easily incorporated into legal judgments (272-3). It is not that judges or other members of the legal establishment intentionally discriminate against women. As Australian Justice Deirdre O'Connor (Senate Standing Committee on Legal and Constitutional Affairs 1994, 22) put it:

> There may ... be difficulties in applying apparently neutral legal principles and concepts to women's experiences when, historically, these principles are based on a male experience of a social world from which women are excluded ...
>
> In my submission, the judicial failure to understand gender issues is not one of intent, but rather one of lack of information and access to changing ideas.

It is naive to presume that by simply increasing the number of women judges the law will be any less gender biased. However, if, as has occurred in Canada, judges with a feminist approach to the law and men sympathetic to women's experiences are appointed to the bench, then there is a much greater likelihood that women's experiences in the public and private spheres will be better understood and will be taken into account in legal judgments.[5]

This is not to argue that the gendered nature of the law is fixed or immune from challenge. In Canada, legal arguments based on feminist jurisprudence have sometimes been used successfully to bring about some changes in how the law deals with women. The following discussion outlines the different experiences of Australian and Canadian feminists with regard to their attempts to unsettle existing constitutional and legal norms.

Engaging with Legal Institutions: Canadian and Australian Feminist Experiences

Canadian and Australian feminists have vastly different experiences of engaging with the legal realm. In Canada, feminists have engaged extensively, albeit cautiously, with legal institutions, including the Constitution and the courts. This engagement has resulted in some positive outcomes, including the provision of sex equality rights in the Charter of Rights and Freedoms as well as the attainment of some important points in law through charter-based litigation. By contrast, Australian feminists have remained relatively aloof from these institutions. Efforts to challenge structural and normative obstacles have been frustrated, and this has reinforced Australian feminists' cynicism about the potential for gaining reform through these institutions.

Anglo-Canadian Feminist Engagement with the Law

Feminists have been involved directly in shaping the nature of rights protection in Canada. They have developed sophisticated positions in relation to the Constitution and the legal system more generally and have engaged in constitutional politics. Before this intervention is discussed, it is important to note that, within the Canadian feminist community, there has not been one unified constitutional position but, rather, a range of views. Some of the divisions within the movement exist along broad linguistic and racial cleavages. On the one hand, Francophone feminists have overwhelmingly supported the stance taken by the Quebec government to reject as far as possible the application of the charter to the province. Aboriginal women's groups have adopted yet another range of positions. Whereas some Aboriginal women's organizations argue strongly in support of the application of the charter to Aboriginal communities, others are more suspicious of an individual rights-based approach to society and fear the charter will interfere with aspirations for self-government (for a full discussion of both positions see Vickers 1993). As is discussed in the following chapter on federalism, these differences have created dilemmas for Anglo-feminists who have wanted to work in coalition with these other feminist groups on constitutional issues.

There have also been important differences between members of the Anglo-feminist community on constitutional questions and strategies. Some feminists have expressed outright opposition to the idea of engaging with the charter and legal institutions on the grounds that they are elite and patriarchal structures and that they offer exclusive access to the wealthy. Others have been ambivalent but demonstrated a willingness to compromise and engage in constitutional politics once it became apparent that the entrenchment of the charter was inevitable (see Dobrowolsky 2000, 69). Still others have embraced the charter, and the litigation opportunities it affords, without reservation. These various positions have been played out throughout the history of charter developments.

Prior to the 1980s Canadian women had little success pursuing their goals through either the Constitution or the court system. Before this time there were no equality rights enshrined in the Constitution. The 1960 Canadian Bill of Rights, a federal statute that guaranteed individuals the right to 'equality before the law and the protection of the law' (in the federal jurisdiction), had created an opening for women to pursue rights claims through the courts. However, women's attempts to use these rights guarantees were stymied. The Supreme Court, which argued in 1928 that women were not persons, continued after the creation of the Bill of Rights to make decisions that had demonstrably negative outcomes for women. Some of the most blatant of these included: the 1973 *Lavell* case, where the court refused to grant 'Indian' status to Aboriginal women marrying non-Aboriginal men;[6] the 1973 *Murdoch* case, which denied wives equal share of their husbands' property regardless of their contribution; the 1978 *Bliss* decision, which found that discrimination on the basis of pregnancy was not sex discrimination; and, the *Pappajohn* ruling, which stated that a man has not committed the offence of rape if he has a mistaken but honest belief that the woman has consented to sexual intercourse (for a full discussion of these and other cases see Mossman 1995, 218-25). According to Bashevkin (1996, 224), all five decisions taken by the Supreme Court of Canada in relation to sex equality during the period between 1973 and 1984 (after which time the equality provisions of the charter came into effect) could be considered to have had a negative impact on women.

The Canadian Bill of Rights (1960) had raised women's expectations about the possibility of using the law to achieve their aims, but in practice it proved to be very disappointing. Decisions taken by the courts after its enactment, which were allegedly based on notions of so-called neutrality, were actually 'constrained by ideas of sameness that used men as the norm' (Mossman 1995, 225). These decisions served to reinforce feminist suspicions about the gendered nature of the legal system, but they did not cause them to reject legal strategies in toto; instead, they 'fuelled feminists' reform activity' within the legal arena (224). Given that, by the late 1970s, the Trudeau government was working towards entrenching a bill of rights within the Constitution, this was a rational response.

The entrenchment of the charter in the Constitution in 1982 was a significant event for Anglo-Canadian feminists. According to Fudge (1989, 447), 'the constitutional entrenchment of equality rights became a symbol of profound political significance around which many disparate feminist organisations and women's groups were able to coalesce.' In engaging in charter debates, Anglo-feminists came to develop their own 'constitutional identity.' Having said this, it is important to note that the influence of the charter on the actions of the movement has not been fixed, predictable, or always positive. As Dobrowolsky (2000, 39) warns, feminists' 'acquisition of equality guarantees cannot be recounted as a narrative of inevitable progress.' Because the charter is itself an 'evolving instrument' that has become 'encrusted' with the experiences and events that have buffeted it since its inception, its impact has varied over time (Cairns 1995b, 196). The position of feminists within the Anglo women's movement in relation to the charter can be seen to have shifted as the charter itself has changed.

Charter Engagement: Phase 1

The involvement of Anglo-feminists in the constitutional debates oc-curred in three distinct phases. The first phase, which occurred during the late 1970s and early 1980s, was both reactive and, to some extent, elitist. It was reactive in that it was driven by the feminist desire to overcome the inadequacies of the existing statute-based Bill of Rights and to have the charter include an unambiguous guarantee of equality for women (see CACSW 1980, 148). Indeed, at the time many feminists were skeptical about what could be achieved through a charter. NAC's submissions pre-sented to the parliamentary committee hearings on the Constitution in 1980 illustrate this ambivalence: 'Given the sorry record of the courts on women's rights cases' issues relating to equality 'should not be left to judicial interpretation' (NAC 1980, 163). Like the support of other femi-nist organizations, NAC's support for the charter was conditional on it including specific, positive equality guarantees for women (163).

This phase of Anglo-feminist involvement was elitist in that those who engaged in the initial round of lobbying were drawn from a relatively nar-row group of activists. According to Billings (cited in Kome 1983, 17), prior to 1980 those engaged in charter politics were 'mostly legal minded women of established organisations.' However, it soon became obvious that this elite-level approach to rights legislation was not sufficient to secure the ironclad equality guarantees that many feminists were looking for. Although the government made some amendments to the charter leg-islation to make men and women equal before and under the law, many feminists felt that this protection did not go far enough. As a result, they began to contemplate using alternative tactics, including mass-mobilization (Dobrowolsky 2000, 50). The need for a new strategy became even more apparent when a forthcoming convention on women and the Constitu-tion organized by the Canadian Advisory Council on the Status of Women was cancelled, with the approval of the minister, Lloyd Axworthy. The can-cellation prompted the resignation of CACSW president Doris Anderson, a well-known and respected feminist. Members of the women's movement rallied around Anderson, established the Ad Hoc Committee on Women and the Constitution, and set about arranging their own conference. Anderson's resignation was very significant with regard to shifting the strategies of the women's movement. As Hosek (cited in Vickers 1993, 198) argues, with her resignation 'the women's movement suddenly had a heroine, a villain and an event, all of which symbolised its exclusion from the constitutional process.'

Charter Engagement: Phase 2

The Ad Hoc Conference ushered in the second phase of feminist organiz-ing around the Constitution. A distinguishing feature of this phase was the level of mass involvement by women activists. Some feminists remained circumspect about how useful a charter would be to the advancement of women's interests because it meant relying on male-dominated courts (see Vickers 1993, 274). Others took a more pragmatic position, being aware of the possible limitations of the charter route but also being willing to try to achieve entrenched equality guarantees. The support for the Ad Hoc Conference on 14 February 1981 provided an indication of the level of interest and concern among feminists regarding the course of constitutional politics. It was expected that 300 women would attend; in the event, 1,300 women registered. The conference outcomes demonstrated the movement's cautious attitude towards the charter: participants agreed to support the charter on the proviso that the government accept their proposed amendments, including an overriding protection of equality rights (Ad Hoc Committee 1981, 165).

The resolutions adopted by feminists at the conference, and the subsequent efforts to bring these resolutions into effect, provide a manifest example of how they were able to take advantage of existing political opportunities and to create new avenues through which they could advance their claims. At one level it can be seen that the charter shaped the behaviour of Anglo-feminists: by opting for the charter route, feminists had, in effect, agreed to work within 'the limits of action set by the federal government' (Burt 1988, 77). In doing so, feminists had to gloss over the many differences between each other and accept that concessions had to be made on some of their major demands, including reproductive rights and equitable political representation (Dobrowolsky 2000, 57, 71). However, operating within these limits, these women demonstrated their agency. In the end, they were able to wield some influence and to make an important difference to the final charter document.

Their influence first became apparent in March 1981, when they secured a federal government agreement to include a general statement on equality rights for women and men. This statement eventually became Section 28 of the charter. Securing government support for the clause came about through the combination of a mass mobilization effort, which included sending information to women across the country about an elite lobbying strategy, which involved Ad Hoc Committee members and the National Association of Women and the Law (NAWL) meeting with senior government members.

The efforts of Anglo-feminists in relation to Section 28 were threatened in November 1981, when at a First Ministers Conference on the Constitution, a decision was taken to subject it to the provincial override clause.[7] Members of the Anglo-feminist community reacted angrily to this move and agitated successfully to have the premiers reverse their decision.[8] While this episode demonstrated to feminists that their hold on events was a tenuous one, it nevertheless convinced them that they could make an important difference to the outcome of constitutional reform. For many feminists, their engagement in the charter debates and, especially, their success in securing the inclusion of Clauses 15 and 28 (both related to sex equality) in the final document, was a radicalizing one (Gotell, 1994). Moreover, it gave them a sense of proprietorship over the charter in general and over these clauses in particular. As Dobrowolsky (2000, 37) notes: 'There was ... a sense that through their efforts, Canadian women had achieved constitutional recognition, something that even their counterparts in a liberal, rights-based society like that of the United States had failed to do.' Their sense of achievement acted as a spur to encourage some feminists to devise a sophisticated litigation strategy once the charter came into effect.

Charter Engagement: Phase 3

The third phase of feminist engagement with the Constitution, which began after the entrenchment of the charter in 1982, saw a return to an elitist strategy, with feminist legal experts involved in developing a legal 'project.' This project had two components: 'Charterwatching' and litigation strategy. Charterwatching involved holding conferences and workshops, writing books and articles, and undertaking an 'audit' of federal and provincial statutes, the aim being to 'pinpoint what needed to be changed to avoid subsequent legal battles over equality and provide women with a catalogue of what may need changing through litigation' (Razack 1991, 39).

Once the equality provisions came into effect, feminist legal activists enthusiastically shifted their effort towards the development of a litigation strategy. In 1985 the Legal Education and Action Fund (LEAF) was created by a group of feminist legal experts with a mandate to initiate and intervene in charter cases affecting women. LEAF members, drawn primarily from professional legal backgrounds, could initially be characterized as liberal feminists – supportive of the 'liberal notion of reasoned argument' (Razack 1991, 44) and having great faith in the transformative power of the law (Gotell 1994, 16). These attitudes were reflected in LEAF's early statements about its ability to take a proactive stance towards the charter by bringing cases of blatant sex discrimination to court – cases that had come to light during the movement's charterwatching activities (LEAF, cited in Gotell 1994, 272-3). It planned to 'approach change incrementally, by using victories in one area as building blocks. A case won, a point of doctrine consolidated, and then the next stage of developing law is undertaken' (cited in Gotell 1994, 273). As one of LEAF's founders, Lyn Smith, explained: 'Our idea was to choose cases which would establish principles with far reaching impacts, instead of a random, unpredictable approach' (Makin 1990, D2).

The provision of public funds through the federal government's Court Challenges Program (CCP) was crucial to LEAF being able to commence its litigation strategy, giving it the financial resources necessary to intervene in court cases. Between 1985 and 1993, the program boosted LEAF's own fundraising activities by up to $250,000 per annum, depending on its caseload. LEAF, as well as other commentators (such as Supreme Court justice Bertha Wilson), saw the CCP as one of the keys to its success (Vienneau 1992, C1; Wilson 1993, 4). When the Mulroney government axed the program in 1992, arguing that by this time a solid body of equality jurisprudence had been developed, LEAF and other equality-seeking groups vigorously opposed the move (see Vienneau 1992). In 1994 the federal government reinstated the program. LEAF continues to be one of the main beneficiaries of the CCP (Allen and Morton 1997, 1).

For a variety of reasons, LEAF's strategy has not been embraced by all Anglo-feminists. After the mass-level activities prior to the entrenchment of the charter, many feminists initially expressed resentment about the return to what was perceived to be an elitist strategy. Criticism has also been expressed about the homogeneity of LEAF itself, especially its preponderance of White, middle-class women and its tendency to downplay issues of race, class, sexuality, and disability (Pellatt 2000, 133). Moreover, many remain skeptical about what can be achieved through litigation so long as the court remains a male-dominated and highly gendered institution. There is a widespread view that placing one's faith in the charter means ultimately putting one's faith in the hands of a judiciary that is viewed as consisting of 'a monopoly of elderly, white men from privileged backgrounds' (Bacchi and Marquis 1994, 102). While some of these critiques remain, others were tempered as LEAF won some important, albeit precarious, legal victories and became more sensitive to representing women from a variety of backgrounds, both within its own ranks and in court.

Anglo-Canadian Feminist Litigation Strategy: An Assessment

During the first few years, LEAF's charter litigation strategy had mixed results. On the positive side of the ledger, the charter had provided LEAF with the opportunity to intervene, albeit in a limited way, to advance a feminist position on various issues within the court system. Moreover, the courts took up some of the arguments presented in LEAF factums, demonstrating that LEAF could have a direct influence upon charter interpretation. On the other hand, LEAF, which had been hampered in its attempt to bring cases to court using the equality clauses, was left to defend those rights that had already been established (see LEAF 1989a, 1).[9]

LEAF experienced a major breakthrough in 1989 with the *Andrews* decision. Although the case did not deal with sex equality directly, LEAF had sought, and was granted, approval to intervene in the case as *amicus curiae*.[10] *Andrews* proved to be a groundbreaking decision and was to have a major influence on the future strategies of LEAF as well as other equality-seeking litigation groups. Its significance rested on two factors: first, it found that 'the purpose of s. 15 was to promote equality for disadvantaged groups rather than to protect the privileged' (LEAF 1989a, 2). In effect, it made it more difficult for groups, including men's groups and corporations, to use Section 15 to challenge existing affirmative action laws – something that had hitherto been a major impediment to LEAF's litigation tactics (see LEAF October 1989). Second, *Andrews* embraced a definition of equality that was substantially different from that which had been applied in the past. Instead of using the 'similarly situated test,' which applied a male standard, the court decided to adopt a 'purposive' definition of equality; that is, one that accepts that women as a group are differently situated from men and that their position of group disadvantage might require specific remedies (Brodsky and Day 1989, 207). In coming to this definition, the court had essentially adopted the view of equality developed within feminist jurisprudence – something for which LEAF claimed the credit (LEAF 1989b, 3).

The *Andrews* ruling was significant because it demonstrated that the feminist litigation strategy had an influence on the application of the charter: feminists, through LEAF, had contributed to a new understanding of how equality was to be applied. It was a sign that feminist intervention could undermine existing gender norms – in this case, the idea that men were the standard against which individuals were to be measured – to influence the operation of legal institutions in a positive way for women. There have also been other court decisions under the charter (in which LEAF has intervened) that have had more positive outcomes for women's equality – the *Morgentaler* decision, which decriminalized abortion, was seen as a major victory by feminists (Allen and Morton, 1997, 10).[11] Other important cases for LEAF include *Butler*, which found that pornography was a form of 'hate speech' targeted at minority women;[12] *Moge* on divorce;[13] *Brooks* on pregnancy discrimination; and *Schachter* on childcare (see various accounts in *LEAFlines* 1987-94; Allen and Morton 1997; Razack 1991, 128).[14] Moreover, LEAF's arguments in these cases have influenced the development of charter jurisprudence, which, in turn, provides a foundation from which LEAF can make increasingly sophisticated equality arguments (Pellatt 2000, 135).

Although these cases mark a turning point in feminists' ability to engage with the law, these gains are by no means secure or uncontested. Decisions in *Egan, Miron,* and *Thibaudeau,*[15] in which the Supreme Court applied 'similarly situated' tests of equality, demonstrate the precarious nature of legal advances. As a result of these rulings, feminists, through LEAF, had to once again find an opening to mount an argument for a return to a substantive definition of equality. This was made possible in the *Vriend* case in relation to sexual orientation, where LEAF was successful in arguing that the courts revert to earlier charter jurisprudence on equality (Pellatt 2000, 142).[16] Some decisions have had contradictory outcomes for women, such as the *Lavalee* case,[17] which used the battered women's syndrome as a defence. Critics have argued that such a defence maintains the notion of women as helpless victims and pathologizes their response to the experience of violence (see Wynhausen 1998). Other cases, such as the *Seaboyer* decision (discussed below), have had a demonstrably negative outcome on women (LEAF 1989b, 6; 1992; 1994).[18]

For some feminists, these reversals and negative decisions have confirmed the futility of engaging with the law and the ongoing bias of judges. For Fudge and Glasbeek (1992), they serve only to demonstrate that the status quo, in terms of class and gender, remains entrenched within the law and court system. Especially in its initial stages, LEAF has also been a target for criticism with regard to its strategy, which assumes that all women share 'a core of oppression' (see Razack 1991, 133; and Gotell 1994). Others have argued that LEAF's feminist jurisprudence is not the breakthrough that some had thought because, in order to win equality, women had to start from a position of disadvantage vis-à-vis men (see Herman 1994, 590; Gotell 1994). One of the problems underlying LEAF's arguments is that, in requiring the women receive different treatment from men in order to augment their overall equality 'is still a claim in relation to the putative position of men' (Jhappan 1998, 74). According to Jhappan: 'It seems that one of the key problems with litigation strategies pursued to date is that women ... have been trying to *win* cases within law's narrow, uni-categorical terms – trying to fit large, complex issues into small simplified categories that judges can understand as abstractions' (106).

LEAF has been alert to these criticisms and has taken some action to address them. It has attempted to develop a more inclusive approach to representation, arguing that 'strategies for equality and legal theory must be developed collectively in order to address the reality of women's lives and ensure that issues of race, heritage and disability are never "add-ons" to the experiences of white women' (LEAF 1992).

It has put these sentiments into action by working in coalition with other women's groups to broaden its understanding of women from a variety of backgrounds. LEAF has also become more careful in its selection of cases, choosing those that reflect women's intersecting identities and diverse experiences. The *Vriend* case, which dealt with discrimination on the basis of sexuality, is a case in point. LEAF and feminists supportive of the litigation strategy have also countered some of these criticisms by arguing that, while by no means perfect, the charter (and the law more broadly) is an important site for political manoeuvre. Rights claims, such as those advanced by LEAF, have pushed the boundaries of the law, and 'the Charter is perceived by many to *at least be capable* of promoting women's equality in Canada' (Herman 1994, 590 [emphasis in original]). As Razack (1991, 130) notes, 'The legal challenge is only the tip of the iceberg, but it may be that crack in the system through which alternative values might seep.' These cautious, but more positive, renderings of the feminist charter litigation strategy do appear to have some basis in practice.

The importance of having a range of strategic devices became starkly apparent under the Mulroney Progressive Conservative government. It was during this period that the litigation strategy pursued by LEAF was able to provide women with protection against negative legislative decisions. At a time when the government was dismantling welfare programs and pursuing a conservative social agenda, feminists were still able to make some progress by appealing to the charter and using the court system. As Bashevkin's (1996, 226-8) research shows, in the period between 1984 and 1993, most of the reforms that advanced women's equality were directly attributable to the charter rather than the legislature. Indeed, it was during this time that the legislature attempted, unsuccessfully, to overturn one of the most celebrated legal victories of Canadian feminism – the decriminalization of abortion.

At the same time, during this period feminists were also made aware of the tenuous nature of a charter-based strategy. This was demonstrated most dramatically in 1989 with the *Seaboyer* judgment. In this case, the Supreme Court struck down the existing rape shield protection that prevented the court from questioning rape victims about their previous sexual history. LEAF intervened in the case, but to little effect. This ruling was seen by feminists who had put their faith in the law as an 'astounding defeat,' not least because it removed an existing protection for women. But the loss within the court system was not the end of the matter. After the decision was handed down, women's organizations, including NAC, mobilized quickly to put their lobbying and mass protest strategies into effect, pressuring the federal Parliament to legislate to maintain the rape shield protection. The then attorney general, Kim Campbell, responded to this pressure by redrafting rape legislation that met some of the activists' demands (see Eberts, cited in Wilcox 1993, 238). While this episode did not lead to improved protections for women rape victims, existing protections were 'saved.'

The problems some feminists have had with LEAF and the litigation strategy more generally cannot detract from the fact that the organization and the strategy have broadened the repertoire of Anglo-Canadian feminists so as to enhance their capacity to make the most of existing institutional arrangements. As Dobrowolsky (2000, 26) argues: 'No matter how persuasive ... arguments against the legal strategy are, the fact remains that the Charter and courts exist and have provided an alternative ground for certain forms of feminist contestation.'

There is no question that charter litigation has limitations and that it alone cannot ensure the equality of all women all the time. As former Supreme Court justice Bertha Wilson (1993, 14) noted: 'The law can only go so far. What is required is the political will to address ... social problem[s] of alarming proportions.' What a decade of litigation experience has demonstrated is that, on its own, this strategy cannot always be relied upon to bring about positive outcomes for women; however, it can sometimes achieve its aims. Moreover, it has shown that, in having a multifaceted strategy, feminists have the potential to take advantage of the opportunities in one institution when they are closed off in another. The importance of having this broad strategic repertoire becomes obvious when we compare it to the situation in Australia, where feminists have avoided engaging with the constitutional and legal realms.

Australian Feminists: The Constitutional and Legal Realms
Australian feminists have not been as preoccupied with constitutional and legal issues as have their Canadian counterparts. Nevertheless, they have engaged in debates about these institutions, especially in relation to the protection of women's rights through constitutional and legal means. Australian feminists' first foray into these debates occurred at the 1890 constitutional conventions on federation. Women's exclusion from full citizenship rights within the colonies (at the time of federation only women in South Australia and Western Australia were enfranchised) led a number of suffragettes to mount a campaign to have universal suffrage written into the new Constitution (Irving 1994, 188). Their lobbying was partially successful. The founders agreed to include a clause (s. 41) that guaranteed women's existing voting rights as well as the federal franchise. Feminist agitation at the federation conferences helped to secure (non-Aboriginal) women's federal voting rights, which came into force in 1902. Yet, despite the best efforts of these feminists, voting rights remained outside the Constitution, with responsibility for electoral laws being left with the legislature (188).

Since the flourishing of the contemporary women's movement in the 1960s, Australian feminists have engaged in internal debates on constitutional issues, especially around the issue of the protection of women's rights. In general there has been concern about existing rights protection; however, unlike in Canada, these concerns have not led feminists to look for constitutional answers to the problem. Australian feminists have been especially ambivalent about embracing the notion of an entrenched bill of rights. Key women's groups such as WEL have not campaigned strongly

on the issue. Where it has been debated – mainly among legal and academic feminists – positions have varied widely. Some support has come from
within feminist legal circles. For instance, feminist barrister Jocelynne
Scutt has argued in favour of entrenched rights because she believes this
would make it harder to manipulate and deny women's rights (Bulbeck
1996, 49). Other advocates for a bill of rights have tended to take a pragmatic position, arguing for a statute-based strategy rather than a constitutionally entrenched one. Such a view has been advanced by Justice
Elizabeth Evatt and feminist legal academics Regina Graycar and Hillary
Charlesworth in the Australian Law Reform Commission (ALRC) report
Equality before the Law: Women's Equality (1994) and at the 1999 Women's
Constitutional Convention (WCC) (see below).

Other feminist academics have opposed such a proposal. Margaret
Thornton has been less willing than some of her female colleagues to
embrace a bill of rights, arguing that it would maintain the male standard
as a benchmark (cited in Larbiestier and Russell 1995, 93). Political scientist Helen Irving (1996, 93) has also argued against a bill of rights,

> partly on the same grounds that opponents of any such bill would
> support (that rights would be determined by judges rather than elected
> representatives, for example), but also specifically on the grounds that
> rights are not fixed and unidimensional, as entrenching them suggests,
> and that disadvantaged groups, including women, need to struggle to
> identify and articulate rights as part of the process of gaining rights.

Political commentators Carol Bacchi and Vicky Marquis (1994) also oppose entrenched rights. Basing their argument on an interpretation of
Canadian women's experience under the charter, they state that 'groups in
power and groups with resources are better placed to exploit the possibilities of entrenched rights.'[19] In their view, 'the risk of rights may then be
too great a risk to take' (107).

These negative opinions appear to be in step with wider views within
the Australian feminist community concerning the problems of working
through what are perceived to be male-biased legal institutions. If the
pages of the feminist journal *Refractory Girl* are any guide, since the early
1970s Australian feminists can be said to have shared a 'cynicism about
the prospect of transforming law to serve the interests of women' (Morgan
1993, 117). As activist Lesley Lynch argued at the first women and law
conference in 1979: 'I worry about all [the] energy and talent being
diverted into exclusively reformist struggles and wonder whether in
twenty years or so the legal structure will still be the instrument of class
and patriarchy that it now is' (ibid.).

Critical views have been expressed elsewhere about the 'numbing dullness of male-centered constitutional law that does not "speak" to us' (Howe 1995, 226). Submissions by women's groups to the ALRC inquiry into gender and the law, and the Senate investigation of gender bias and the judiciary, suggest that there is an enduring suspicion among Australian feminists concerning just how effectively the courts would advance women's interests (see ALRC 1994, esp. chap. 2; Senate Standing Committee on Legal and Constitutional Affairs 1994).

The recent Australian republican debate saw contemporary feminists focus once again on broader constitutional questions. Their intervention occurred both at an intellectual level (e.g., see Curthoys 1993, 28; Irving 1996, 90) and at a practical level. In February 1998 various women's groups, including specifically feminist organizations, came together to organize the Women's Constitutional Convention (WCC). The WCC was strategically timed, meeting immediately prior to the formal Constitutional Convention (CC). (The latter was charged with the task of formulating the referendum question pertaining to whether or not Australia should become a republic.) WCC participants expressed a spectrum of opinion on changes to the Constitution, ranging from those who supported minimal change through to those who wanted a complete overhaul of the existing political system. Despite these differences, the WCC produced a statement and presented it to the chair of the CC, Ian Sinclair. The document indicated that most women at the WCC supported the move to a republic provided that 'the new system promote[ ] women's equality in future decision making ... and recognise[ ] indigenous Australians.' It called on the CC to accept an appointment process for selecting a head of state – one that involved women to the same extent as it did men – and to adopt a new constitutional preamble that included a statement on the equality of the sexes (for a full transcript of the WCC outcomes and debates see <http://www.womensconv.dynamite.com.au>).

If feminists were hoping to exercise significant influence over the outcomes of the CC, then they were to be disappointed. In step with what occurred a century earlier, the voices of Australian feminists were stifled at the main convention and their views had little impact on its outcome. Two prominent feminists delegates to the CC, Aboriginal activist Pat O'Shane and human rights advocate Moira Rayner, managed to convince the convention to address process issues by adopting a committee structure that took account of gender equality. And this, by one account, was no mean feat (Vizard 1998, 130-2). However, other substantive issues, including the issue of equal gender representation in the pre-selection process for a future president, failed to make it onto the CC agenda. The difficulties confronting Australian feminists at the formal convention, their inability to influence the CC agenda, and the eventual defeat of the referendum in November 1999 all stand in direct contrast to what happened during the Canadian constitutional debates of the early 1980s.

Australian feminists have differed from their Anglo-Canadian counterparts not only in terms of the degree and efficacy of their engagement in constitutional and rights debates, but also with regard to their use of the court system. The most prominent Australian court case concerned a sex-discrimination claim by over 700 women from non-English speaking backgrounds against Australian Iron and Steel Pty. Ltd.[20] The case was upheld in 1989 by the High Court. Although ultimately successful, the Jobs for Women Campaign, as the action came to be known, took an inordinately long time to settle. As the women's lawyer stated at the conclusion of the case: 'The fact that it took fourteen years to resolve indicates an urgent need for serious examination of what changes can be made to ensure that other complainants will not have to endure the inexcusable delay and hardship that these women went through to obtain justice' (Burnstein 1994, 12).

The complainants also experienced significant difficulty in obtaining any funding to support their case. Unlike Canadian feminists, Australian feminists have not had access to a court challenges program and have had to rely on the limited federal Legal Aid Program. After an application for funding was initially refused, feminist lawyers engaged in the case undertook an extensive lobbying campaign and eventually received some support through the program. According to the lawyers, although limited, legal aid made all the difference to their success in the case (Anderson 1994, 108).

Aside from not running test cases, Australian feminists have not often intervened as *amicus curiae* in cases that are of broad concern to women. There are two reasons for this. First, historically, Australian judges have been reticent to approve *amicus* standing for any advocates, including those wanting to intervene on behalf of women. There are a few exceptions,[21] but most applications from feminists and other supportive parties to be heard in court have been unsuccessful. A recent failed attempt concerns a request by the Public Interest Advocacy Centre (PIAC) to intervene as *amicus curiae* on behalf of four equality-seeking groups, including WEL and the Association of Non-English Speaking Background Women (NESBW), in the *Brandy* case, which was being heard before the High Court.[22] The case related to the issue of the enforceability of determinations made by the Human Rights and Equal Opportunity Commission (HREOC), which had implications for the Racial Discrimination Act, the Sex Discrimination Act, and the Disability Discrimination Act. PIAC's application was, according to the PIAC deponent, a 'remarkable failure' (interview with author, 1998). The court refused to hear PIAC and provided no reason for its decision (PIAC officer, interview with author, 1998; ALRC 1994 nn. 92, 125).

Australian feminist legal groups have campaigned against the limited standing and *amicus* laws. In 1993 the short-lived feminist litigation organization, Women Advocates for Gender Equality, made a submission to the ALRC inquiry into equality before the law, urging it to recommend 'that the laws of standing in Australia be reformed to accommodate interest groups, permitting them to intervene where the issues in dispute have ramifications for women in general' (PIAC 1995). Feminist lawyers Roxon and Walker put a similar submission to the commission, arguing the need for an extension of *amicus curiae* provisions (ALRC 1994, 116). Despite these calls for reform, and the follow-up recommendations of the ALRC inquiry, these laws remain unchanged.[23]

The courts' reluctance to hear women's voices has been matched by a reluctance on the part of feminists to organize themselves to intervene in court cases. An interesting feature of the PIAC application in the *Brandy* case was that it was PIAC that approached WEL and NESBW to support its intervention in the proceedings rather than the other way around. According to a PIAC officer, *Brandy* was a critical case because of its potential ramifications for the treatment of sex discrimination by the Human Rights and Equal Opportunity Commission. It wanted to intervene, but it wanted its application to include 'authentic voices' from the communities that might be affected by the case, so it sought the support of groups that represented them (interview with author, 1998).

Australian feminists' lack of emphasis on the courts as an avenue for political contestation was illustrated again in 1996, when the High Court heard an abortion case, *Superclinics Australia Pty. Ltd.* v. *CES and ORS*.[24] When this case came before the High Court it seems that few members of the women's movement were aware of it. Among those who were, most wanted to treat it as a case relating to medical negligence rather than to run the risk of having a 'showdown' over abortion (Graycar, personal communication, 2 March 1998; see also Wainer 1997, 136). No women's group organized to become involved in this case until, in a highly unusual and somewhat controversial move, the High Court granted the Australian Catholic Health Care Association and the Australian Catholic Bishops' Conference *amicus* standing (the presiding chief justice, Gerard Brennan, was known to be a practising Roman Catholic). Even the Abortion Providers Federation (APF) were better organized than was the women's movement on this issue: following the High Court's decision to allow the Roman Catholic Church intervenor status, the APF immediately sought, and received, the same standing. It was only after these two groups had become involved that feminists began to rally and look to WEL to develop a strategy (Wainer 1997, 137).

WEL was totally unprepared for a litigation strategy: as one of the participants in the campaign noted, 'we had no money, no campaign group on the issue, no legal team, no time' (Wainer 1997, 137). After some frantic organizing that drew on feminist networks, WEL applied to be heard as *amicus curiae* before the High Court (137-8), only to withdraw its application when the case was settled out of court (WEL 1996). One of the lessons learned by Australian feminists from the *Superclinics* case was that their lack of focus on the legal and constitutional sphere had left them unprepared to take advantage of the opportunities they sometimes afford.

Australian feminists have not looked to the Constitution and legal realm to advance women's rights issues. However, it would be wrong to assume that they have ignored rights issues entirely; rather, they have adopted the modus operandi of most Australian interest groups and looked to other arenas to advance their claims. Chapter 4 notes how feminists have used the bureaucracy. Women's groups, together with femocrats, have brought to light serious violations of women's rights and have campaigned to bring about statute law reform in areas such as discrimination in the workplace, domestic violence, sexual assault, control over reproduction, matrimonial property law, and family law.[25] Women's organizations and feminists within the bureaucracy have also been active in lobbying the government to ratify international conventions such as the Convention on the Elimination of All Forms of Discrimination against Women (CEDAW) and, once introduced, have sought to ensure that these conventions are upheld (see Wills 1995).[26]

But not all Australian feminist efforts to improve women's rights have been directed towards the bureaucracy. Like other Australian rights activists, feminists have also been able to take advantage of openings in other quasi-judicial institutions. The Conciliation and Arbitration Commission (and, more recently, the Industrial Relations Commission) has been a particularly important arena for them. Created as what Miller (1964) describes as an 'organ of syndical satisfaction' for working-class interests, the commission has sometimes been open to the demands of women. The expansive standing provisions have provided an opening through which women are able to intervene in wage cases in order to put forward equal pay claims, often with positive outcomes. As Scutt argues: 'Advances in wage relativities have come about only where women have intervened' (see ALRC 1994, 117). It is also the case that advances have come about when government has intervened on behalf of women (e.g., when, after its election in 1972, the Whitlam Labor government successfully lobbied to have the equal pay case reopened).[27]

Another quasi-legal avenue opened up for women in 1984, when the Hawke Labor government enacted the Sex Discrimination Act (SDA). The SDA, which partially activated the UN CEDAW in Australian law, created the position of the Sex Discrimination Commissioner in the Human Rights Commission (later to become the Human Rights and Equal Opportunity Commission [HREOC]) and accorded the commissioner the power to conduct quasi-judicial inquiries where conciliation had been unsuccessful (Ronalds 1990). The provisions of the act have not been immune from feminist criticism, particularly with regard to the 'sameness' notion of equality and the limitations of complaints-based legislation. Nevertheless, since coming into effect, the SDA has 'greatly assisted women to seek redress for immediate and direct discrimination' and has been well utilized.[28] Moreover, despite these concerns there has been no effort on the part of women's groups to shift their attention towards a greater emphasis on court litigation; rather, the most common response has been to call for a strengthening of existing legislation (see Sawer 1990, 210; House of Representatives Standing Committee 1992, 59-69).

Australian feminists have undoubtedly made some gains using these extra-legal institutions to pursue rights issues, but their strategy has its limitations – limitations that have become increasingly obvious under the conservative Howard government. Since coming to office in 1996, the government has shown little support for anti-discrimination legislation and the executive machinery established to enforce it. It did not support changes that would have strengthened the provisions of the SDA. In fact, in 1997 Attorney General Daryl Williams took to Cabinet a plan to abolish the sex discrimination commissioner. Furthermore, in its 1997 budget, the federal government cut funding to the commission by 40 percent and left the position of sex discrimination commissioner vacant for over twelve months after the incumbent, Sue Walpole, resigned (Jamal 1998, 2).[29] The Howard government's attack on the UN for venturing too far into domestic issues, its decision to review Australia's commitment to UN treaties, and its refusal to make Australia a signatory to the CEDAW Optional Protocol sends a further signal to Australian feminists that relying on existing institutions to achieve adequate rights protection would be a risky strategy indeed.[30]

In line with Australian feminist resistance to formal organizational structures, unlike the Canadian LEAF, feminist groups have not expended a great deal of effort on developing litigation organizations. Their decision not to create such an organization is also no doubt, in part, the result of barriers in the legal realm. While some advocacy organizations have emerged – such as the Women's Legal Action Fund in Victoria and WAGE in New South Wales – they have not been able to sustain themselves over time. The ALRC (1994, 131) inquiry into women and the law described existing women's advocacy organizations as 'no more than small groups of volunteers seeking resources.' As noted in relation to the *Superclinics* abortion case and PIAC's intervention in the *Brandy* case, outside legal circles feminist groups have made little effort to orientate themselves towards the legal system.

Australian feminists' reluctance to engage with the constitutional/legal arena or to create sustainable legal organizations leaves them at a disadvantage vis-à-vis their Canadian counterparts. Whereas in Canada during the Mulroney period feminists could look towards the charter and the legal institutions to compensate for negative decisions within the legislative arena, in Australia feminists do not enjoy such an option. Until they have access to a bill of rights and are able to establish a litigation strategy, feminists in Australia will be unable to take full advantage of the benefits that arise from being able to engage in the full spectrum of political institutions.

Political Opportunities in the Canadian and Australian Constitutional and Legal Arenas

In Canada and Australia the POS available to feminists in the constitutional and legal arenas has been shaped by five central factors: (1) legal principles, (2) the prevailing rights culture and access to a bill of rights, (3) funding for court challenges, (4) existing standing provisions, and (5) the presence of feminist judges. In relation to each of these variables, Canadian feminists have enjoyed substantially more positive opportunities than have their Australian counterparts.

Rights Culture and a Bill of Rights

Constitutional questions have long been a focus of legal and political discourse in Canada. As Trudeau (1968) pointed out: 'Of all the problems Canadian public opinion is currently concerned with, the one that is most frequently debated, the one that brings forth the strongest expression of view, is that of constitutional reform' (52).

Although historically the Constitution was a focus of attention, rights issues were not. Unlike in the United States, in Canada provisions for the protection of rights were originally not a major concern. As with other countries with Westminster systems, in Canada there was a fundamental assumption that the common law, federalism, and the legislature would act as a bulwark against rights abuses (see Cairns 1995b, 203).

Initially, rights were not a priority for Trudeau either. On coming to office, he showed no interest in using the existing bill of rights to advance rights issues. However, by the late 1970s, this had changed. In pursuit of his national unity goal, Trudeau embraced the notion of rights in general and a bill of rights in particular. According to Simeon (1988, S14), the charter 'was an explicit attempt to foster a national community based on shared rights, enforced by a national institution and thus able to undermine provincial identities and provincial particularism' (see also Cairns 1995b, 198; Dobrowolsky 2000, 66).

Using the charter for political goals has had profound flow-on effects for the constitutional culture in Canada. Most particularly, there is evidence of the emergence of a rights-based culture throughout the country in general, and within certain identity groups in particular (see Simeon 1994, 31). As Cairns (1992, 68) argues, alongside federalism 'the Constitution is now also about women, aboriginals, multicultural groups, equality, affirmative action, the disabled, a variety of rights and so on.' My earlier discussion illustrated how Canadian feminists have taken advantage of this emerging culture and of the charter itself. It is also important to note that the flow of influence has not always been in a top-down direction (i.e., from the charter to feminist activists). The budding rights culture and the existence of the charter have indeed influenced feminists; however, in turn, feminist strategies have helped shape the nature of the charter. As noted, Anglo-feminists have not only been successful in lobbying the government to agree to include sex equality clauses in the charter but, once these were in place, they have also been able to intervene in a number of critical cases to influence charter jurisprudence. The court's acceptance and application of feminist arguments have set important precedents for future charter-based cases. Through this interaction Canadian feminists have gained for themselves a constitutional identity. At the same time, they have come to be seen as legitimate constitutional activists with valid constitutional claims.

In Australia, there has been a comparatively low degree of interest in constitutional issues, especially those issues related to individual rights. Australia is one of the few liberal democratic nations not to have either a legislative or a constitutional bill of rights. Various ALP governments have attempted to create a statutory bill of rights,[31] but with no success. Aside from supplying a few express rights protections,[32] it was the view of the framers of the Australian constitution that the system of responsible government – in which Parliament is sovereign – combined with the common law, would act as a buffer for the protection of individual rights (Kennett 1994, 582). Support for parliamentary and common law rights protections, rather than an entrenched bill of rights, has remained strong since federation (Maddox 1996, 243; Connolly 1994).[33]

To some degree, the reluctance to address rights issues has been influenced by the broader Australian political culture. From the time of White settlement, the question of individual rights has been subordinated to other issues. In Australia, the perception of government as 'a source of services,' or as a 'provider,' has been far more common than the perception that it is a protector of rights (Colebatch 1992, 4). To the extent that 'rights talk' has taken place, it has inclined towards a Benthamite view, emphasizing majoritarian rights rather than those of minority or disadvantaged groups. According to Charlesworth (1993, 201):

The Australian suspicion of constitutionally entrenched rights has been enduring. It has been supported by arguments that constitutional rights could both politicize the judiciary and legalize public policy, thus undermining our legal culture. The suspicion also rests on regional instincts of preserving states' rights. At a more fundamental level, reservations about rights are linked to a utilitarian confidence in our existing governmental structures.

The emphasis on responsible government in Australia has meant that, to the extent that individual rights protection does exist, it has been the product of a patchwork of executive and legislative measures rather than of the Constitution (Thompson 1997, 99). Combined with the fact that there is no bill of rights instrument in Australia, the absence of a rights culture has had a fundamental negative influence on the strategies of Australian rights activists, including feminists. Feminists have been encouraged to look elsewhere – primarily to the bureaucracy and the legislature – in an attempt to advance their objectives.

Funding
Another important influence on the POSs open to Canadian and Australian feminists wanting to engage with the constitutional and legal arenas concerns the availability of litigation funding. In Canada, the federal government's funding for court challenges cannot be underestimated. Under Trudeau, Ottawa increased the level of funding available for charter litigation under the Court Challenges Program and extended its terms to allow certain 'equality-seeking groups' to 'participate in the process of defining and interpreting the meaning of the Charter's Equality provisions' (Canadian Council on Social Development 1987). As noted above, LEAF has been a major recipient of these funds, and its litigation strategy has depended heavily upon their availability.

In Australia, funding, or, more precisely, the lack of it, has been a crucial factor in feminists' non-engagement in the legal and constitutional realms. The Australian Legal Aid Program, which has been in place since 1973, and which was designed to provide funds for advice and support in litigation procedures, has not worked to improve women's access to the law. This is in part because legal aid defendants in criminal cases, most of whom are men, have been given priority with regard to funding (ALRC 1993, 53). The emphasis on criminal cases has been accepted by the Attorney General's Department as a form of indirect discrimination against women (Attorney General's Department 1994, 41).[34] Despite the findings of these bodies with regard to the allocation of aid, in recent years the situation for women has been further exacerbated. This is the result of two factors. The first relates to the 1992 High Court's ruling in the *Dietrich* case.[35] In *Dietrich* the High Court ruled that the right to a fair trial is 'fundamental' to the criminal justice system. One of the ramifications of this ruling is that it puts 'a positive duty on the executive to provide counsel' for the accused. In other words, it has meant that legal aid funds have continued to be weighted in favour of criminal cases (Kennett 1994, 596). Second, since coming to office in 1996, the Howard coalition government has made substantial cuts to the legal aid budget.[36] Without access to legal aid, or an equivalent to the Canadian CCP, women's groups have been faced with a serious impediment in developing a litigation strategy – a point not lost on feminist activists. As the incipient WAGE told the ALRC inquiry into Equality before the Law: 'The major stumbling block to the pursuit of our legal action is funding ... The importance of considerable financial support is central to the success and the valuable results which groups like LEAF, WAGE and the Women's Legal Action Fund can achieve' (ALRC 1994, 131).

Standing

Gaining access to the legal system, either to commence a court challenge or to intervene in a case to present arguments that are pertinent to the case, is another crucial variable influencing the experiences of feminists in Canada and Australia. In Canada, the Supreme Court has frequently used its broad discretionary powers to allow public interest groups to intervene as a party in constitutional cases. The Canadian courts have also adopted a generous approach to those seeking *amicus curiae* status,[37] often allowing interested individuals the opportunity to present twenty minutes of oral argument and a twenty-page written argument to assist the court in its deliberations (ALRC 1995, 66, 71).

These provisions have been extremely beneficial to LEAF. Initially, in its proactive mode, LEAF expected to be able to make use of the generous standing provisions to mount its own cases in order to test them under the equality clauses of the charter (Allen and Morton 1997, 1). Due to challenges to existing affirmative action provisions, mostly by men, it quickly found itself adopting a more reactive strategy, intervening as *amicus curiae* in a range of cases (i.e., not just those related to Sections 15 or 28, the equality sections) (see Razack 1991, 62). Since the *Andrews* case in 1989, LEAF has continued to rely on intervening as 'a friend of the court.' Although reactive, this intervention strategy has provided an opening that has enabled LEAF to advance a feminist position on various issues – including abortion, equality, sex discrimination, and childcare – within the court system.

In their study of interest groups in Australia, Matthews and Warhurst (1993) identified three barriers that limit interest group litigation in Australia: (1) cost, (2) the rules of standing, and (3) the limited approval of *amicus curiae* applications. Each of these factors is particularly relevant to Australian feminists. Problems arising from prohibitive costs and the absence of government financial assistance have already been noted. In addition to the financial barrier, Australian women's groups have, like other equality-seeking groups, also found it difficult to gain access to the court system because of the rules pertaining to who can be given standing. Unlike in Canada, in Australia it is very difficult to run test cases. Australian law on standing requires that parties to a legal case must have a personal, or 'special,' interest in the proceedings. What constitutes a special interest has been left to the discretion of the court, with the consequent result that rulings related to standing have been 'uncertain, complicated, inconsistent and overly dependent on subjective value judgments' (ALRC 1995, 5).

The problem standing rules have created for the development of a feminist legal strategy was acknowledged by the ALRC (1994, 4.37, 70) in its report, *Equality before the Law*:

> Court rules presently restrict those who can commence legal proceedings or intervene in legal proceedings. These rules mean that women's experiences and perspectives often do not come before the courts. This limits the opportunities for the courts to develop the law to take better account of women's needs.

NSW Supreme Court judge Jane Mathews has also identified these rules as an impediment, stating that 'eliminating the restriction on group intervention in gender sensitive cases would be a major step in reforming the system' (Lewis 1993, 3).

Aside from restrictions on who can commence legal proceedings, Australia has also had prohibitive laws relating to who can intervene in cases as *amicus curiae*. Australian feminist lawyers are aware that this leaves them at a distinct disadvantage compared to their Canadian counterparts (ALRC 1993, 37). Canadian feminist legal expert, Mary Jane Mossman (1993, 30), has pointed out how access to *amicus curiae* could have worked to the advantage of Australian feminists in the *Dietrich* case on legal representation:

> While Brennan J (and Dawson J) recognised that legal aid funding is a political issue to be decided by the government of the day because of competing claims on limited resources, noticeably absent was an acknowledgment that the priority given to criminal law had a gendered impact ... The situation may well have been different had an organisation similar to Canada's Women's Legal Education Fund intervened to apprise the court of the gendered consequences of its decisions.

The experience of PIAC (noted earlier) has further demonstrated the effect of limited *amicus* rulings for those wanting to intervene in cases related to women. In an ironic twist for feminists, the High Court's decision to grant the Roman Catholic Church *amicus* standing (to argue against abortion services) in the *Superclinics* case has possibly eased the path for women's groups to intervene in future cases. However, the ruling has yet to be tested.

Given their troubled history in attempting to be heard in the legal arena, Australian feminists may need more than changes to intervention laws to make them shift their resources and energy towards this institution. As the Canadian example indicates, a bill of rights and adequate funding arrangements are important prerequisites for a successful feminist litigation strategy. The presence of women on the bench – women who are willing and able to espouse feminist views – can also make an important difference.

Feminist Judges

The presence of women judges can make a difference to the POS open to feminist activists. As the feminist legal literature cautions, merely adding women to the bench (or to the jury or bar, for that matter) does not mean that the underlying gender assumptions of the law will unravel (see Neave 1994; Graycar 1995). However, when *feminist* judges are appointed – judges who then have access to evidence supplied by *feminist* legal advocates – it is possible to sometimes challenge the law's hidden gender assumptions. Again, the Canadian case is illuminating here. The decisions of Canada's Supreme Court justice, Bertha Wilson, often applied feminist principles to underlying legal gender norms, including the public/private distinction and the use of a male standard to judge individuals. For instance, in the *Betcherman* case Wilson (1993, 10) argued: 'Some aspects of criminal law ... cry out for change since they are based on presuppositions about the nature of women and women's sexuality that in this day and age are little short of ludicrous.' In the *Morgentaler* abortion case she argued that only women should have the right to decide whether or not to have an abortion; while in *Andrews* she argued firmly in favour of a contextual approach to equality (see Pearlman and Dawson 1989, 8). Other female justices, including Donna Hackett and Claire L'Heureux-Dubé, have also expressed feminist opinions in their judgments, including the need to contextualize the law to take into account the experience of women (and other identity groups) (see Hackett 1998). These judgments, which reflect feminist jurisprudence, have given encouragement and further impetus to the feminist legal project because they have demonstrated to feminist advocates that they have a chance to be heard in an otherwise overwhelming nominal and substantive masculine institutional environment.

Australian feminists have not enjoyed the same access to feminist judges as have Canadian feminists. This is not to say that none of the (still relatively few) women who sit on the bench are feminists. Female judges have at times expressed feminist sentiments and demonstrated an understanding of feminist concerns. For instance, in a speech to Australian women lawyers, Mary Gaudron (1997), the first and only woman High Court justice, demonstrated an overt commitment to such key feminist principles as the inherent gender bias in the law. She made note of 'the feminist legal academics and legal theorists who have drawn attention to the ways in which the law fails to address women and fails to respect their equality, and thus, denies equal justice' (5). Even though, as Gaudron's comments suggest, there is some support for feminist views among women judges, they have been unable to make a demonstrable difference to the POSs available to feminists in the legal arena. Without any express constitutional sex equality guarantees within the Australian constitution, these judges must continue to work within the confines of the precedent-based common law. To date, the common law in Australia has maintained a limited 'similarly situated' understanding of sex equality, and it has been difficult for judges to change this understanding from the bench, in part because equality rights activists have been reluctant to test their claims in court. Further, these judges have not enjoyed the benefit of having other women,[38] let alone feminist legal advocates, present cases or arguments before them. Without these prerequisites, the presence of sympathetic judges has made little difference.

Furthermore, in Australia any differences made by the presence of female judges continue to be counteracted by the deeply entrenched gender biases expressed by some of their male colleagues. As recently as 1992, Justice Bollen of the South Australian Supreme Court argued that 'there is nothing wrong with a husband, faced with his wife's initial refusal to engage in intercourse, in attempting, in an acceptable way, to persuade her to change her mind, and that may involve a measure of rougher than usual handling' (cited in Raman 1997, 347).[39] This statement was widely condemned and contributed to the decision of the Senate Standing Committee on Legal and Constitutional Affairs to commence an inquiry into gender bias and the judiciary (Senate Standing Committee on Legal and Constitutional Affairs 1994, ix). While the report noted that the statements of some judges had been taken out of context and had been sensationalized by the media, it nevertheless confirmed that Justice Bollen's statement was not an isolated example of gender bias in Australian judgments.[40]

The strategies pursued by Canadian and Australian feminists have been directly shaped by the existing opportunity structures. If we return to Table 5.1, we see that it is apparent that Canadian feminists have faced a relatively more positive POS in relation to the legal and constitutional arenas. Significantly, as far as my argument is concerned, the engagement of Anglo-Canadian feminists with the law has occurred not simply in one direction. While they have exploited existing POSs through their intervention in the constitutional and legal realm, feminists have also helped shape these structures. Their involvement in constitutional debates ensured that equality provisions were included in the charter, while their litigation strategy has, at times, influenced the interpretation of the charter in ways that have produced demonstrable advances in women's rights. The *Andrews* decision arguably gave feminists the most significant breakthrough in terms of challenging entrenched gender norms, but they have also been able to challenge existing court rulings in relation to reproduction, employment, and sex discrimination.

Australian feminists have faced greater structural and normative constraints than have Canadian feminists when engaging with constitutional/legal institutions. In structural terms, Australian feminists are obstructed by the absence of a constitutional or legislative rights instrument, a lack of public funding for legal challenges, restrictive standing laws, and the inability of sympathetic judges to make their views known. Without tools to engage with legal institutions, entrenched masculine norms go unchecked. Even when feminist judges are appointed, they do not have access to the means to challenge common gender-biased assumptions, while the rulings of certain male judges continue to perpetuate myths and stereotypes about the nature of women and their experiences.

While the absence of rights protection in the Australian Constitution has functioned to constrain feminist aspirations, the federal aspect of the Constitution has provided them with a more positive POS. As the next chapter demonstrates, the nature of Australian federalism has, under certain conditions, offered some openings that have enabled feminists to advance their claims.

6
Feminists and Federalism: Playing a Multi-Level Game

In the preceding three chapters we have seen how opportunities and constraints within legislative, executive, and constitutional and legal realms have shaped Australian and Canadian feminist strategies. Feminists have engaged across these institutions with varying degrees of success. For instance, in both countries they have faced a range of constraints within the party, electoral, and parliamentary realms, leading them to pursue their aims in other arenas. Australian feminists have exploited a positive political opportunity structure in the bureaucracy, while their Canadian counterparts have taken advantage of openings in constitutional and legal institutions. This chapter considers a fourth institutional arena – federalism – in order to assess how it has influenced the strategies of feminists in the two countries under consideration.

As a key feature of the political landscape in both Australia and Canada, federalism is gradually beginning to receive attention from feminist scholars. In Australia, Gwendolyn Gray (1998) mentions federalism as a positive factor influencing the development of the women's health sector, while Helen Irving (1994) considers the significance of federal design features at the time of federation. In Canada, Jill Vickers (1990, 1993, 1994) and Alexandra Dobrowolsky (2000) give federalism some attention, but both suggest that it is an area that needs further exploration. In an important article, Canadian feminist political scientists L. Pauline Rankin and Jill Vickers have undertaken to compare three Canadian provinces – Alberta, Ontario, and Newfoundland – in order to illustrate the importance of federalism for feminist activists. Their work focuses on the importance of space for feminist activism and demonstrates 'the way patterns of political activism differ significantly from place to place' (Rankin and Vickers 1998, 342). Recently, Sawer and Vickers (2001) have also contributed a comparative study of constitutional politics in Australia and Canada, which includes a discussion of federal relations.

Although not addressing the particularities of Australia and Canada, one other significant comparative study that considers how federal structures shape the choices of feminist activists is Banaszak's (1996) research into the suffrage movements in the United States and Switzerland. Banaszak is particularly interested in how federalism has influenced the POS for those struggling to gain the women's vote. An important point to emerge from her account is that differences in feminists' engagement with federal institutions can affect their strategic choices. She notes how the US suffrage movement was influenced by existing federal arrangements when creating its own structures and how it 'took full advantage of its own federal structure to spread the knowledge and information about tactics to local areas' (217). By contrast, Swiss activists were less inclined to work with federal structures or to organize themselves along federal lines and, thus, missed an important opportunity for garnering support for their cause (67).

Although Banaszak's work can be seen to be groundbreaking in the feminist literature, it fits within a more general and extensive literature on the engagement of social actors with federalism (e.g., Coleman 1987; Bakvis and Chandler 1987). Moreover, her argument that federalism can create opportunities for 'trailblazers' (in this case, US suffragettes) who can use federalism to their advantage also has a long heritage. Pro-federalists have long advocated this form of political system on the grounds that it promotes innovation and can lead to flow-on reforms across jurisdictions (see Nathan 1992; Gagnon 1995).

Other arguments in favour of federalism are also relevant here. Many of its defenders begin from a liberal democratic position, advocating federalism because of the way it disperses political power, limits government, and breaks up majority rule (see Galligan 1995, 35-53). As well as stimulating innovation, it is seen to protect against central tyranny, reconcile unity and diversity, and increase citizen participation in the political process (for a summary, see Nathan 1992, 97). Most relevant from a social activist point of view are those arguments that suggest that federalism enhances participation in political decision making. Proponents argue that this multi-tier system of government 'establishes a system of dual citizenship or double democracy' (Galligan 1995, 51).

These arguments have not been accepted unquestioningly. Federalism's critics respond by arguing that it creates waste and duplication, replaces a tyranny of the majority with a tyranny of the minority, and leads to conservatism and parochialism (see Maddox 1996; Riker 1964). The latter is seen as a particular problem for those promoting 'progressive interests.' Adopting a pro- or anti-federalist stance is perhaps too simplistic. As Paul Pierson (1995, 450-1) notes, it is important not to make generalizations about the consequences of federalism for social policy because of the 'substantial variation among federal systems in crucial features of institutional design.' The same can be said for making assumptions about the effect of federalism on social actors, including feminists. In Pierson's view, there are three important design features that influence the operation of federal states: (1) the distribution of powers between the constituent units, (2) the representation of these units at the national level, and (3) the extent of commitment to fiscal equalization across units. As this chapter demonstrates, the federations of Australia and Canada are different from each other in each of these crucial design features and, as a result, offer feminist activists different opportunities and constraints.

This chapter considers the features of the Australian and Canadian federal systems and asks two key questions. First, have feminists found, as Banaszak notes in relation to suffragettes in the United States, that a two-tier system has enhanced their ability to achieve their aims? Second, can feminists in either or both countries take advantage of a system of 'double-democracy,' as Galligan suggests?

Engaging with Federalism: Australian and Canadian Experiences

Australian and Anglo-Canadian feminists have not only had different experiences with regard to engaging with the 'rights' aspects of their respective constitutions, but they have also had different experiences with the federal government. Whereas Canadian feminists outside Quebec faced a mostly positive POS in relation to the former, their relationship with, and attitude towards, federalism has ranged from outright hostility to ambivalence. By contrast, Australian feminists have generally reflected a favourable attitude towards federal arrangements and have taken advantage of the political leverage offered by the multi-level system by shifting their attention between the federal and state levels as opportunities arise.

Australian Feminists and Federalism: Playing the Two-Level Game

Federalism has not been an issue central to Australian feminist discourse. To the extent that they have focused on it, feminists have tended to adopt a relatively sanguine attitude towards the institution. On the one hand they have supported the arrogation of power to the central government in areas such as welfare, childcare, and family law (Sawer and Vickers 2001). On the other hand, they have tended to espouse the view that federalism offers them multiple opportunities for pursuing their objectives. Long-time feminist activist Eva Cox (1995, 48) advances a positive assessment, arguing that, under federalism 'feminists and other lobbyists [can] play off the different levels of government to gain advantages for the less powerful.' Cox goes on to defend the federal status quo:

> There are claims in Australia that we are over-governed and that we have too much reliance on government. There are those who want to abolish the states and those who are always suspicious of the Commonwealth.

However, as an activist over the past two decades, I am happy to see what we have remain and even stay a little confused and overlapping. The demonising of state and public power ignores the possibilities of using these powers to mediate and control the powerful. (49)

Carmel Flask and Betty Hounslow (n.d.), feminists active in the women's services sector, echo Cox's sentiments:

The Australian federal system, with its different tiers of governments, not only creates complexity, it also allows further opportunity for manoeuvring. Times can be instanced when some battles have been won (and lost) because of the complexity of state and federal funding systems and the negotiations that occur between bureaucrats across departments.

As Sawer (1990, 140) notes in relation to the femocrat strategy, having a federal system has meant that 'when progress has been blocked at one level of government, it has been possible for them to continue at another.'

As has been seen some feminists espouse the idea that federalism allows them to exploit openings at different levels of government – an idea that has been largely borne out in practice. This has been made most obvious in relation to the femocrat strategy. As was outlined in Chapter 3, femocrats began their work at the federal level in 1974 under the Whitlam ALP government, but the network spread quickly as opportunities arose to enter state bureaucracies. During the 1970s and early 1980s, when the Fraser Liberal coalition government was paring back women's policy machinery at the federal level, state Labor governments were opening up opportunities for femocrats to enter the bureaucracy. This occurred in South Australia (1976), Tasmania (1976), New South Wales (1977), and Western Australia (1983). Women's advisory positions were also established under conservative governments in Victoria (1976) and the Northern Territory (1982). These developments can in some ways be seen as analogous to the case of US women's suffrage campaigns mentioned earlier. Once women's policy machinery had been entrenched federally, it set an example for other governments to follow. Femocrats at the federal level had been the initial trailblazers. When key states such as New South Wales and Victoria came on board by creating openings for this strategy, they set an example that other states (with the exception of Queensland),[1] were willing to follow.

Feminist lobbyists have also been able to take advantage of Australian federalism by shifting their focus between different levels of government, depending on where they perceive they can make the greatest inroads. For the most part, this has been where there have been ALP governments in office. Lobbying around the issue of women's refuges provides an excellent example of how feminists have made the most of having a two-tiered government system. The refuge movement is a good case to consider when examining the effects of federalism because it shares a number of features with other women's groups: it aims to provide services to women based on feminist principles, it is dispersed throughout the country, and it must relate to both levels of government.

During the early 1970s much of the feminist effort around women's refuges was directed towards the central government. Feminist activists needed financial support and realized that, with the reformist Whitlam government in office, they were most likely to find it at the Commonwealth level (Dowse 1984, 145). After securing in 1974 funding from the federal government for 'Elsie,' the first Australian women's refuge (located in Sydney), femocrats within the federal bureaucracy worked with feminists on the outside to lobby the Whitlam government to provide a national program. In June 1975 Canberra responded, providing over $200,000 in direct funding to eleven refuges throughout the country (Townsend 1994, 3). Once the national program was in place, femocrats put pressure on the refuge movement to become a national organization, thus enabling it to deal more effectively with the federal government. It refused, arguing that such a move would threaten its autonomy and grassroots strategy (McFerren 1990, 194).

As it happened, the refuge movement's decision not to focus on Canberra was a prescient one, as, in 1976, the incoming Fraser coalition government devolved primary responsibility for administering refuges to the state level. From this time on, feminists divided their attention between the Commonwealth government, which continued to provide the bulk of the funds for the refuges, and the state governments, which oversaw the administration of these funds. On those occasions when Canberra made changes in its policy on refuges, feminists targeted the federal government. For instance, in 1977, when the federal Cabinet stalled on its commitment to refuge funding, femocrats and external women's activists alerted the media and convinced the Australian Broadcasting Commission (ABC) to produce a Four Corners documentary program on the issue (Dowse 1984, 152). In 1981, when responsibility for refuges was further devolved to the states, members of the women's movement staged a protest in Parliament House in Canberra (Healy 1991, 193).

However, not all the attention has focused on the Commonwealth government. Because of the states' role in administering refuges, feminist refuge groups have also been active at this level. For instance, throughout the 1970s and 1980s, activists lobbied intransigent governments in Western Australia and Queensland to change their policies (see McFerren 1990). Within state bureaucracies femocrats have attempted to influence the development of policies in this area. A case in point relates to the NSW femocrat, Carmel Niland, who encouraged external women's organizations to pressure the Wran Labor government to not only pick up the Commonwealth shortfall for refuges, but also to fund its own (see Sawer 1990, 155).[2] In Victoria too, under the Cain Labor government, femocrats were able to make some headway in securing state funding for refuges. By the mid-1980s, Melbourne's most prominent feminist refuge, Halfway House, felt that state funding was secure enough to discourage it from 'join[ing] in with other refuges in a campaign to restore federal control over refuge funding' (Dowse 1984, 156).

The experiences of the refuge movement provide a good example of how federalism has shaped the strategies of Australian feminists. Similar stories can be found in relation to childcare (see Brennan 1994) and the women's health care movement (Gray 1998). Rather than focusing on one level of government, feminist activists have shifted their efforts between the two, according to when and where new opportunities or constraints arise. Their capacity to keep their issues on the agenda by exploiting the openings at federal and state levels suggests that Australian federalism has, at various times, afforded them a system of 'double democracy.' It cannot be assumed, however, that all federal systems provide the same positive POS. As the experiences of Anglo-Canadian feminists attest, federalism can also function to frustrate feminist objectives.

Anglo-Feminists and Federal Structures

Along with the rest of Canada, since the late 1970s feminists have been heavily engaged in constitutional debates, which have included issues related to federalism. As a result, Anglo-Canadian feminists have articulated their attitudes towards federalism much more fully and frequently than have their Australian counterparts. Nevertheless, feminists are far from having reached a consensus within this institutional arena. As noted below, Quebec feminists tend to take a pro-provincial stance, while Aboriginal women tend to take a stance that is in line with their own nation-building objectives. Within the Anglo-feminist community itself there is a variety of positions. As the work of Rankin and Vickers (1998) shows, women activists in Alberta, Ontario, and Newfoundland all respond differently to the question of engaging with national/subnational political spaces, depending upon the opportunities, history, and culture of each province. Despite this diversity, the position most strongly articulated from within the mainstream Anglo-movement, especially through NAC, has been a strong preference for strengthening Ottawa's power vis-à-vis the provinces.

Anglo-feminist attitudes towards federalism were highlighted most clearly in the late 1980s and early 1990s during the debates surrounding the Meech Lake and Charlottetown constitutional accords.[3] Most Anglo-feminists adopted a 'no' stance towards both accords. The reasons for their position are enlightening. First, they objected to the processes by which the accords were devised and how they were to be ratified. After being so directly involved in influencing the provisions of the charter in the early 1980s, members of the Anglo-women's movement were outraged when the Meech Lake Accord was drawn up in secret and presented to the community as a *fait accompli* (see *Action Now* vol. 2, no. 7, 1987). They were also critical of the fact that it was to be ratified by provincial legislatures rather than by the people.

Second, many Anglo-feminists feared that the adoption of the Meech or Charlottetown accords might threaten women's rights in Canada by creating a hierarchy of rights – with Aboriginal people and multicultural groups gaining protection at the expense of women (see *Feminist Action* vol. 3, no. 2, 1988; McLellan 1991). The third, and most pertinent, reason for opposing the accords had to do with not wanting any further devolution of spending powers to the provinces. Feminist organizations, including NAC and LEAF, presented submissions to the parliamentary committee on the Meech Lake Accord, arguing that women were especially dependent upon the provision of social services such as health care, which were provided through federal grants and cost-sharing programs (see *Feminist Action* vol. 3, no. 3, 1988). In their view, as Judy Rebick argued in the *Globe and Mail* on 25 August 1992, enabling provinces to 'opt out' of ·federal programs would create 'a checkerboard of social programs across Canada, leaving women in small provinces without access to programs available in larger provinces' (see also Dobrowolsky 2000, 86).[4] Many Anglo-feminists were also conscious that universal projects, such as a national childcare program (which had been on the agenda since the RCSW), would be in jeopardy if greater decentralization occurred. In a speech on the Charlottetown Accord, NAC president Judy Rebick (1993, 105) voiced a common concern:

> Let us say that we were successful in electing a national government committed to publicly funded childcare ... They would be unable to implement such a reform under this agreement because as a national government they would be unable to set the standard for public child care. The government would have to go to the first ministers and try to negotiate it. Even if it were negotiated, Alberta or Ontario could opt out with compensations and say that its program was compatible with national objectives.

A further problem for Anglo-feminists during the Meech debates related to granting greater autonomy to Quebec. Some feared that any future retrograde decisions made in that province on issues such as family law and abortion might set precedents that could be upheld by the Supreme Court of Canada and, therefore, have flow-on effects for women's rights across the country (McLellan 1991, 19). In other words, they feared the consequences of successful conservative trailblazers in Quebec.

Underlying feminist claims were long-standing anti-provincial sentiments that were driven by the belief that the second tier of government was intolerant of women's issues (McLellan 1991, 26). As one feminist put it: 'As a woman from B.C., a province which has suffered government by car dealer for all but four of the past forty years ... I fear ... powers being devolved to my province' (Day, cited in Vickers 1993, 269). Vickers (1990, 22) summarizes the position of these women: 'Relatively few Canadian women outside of Quebec would accept the proposition that provincial governments, as they have been constituted to this point, have been particularly responsive to the attitudes and aspirations of their women citizens.' However, as Rankin and Vickers (1998) also point out, there are some exceptions to this rule. For example, in Newfoundland feminists have been active at the provincial level and have found it to be supportive of some of their aims, especially under the Peckford PC government.

The differences between feminists inside and outside Quebec with regard to the issue of federalism and decentralization could not have been more divergent. As Busque (1991, 160) explained during the Meech debates: 'While Quebec women had (and still have) a tendency to distrust federal intrusion in areas that are exclusively provincial jurisdictions, and are favourable to the possibility of opting out with financial compensation, women in other provinces feared negative use of power to opt out.' In her view, this was because Anglo-feminists 'were concerned that federal standards would not be applied and even feared that the money recovered would be used improperly. This attitude on the part of (Anglo) women appears to us to stem from having higher expectations of the federal government than of provincial governments' (160).

For a number of reasons, Quebec feminist support for provincial funding arrangements was not surprising. First, Francophone feminists in that province have always hitched their cause to that of Quebec nationalism. The slogan, 'No Women's Liberation without Quebec Liberation, No Quebec Liberation without Women's Liberation,' which became the catch-cry of Québécois feminists during the early 1970s, indicates the strength of this link (Dumont 1992, 76). Unlike the goals of feminists in the rest of Canada, the goals of feminists in Quebec are not at odds with territorial claims but, rather, are wedded to them. Rankin and Vickers (2001, 17) note that 'successive Quebec governments have been eager to draw women's movements into the nationalist cause and have often responded positively to women's advocacy as an element of the nationalist struggle.'

The second reason why Quebec feminists have adopted such a positive view of decentralization relates to the fact that they face entirely different institutional and political arrangements than do their sisters in other parts of the country. This has resulted in Quebec feminists achieving some of their key goals at the provincial level. As noted in relation to the bureaucracy, the Quebec provincial government has provided ongoing funding for the Conseil du statut de la femme, which is well supported by the feminist community (Rankin and Vickers 2001, 17). It has introduced a legislatively based bill of rights and has introduced reforms in key 'women's policy' areas, such as equal pay and childcare (for a discussion of the role of feminists in Quebec politics see Tremblay 1997).

The position of Quebec feminists reflected the view that federalism can provide feminists with a multilayered opportunity structure, providing their goals are compatible with those of the provincial government. As Sawer and Vickers (2001, 19) note, within the Franco-Quebec women's movement 'decentralization [and] diversity' has been favoured over centralization as a way to achieve feminist goals. The significance of these points was not lost on Anglo-Canadian activists who, during the constitutional debates, were forced to rethink their position on federalism so as to incorporate the views being expressed by their Quebec and Aboriginal sisters. They responded with their own asymmetrical 'three nations constitutional vision.' This 'vision' recognized the right of Quebec and Aboriginal women to a separate constitutional identity while at the same time acknowledging that Anglo-women perceived the federal government as a better protector of their rights than the provinces. NAC presented this vision in the following terms: 'NAC's policy has been support for the right of Aboriginal peoples to self-government, support for the right of the people of Quebec to self-determination in defining their relationship with the rest of Canada, and support for strong, central government in the rest of Canada' (*Action Now*, vol. 5, no. 1, 1995).

Much to the dismay of many Anglo-feminists, the failure of the Meech Lake and Charlottetown accords has not stopped the trend towards greater decentralization within Canada. NAC, and Anglo-feminists more generally, have continued to oppose this trend. In a 1995 press release, NAC (1995, *A Very Political Budget*) criticized the Chrétien government's reduction in social program transfers to the provinces, the minimization of national standards on transfer payments to the provinces, and the shift towards block funding: 'The politicians are implementing ... the Charlottetown Accord through the back door despite the "NO" vote to the constitutional referendum. Our social safety net will collapse as provinces compete to run the cheapest programs.'

The anti-provincial views expressed by Anglo-feminists have been reflected in their practice. In the main, they have attempted to circumvent the effects of living in a decentralized federal system by maintaining a focus on Ottawa, using the charter, and being 'centrist' in their demands (Dobrowolsky 2000, 25). At the same time, feminists have, on occasion, been heavily engaged in lobbying at the provincial level. One notable example occurred during the charter debates when Anglo-feminists successfully mobilized to pressure provincial premiers to protect the proposed sex equality guarantees. Feminist success in this endeavour demonstrated that the federal system could provide 'some leverage for women' (65). However, it must be noted that feminists feared provincial interference in sex equality issues and were lobbying to have the premiers agree to leave this area of rights outside provincial jurisdiction. In other words, through these efforts Anglo-feminists were seeking a way to counter, rather than harness, the centrifugal dynamic within Canadian federalism.

The centralist stance of the Anglo-feminist community has not stopped its members from engaging with subnational governments. However, this engagement is less uniform in Canada than it is in Australia. The willingness of feminists to become involved in provincial-level activism has varied markedly between the provinces; and within the provinces it has varied markedly between institutions. As Rankin and Vickers (1998, 348) illustrate, in Alberta, feminists made some early strides in entering the parliamentary arena but have since become disengaged from mainstream politics; in Newfoundland, as femocrats, they found opportunities within the bureaucratic realm; and in Ontario they have tended to shun provincial institutions in favour of federal ones. In British Columbia, under the NDP government, feminists also made some headway by working within bureaucratic institutions (Teghtsoonian 2000).

Signs are that, in the future, there will be a stronger imperative for feminists to engage with provincial institutions. Even with the counterweight of the charter, the reality is that, in Canada, provincial governments are becoming increasingly powerful. Consequently, in order to remain effective, feminist organizations must turn their attention to this level of government. As Arscott, Rankin, and Vickers (n.d., 41) argue: 'As the effects of decentralization are felt more acutely, provincial and territorial governments inevitably will loom larger as important sites for women's struggles for equality.' There is some evidence that NAC is responding to this reality by reassessing its stance towards provincial politics. In 1995 incoming NAC president Sunera Thobani made it clear that, in order to deal with the shift of power to the provinces, efforts were being made to have the organization adopt a more provincial focus and to structure itself along regional lines.

There are obvious differences between how Australian feminists and Canadian Anglo-feminists approach federalism. In neither country is there a unified position with regard to which level of government is the most conducive to feminist aims. The feminist community in Australia has tended to be more optimistic about the opportunities afforded by federalism than has the Anglo-feminist community in Canada. Regardless of where feminists reside, they have attempted to make use of the political leverage afforded by multilayered government, switching their focus between state and federal arenas as opportunities arise. In Canada, while there is diversity of opinion within the Anglo strand of the movement with regard to where best to concentrate feminist efforts, the major focus has been towards the federal government, with a great deal of skepticism towards the opportunities available at the provincial level. These responses suggest that federal institutions do not offer the same opportunities for political activists, that the specific features of a given federal system make a difference with regard to the available POSs.

Political Opportunities and Constraints in Australian and Canadian Federalism

Differences between the Australian and Canadian federal systems are evident at both a structural level and a normative level. Important structural differences include the division of political and fiscal powers between the levels of government as well as intergovernmental mechanisms. Normative differences, especially the degree of emphasis on territorial claims, are also obvious. These attitudinal differences have been largely influenced by feminists' experiences with federal institutions. (See Table 6.1.)

Division of Political and Fiscal Authority in Australia

The foundations of Australian federalism are quite different from those of Canadian federalism. The Australian federal compact was neither an attempt to unite disparate ethnic groups nor an attempt to protect distinct regional identities. The driving force behind Australian federalism was a political imperative: it was a compromise struck between pre-existing political entities in order to advance their common economic and defence interests. The objective of the initial compact was to constrain the power at the centre and to leave most of the authority with the states. The Australian Constitution enumerated a limited range of powers for the federal government, including customs and excise; provided for concurrent powers between the federal and the six state governments; and left the residual powers with the states.

Canberra's revenue-raising capacity has been at the heart of its control. In essence, it has been able to secure 'a monopoly over the lion's share of revenue sources,' while the states and local government have been left with separate tax bases, which are 'grossly insufficient for their expenditure needs' (Galligan 1990, 25).[5] High fiscal capacity has enabled the federal government to intervene in state policy areas that are technically outside its constitutional jurisdiction. Since the 1970s it has done this

Table 6.1

Federalism and political opportunity structures

	Australia	Canada
Division of political and fiscal authority	*Structures* **Positive** High federal political and fiscal capacity combined with moderate state political capacity	*Structures* **Negative** Moderate federal political and fiscal capacity combined with high provincial political and fiscal capacity
Intergovernmental mechanisms	*Structures* **Negative** Nominally male **Positive** Creation of effective national women's policy machinery	*Structures* **Negative** Nominally male **Moderate** Creation of women's policy machinery *Norms* **Negative** Perceived to be undemocratic and elitist
Salience of territoriality	*Norms* **Moderate** Ameliorated by political and fiscal division of powers and party system	*Norms* **Negative** Territoriality strong at expense of gender interests **Positive** Ameliorated by politicization of non-territorial identities through the Charter of Rights and Freedoms
Intervening institutions	*Structures* **Positive** Symmetrical, class-based party system reduces salience of regional interests *Norms* **Positive** ALP representation Protection of gender interests	*Structures* **Negative** Asymmetrical party system reinforces importance of regional concerns at the expense of non-territorial ones

primarily through Section 96 of the Constitution, which provides the Commonwealth with the power to make Specific Purpose Payments (SPP) to the states. These payments specify the policy terms and conditions under which the grants can be used.[6]

One effect of Canberra's fiscal dominance was to bring about a high level of equalization between the states. Through the auspices of the Grants Commission, the Commonwealth government has allocated SPPs and unconditional grants to the states. The philosophy underlying the formulae used to allocate grants is, according to Painter (1997b, 203), 'one of a "fair go": the right of all citizens to an equal opportunity of being provided with an equivalent range of public services.' To a large extent, equalization has been achieved through the subsidization of the smaller states by the larger ones – much to the chagrin of the latter. The equalization principles pursued in Australia go much further than do those of other federations, including Canada and the United States. In these other federations, states are compensated for disabilities to their revenue-raising capacity but not for the differential in costs related to the provision of services. In Australia equalization funding takes both factors into account. According to Self (1989), these measures have had a profound influence on the nature of Australian federalism. In his view, they 'reduce the incentive and the need for states to pursue different policies' (80). Moreover, he suggests, Australia's 'equalisation policy can be seen as one way of seeking to approximate federalism to the conditions of a unitary state.'

Self's argument is, however, somewhat overstated. Although centralization and equalization are key characteristics of Australian federalism, it would be incorrect to assume that the states operate merely as the agents of the Commonwealth. Despite their weak fiscal capacity, they do exercise a level of political capacity. An important characteristic of Australian federalism is that there exist 'active, vigilant, rival governments' who have 'the capacity and the will to assert their autonomy and their difference' (Painter 1996, 86). It may be the case that the Commonwealth has the ability to set policy guidelines and has control over finance; nevertheless, 'the key to implementation of a policy is frequently in the detail. This is more likely to remain in state hands' (Gillespie 1995, 168). The states, thereby, retain an independent role within Australian federalism.

In line with my central argument regarding the importance of gender norms, it is interesting to note here what Australian feminist and political scientist Helen Irving has to say about Australian federalism. According to Irving (1994, 196), there is a gender division at the very heart of the Constitution:

When we look closely at the ... 1901 Constitution ... a pattern emerges where the public and external become identified as national and thereby as appropriate to the Commonwealth jurisdiction. For the most part, the domestic and familial – the sphere which constituted the greatest sources of interest to women activists – is left to state jurisdiction, often meaning in this period, to the private sphere. The nation, it might seem, is public and male, and the state the sphere of the female.

The division of powers in Australia may have gendered foundations, but these have, to a large extent, been eroded. Over time the intent of the constitutional founders has been reversed. Through High Court decisions and the Commonwealth's creative use of existing powers (especially in areas related to arbitration and conciliation, defence, tax, and external affairs), the federal government has come to be the dominant partner in the federation (Gray 1991, 18). Since the 1940s the arrogation to the federal government of powers that were previously the exclusive responsibility of the states – especially in the welfare field – has also helped to tip the balance in the Commonwealth's favour. While the states still have some responsibility for 'the domestic and familial,' many of these are now shared with the Commonwealth.

The political and fiscal features of Australian federalism can be seen to have contributed to feminist strategy about how and where to agitate for reform. For a start, it has been logical for them to target the federal arena. The Commonwealth has responded to pressure from feminist activists to intervene in women's policy areas that are within its own jurisdiction as well as in areas that would otherwise be the responsibility of the states. Canberra has used its external affairs powers (s. 51 [xxix]) to develop sexual discrimination legislation, and it has used its conciliation and arbitration powers (s. 51 [xxxv]) to develop equal pay legislation.[7] It has legislated for the maternity allowance, child endowment payments, widow and sole parent pensions, and federal public service equal opportunity policies. The federal government has also relied upon its fiscal clout to act unilaterally, or jointly with the states, to gain a foothold in policy areas that are not enumerated under the Constitution. Such areas include women's refuges and domestic violence, women's health, and childcare.[8]

The degree of equalization inherent in Australian federalism has also shaped the strategic focus of Australian feminists. Through fiscal and legislative means, Canberra has sometimes been able to respond to feminist lobbying and so bypass recalcitrant state governments. For instance, through its enactment of the Sex Discrimination Act, the federal government was able to ensure that women in Queensland and Tasmania – two states that had refused to develop their own anti-discrimination legislation – had some degree of protection with regard to sex discrimination (Simms and Stone 1990, 289). When these two states also failed to create their own women's policy agencies, the Commonwealth stepped in and funded women's information services in both through the federal Office of the Status of Women (OSW 1989).

In Australia, the degree to which the Commonwealth has been able to become involved to create national women's policy issues, either through its constitutional authority or its financial capacity, has meant that Australian women are less likely to be treated differently because they live in one state rather than another. In contrast to their Canadian counterparts, they have therefore had less reason to fear the development of a checkerboard of policies across the country. But it would be wrong to assume that it is only central control and uniformity – two 'anti-federal' tendencies – that have shaped feminist responses. Another important influence, one that arguably offers them the opportunity to enjoy a system of 'double democracy,' has been the states' political capacity and willingness (on occasion) to 'go it alone' in a range of policy areas, including abortion, equal employment opportunity, domestic violence, sexual assault, and childcare. For instance, during the Fraser coalition government period, when the Commonwealth 'dilly-dallied' on sex discrimination legislation, most of the states took action to introduce it (Simms and Stone 1990, 289). State governments have also been prepared to take the initiative in providing support for some women's services when they have been stalled at the national level. This occurred in the late 1970s in New South Wales when the Wran ALP government started funding women's health services after the federal Liberal government withdrew Commonwealth funding for these programs (Smith 1984, 4). Again, during the 1980s, when conservatives held power in Canberra, the South Australian government agreed to provide 100 percent of the funding for women's health centres (Sawer 1990, 13).

Division of Political and Fiscal Authority in Canada

The Canadian federation is markedly different from the Australian federation. It is asymmetrical, built on an underlying multi-ethnic and multilingual foundation, with Francophone Quebec existing alongside predominantly Anglophone provinces. It is also based on strong economic and geographical regional cleavages, with the Maritimes, the Prairie provinces, and western Canada defining themselves against the centre; that is, Ontario and Quebec. The ethno-regional nature of the Canadian federation has meant that it has developed as a relatively decentralized system, which can be seen to run counter to the intentions of its constitutional founders. It was their aim to create a federal system that had a strong central government, vesting Ottawa with innumerable powers and the ability to override conflicting provincial laws. However, over time the balance of power within the Canadian federation has shifted towards the provinces. This has occurred in part through judicial interpretation that 'gave broad reading to provincial jurisdiction over property and civil rights and a narrower interpretation than originally intended to federal powers' (Hurley 1997, 115). Quebec's claims to sovereignty have also contributed to greater decentralization and paved the way for other provinces to make their own claims for increased autonomy (Corbett 1990, 301). In recent years, the provinces have come to reject any notion that the national government is a superior level of government, instead claiming that Canada has eleven equal governments (ten provincial and one federal) (Simeon 1988, S14).

The strength of the Canadian provinces has been enhanced by two factors: their constitutional authority and their fiscal capacity. Provinces have jurisdiction over many policy areas, including local government, primary and secondary education, and most areas of non-criminal law. They also control key social policy areas, including health care, social welfare, and tertiary education. Since the 1950s the growing cost of these programs has led the provinces to depend increasingly on federal coordination and financial support (MacIver 1995, 220). Through the use of federal spending power, Ottawa was able to assert some control over such provincial policy fields as health and social welfare. However, in recent years, the role of the federal government in provincial affairs has been challenged. Interference by the federal government through tied funding has been highly contentious, with many provinces asserting their claim to autonomy (Watts 1996, 41). Political pressure from Quebec and other provinces has led to the federal government's gradual withdrawal from shared-funding programs in areas such as health, social services, unemployment insurance, training, and the labour market. In their place, provinces have been granted unconditional block funding (Maslove 1992, 170). While Ottawa continues to have some hold over the purse strings, it has gradually lost control over directing how provinces spend their money.

Subnational autonomy has been further enhanced as a result of the provinces' extensive fiscal capacity. Unlike the Australian states, the Canadian provinces can operate in every tax field except customs, excise, and domestic property (MacIver 1995, 226). The move by the provinces to re-enter the field of income taxation after the Second World War, and to collect rents from their own resource base, has significantly contributed to their vitality.[9] Cullen (1992, 129) summarizes the position of provinces as having 'considerable scope to develop (and protect) their own economies (and identities). Although not entirely fiscally independent, the provinces also enjoy significant, provincially based, revenue raising capacity.' Not all provinces enjoy the same degree of fiscal autonomy. Indeed, significant discrepancies exist between the provinces in terms of their revenue-raising capacity. For instance, oil-rich Alberta is able to raise much more revenue than are the less prosperous Maritime provinces. Efforts have been made to minimize these differences through federal government transfers.[10]

Because these efforts have focused only on adjusting for differences in the revenue-raising capacity of the provinces (and not on the cost of expenditure), the effect of federal transfers has been nowhere near as dramatic as it has been in Australia (Watts 1996, 47). As a result, greater regional variations have developed in Canada than in Australia.

Centrifugal pressure has undoubtedly been the strongest dynamic in Canadian federalism. However, countervailing tendencies also exist within the federation. Just as in Australia, where federal strength has been checked by state autonomy, so in Canada centralizing forces have countered provincial autonomy. The most obvious and powerful of these has been the Charter of Rights and Freedoms.[11] The main political purpose underlying the charter was Trudeau's pan-Canadian nationalizing vision. Trudeau (1968, 54) made his intentions clear in 1967 in a speech on constitutional reform: 'The adoption of a constitutional Bill of Rights is intimately related to the whole question of constitutional reform. Essentially we will be testing – and, hopefully, establishing – the unity of Canada.' It was introduced in an attempt by Ottawa to bypass provincial governments and to speak directly with the citizenry (Cairns 1995b, 200). To some extent, it can be argued that the charter has been successful as it has helped foster the development of a national rights community. As discussed below, feminists, along with Aboriginal groups, have certainly taken advantage of this opening. In other ways though, the charter and Trudeau's constitutional vision have failed. Because it did not successfully deal with either the duality issue with regard to Quebec or address regional concerns (especially in the west), constitutional reform has contributed to the tension between Ottawa and the provinces (MacIver 1995, 236). Rather than stemming centrifugal forces, constitutional reform arguably served to encourage them.

In Canada, federal political and fiscal arrangements have influenced Anglo-feminist strategies, albeit in a negative way. Despite the presence of strong centrifugal and regional pressures, Anglo-feminists have been reluctant to look towards the provincial level. As noted earlier, there has been some engagement with provincial institutions (e.g., in British Columbia and Newfoundland and, in earlier periods, Alberta). However, many Anglo-feminists and the key feminist organization, NAC, have preferred to maintain their focus on Ottawa. The federal government, especially during the Trudeau era, has helped encourage this effort in two ways: through Women's Program funding and the Charter of Rights and Freedoms.

Since the 1940s the Canadian federal government has been involved in providing financial support for the creation of interest groups. The purpose of this funding has been twofold: (1) to be able to communicate easily with the public it serves and (2) to strengthen the allegiance of certain interest groups with the central government rather than with the provinces.

The Trudeau government, which came to office in 1968, can be seen to have overtly focused on the latter task. Governing at a time when centrifugal forces were at their peak, it saw funding interest groups as a way to advance its own vision for Canadian unity and explicitly linked this to notions of 'participatory democracy,' national unity, and citizenship (Phillips 1991, 190). The Women's Program, established in 1974 by the Department of Secretary of State, was part of this effort (Pal 1993, 14).

The program was established to help and support the development of groups involved in promoting understanding and action on Status of Women issues. The program has funded not only national groups, but also groups that are provincially and municipally based.[12] The program has established offices in all major regional centres to administer funding applications and to make recommendations to head office with regard to grant allocations. Although the program cannot provide money for women's services, as this is a provincial responsibility, it has provided funds to enable organizations to lobby the provincial governments on matters that relate to legislation or funding for these services. According to a senior Women's Program officer, 'the regional nature of the program has created an interesting situation where in some cases the program is funding groups to protest against provincial policies. An example of this occurred when the program funded women's groups to lobby the Alberta government to stop its changes to the health system' (interview with author, 1995).

The Women's Program has been crucial in encouraging Anglo-feminists to look towards Ottawa. As Vickers (1990, 22) argues, the program's funding made it logical for women's groups to 'construct themselves as part of the federal government's community of clients,' even if their main activity related to the provinces. Its influence as a centralizing force for feminists was weakened under Mulroney when he cut funding levels and provided financial support to the anti-feminist REAL women's organization – a trend that continued under the Chrétien Liberal government (see Phillips 1991, 201).[13] Nevertheless, the program's legacy is still obvious. In Phillips's view, 'the expectation has been created that the funder of minority interests will also be their protector' (205).

The charter, which was introduced in an attempt to counter decentralizing forces, has also influenced the strategies of Anglo-feminists. Chapter 5 illustrated how it has provided them with the ability to engage in a litigation strategy. The charter has also helped Anglo-feminists avoid the 'patchwork' effect they so fear will result from greater devolution of services. According to McLellan (1991, 11; cited in Vickers 1993, 271), many Anglo-feminists have come to perceive the charter as an instrument they can use to ensure 'a comparability of benefits, legal conditions and support programs wherever they might end up living.' As noted earlier, they have been able to use the charter to good effect, winning important cases pertaining to equality, reproductive, and employment rights – rights that affect women regardless of where they live. In short, the charter has given Anglo-feminists an instrument with which to counteract increasing forces of decentralization and, even at a time when provinces are increasingly important, a reason to maintain a national focus.

Intergovernmental Mechanisms

Over the course of the past two decades in Australia and Canada, federalism has increasingly taken on an executive form. In both countries a vast array of formal and informal intergovernmental mechanisms has been created to facilitate communication and joint action between elected and non-elected officials at the national and subnational levels of government. Canada's federal-provincial forums, which include conferences between first ministers as well as meetings between ministers and bureaucrats responsible for particular policy areas, are mirrored in Australia by the Special Premiers' Conference, the Council of Australian Governments (COAG), and ministerial councils (for a discussion of intergovernmental machinery in Canada see Hurley 1997; in Australia, see Painter 1997b, 204-7). Although the Canadian intergovernmental system is vast, according to Watts's (1996, 52) comparative survey of federation, they are more formalized in Australia.

Intergovernmental mechanisms have, at least in a nominal sense, been highly gendered. In both countries, women have been poorly represented in most of the machinery of executive federalism.[14] The uneven gender balance may not be a function of federalism per se but, rather, a reflection of the under-representation of women in political leadership positions, in Cabinet, and in the upper echelons of the public service. Nevertheless, it has meant that women have been mostly absent from the leadership positions in these increasingly important institutions. On a more positive note, executive federalism has also opened up some opportunities for the advancement of women's policy. In Australia and Canada intergovernmental women's policy machinery has been created, and this has included meetings between national and state/provincial Status of Women's ministers and bureaucrats. This machinery has been especially important in the Australian case. During the late 1980s and 1990s femocrats in state jurisdictions cooperated with those at the federal level to fashion national polices concerning childcare, domestic violence, women's health, and other areas that required joint government action. Most recently, the Howard Liberal government has joined with the states to implement the national Partnerships against Domestic Violence Program, which provides funding for research on domestic violence at the Commonwealth level as well as in each state (Chappell 2001).

In line with their general attitude towards federalism, Canadian Anglo-feminists have tended to be more wary of these intergovernmental institutions than have Australian feminists. They have joined with others in criticizing these institutions as undemocratic and elitist.[15] Their opposition to these structures was most obvious during the debates around the Meech Lake Accord. They were highly critical of the elitist process used to devise the accord. NAC's anti-Meech slogan – 'Don't let eleven men threaten the legal rights of over half the population' – summed up the mood in the Anglo-feminist community with regard to the workings of executive federalism (*Action Now* vol. 2, no. 7, 1987).

It may also be the case that the link between feminists and executive federalist institutions has been weaker in Canada that it has in Australia because of Canada's less institutionalized 'femocracy.' Without comprehensive or entrenched women's policy machinery, Canadian feminists have found it difficult to utilize the executive federal structures at their disposal. Rankin and Vickers (2001) support this view, at least in relation to anti-domestic violence policy making. Their research found that the links between Canadian femocrats at all levels of government working in this policy area were very weak and that federal arrangements were so complex that it was difficult for those working either inside or outside the state to develop a coordinated approach to the issue of domestic violence (57).

Federal Norms

As with other institutions, it has not only been structures but also underlying norms that have played a role in shaping the POS open to feminists within federalism. The very term 'federalism' is, as Watts (1996, 6) notes, 'basically not a descriptive but a normative term.' It is, as he points out, 'based on the presumed value and validity of combining unity and diversity and of accommodating, preserving and promoting distinct entities within a larger political union.' However, it is important to note that federalism seeks to accommodate and to preserve a distinct form of diversity – one based on territory. In Whitaker's view: 'The essential organising principle of federalism is territoriality ... Federalism as a system of representation ... is predicated along the axis of space and its political organization' (cited in Gagnon 1997, 193). Gagnon agrees, arguing that, 'central to any view of federalism is the respect for diversity, which implies the maintenance of territorially based communities with specific identities' (28).

The strength of territorial representation as an underlying norm of federalism has some profound consequences. While it empowers certain ethno-regional groups, it does so at the expense of other 'non-territorial' groups. As White (1997, 18) argues, 'the most marginalised will be as marginal in a federal system as they are anywhere else; neither the theory nor the practice of federalism is about equalising democratic weight beyond the perimeters of its recognised territorial structures.' The significance of this point has not been lost on the Canadian Aboriginal community, which has pushed strongly for a vision of federalism that is not based on territorial boundaries but, rather, that is able to embrace group identity as a form of representation (see Rocher and Smith 1995, 56). Feminists have also been alert to the significance and limitations of privileging territorial concerns. For Vickers (1994, 14), 'the territorial organization of politics suppresses interests and needs which are not territorially contained.' She notes that federal arrangements might suit certain groups of women, such as Francophone feminists living in Quebec, who have been able to use their unique ethno-regional position to further gender-based interests. However, outside these exceptional cases, women (and, more specifically, sex/gender interests) are not politically relevant. The problem for feminist activists in federal systems is that 'political institutions are structured to represent geographically organized political interests, while women are geographically dispersed' (Vickers 1990, 20).

How has federalism's emphasis on territoriality influenced the POS open to Australian and Canadian feminists? In Canada, because the provinces have enjoyed more political and fiscal autonomy than have the Australian states, and because of the ethno-regional character of Canadian federalism, the politics of territory has been particularly salient. The consequences of this have been that gender (and other identity) interests have been downplayed, if not ignored, within federal debates. The emphasis on territorial issues has no doubt contributed to women activists' disinclination to engage in provincial politics (on this point see Vickers 1990, 22). However, as noted, a parallel force is at work in Canada – the centralizing dynamic of the Charter of Rights and Freedoms. To some extent it can be argued that the entrenchment of the charter has provided space for representation of cleavages that are nationwide and non-territorial, such as those based on race and gender identities (Rocher and Smith 1995, 63). The charter not only offers the women's movement opportunities to engage in a litigation strategy to advance its interests in the face of legislative barriers, but it also provides it with an instrument (albeit a limited one) with which to challenge the politics of territory that inhibits the representation of gender concerns.

Territorial interests are also important in Australia. Turf wars between the federal and state governments are a feature of the political landscape and, at times, dominate the political debate. In Australia, though, these interests are ameliorated to some extent by the fact that regional cleavages are less obvious than they are in Canada and the fact that there is no imperative to embrace a second majoritarian culture. Furthermore, the nature of the party system and the presence of a progressive political party, which has traditionally been focused on class issues, have acted as counterweights to territorial concerns. As has been noted in previous chapters, feminists in Australia have made gains at both the state and federal levels when there has been an ALP government in office. It would be incorrect to assume that these mediating factors have meant that gender interests are central in Australian political debates. Nevertheless, exploiting the opportunities provided by a progressive party at both levels of government, Australian feminists have, at certain times, taken advantage of federalism's multiple access points in order to influence policy and services for women.

The experience of Australian and Canadian feminists with regard to federalism provides some support for the arguments of Banaszak (1996) and Galligan (1995); that is, that it can open new spaces for political activists and provide a system of 'double democracy.' The Australian case demonstrates that, where feminists face a system within which both levels of government have some political and/or fiscal authority, and within which territorial concerns are ameliorated by equalization concerns and the presence of a progressive political party, opportunities for dual citizenship can emerge. However, as Paul Pierson (1995) makes clear, different federal systems can produce different results. This is obvious from the comparison presented here. Anglo-feminists confront a highly decentralized system, with the norm of territoriality being strong and with mediating party structures being weak. Operating within these conditions, Canadian feminists have not always found that federalism offers them a system of double democracy; rather, they have found that it is better to direct their effort towards the national government and to use the charter to advance their nonterritorial claims. There are signs that centrifugal forces will lead to greater decentralization in Canada. These forces, along with evidence that certain provincial governments (e.g., the former NDP governments in British Columbia and Ontario) can be supportive of feminist demands, might lead Anglo-feminists to look more closely at the experience of their Quebec counterparts and find new ways to engage with federal institutions.

7
Feminists and Institutions: A Two-Way Street

Gendering Government advances three central arguments. First, it posits that the choices of feminist strategies in Australia and Canada are influenced by the nature of the institutional environment within which feminists operate. In line with the neo-institutionalist and political opportunity literature, it suggests that political institutions play an important role in shaping how social actors, including feminists, engage with the state, which, at different times, provides them with both openings and obstacles. Second, it argues that institutional norms as well as institutional structures influence the political opportunity structure open to feminist activists. It highlights the importance of the operation of entrenched gender norms (often parading in a neutral guise) for feminist engagement with the state, and it shows how the operation, or 'fixity,' of gender norms within an institution influences the extent to which it is open or closed to feminist aims. Third, it argues that the interaction between institutions and feminists is co-constitutive; that is, just as feminists' choices have been shaped by their engagement with institutions, so have the latter been shaped by the former. The argument further suggests that feminist goals have been constructed through the process of engagement.

Ideological and Institutional Variables
Gendering Government began by suggesting that feminist strategies cannot be explained by ideological factors alone. As Chapter 2 notes, there have been ongoing debates within the two women's movements concerning engagement with the state. Nevertheless, in both instances these differences have often been put aside and a pragmatic position has emerged. In the main, the ideological position of Australian and Canadian feminists can be characterized as being pro-statist. This explains why feminists in the two countries have been willing to engage with the state, but it does not explain the important differences between their choice of strategies and structures. Ideology alone does not explain why Australian feminists

have pursued a femocrat project while Canadian feminists have relied on lobbying and mass mobilizing tactics (and, increasingly, on litigation). Nor does it reveal why Australian feminists have resisted all attempts to create a peak body, while Anglo-Canadian feminists have successfully maintained the National Action Committee on the Status of Women and other organizations. These differences require an additional explanation, which is: Within each polity, feminist strategy is shaped by institutions and the political opportunities and constraints they afford.

Political Institutions, Political Opportunities, and Feminist Activists

At first glance it appears that the Australian and Canadian political systems are very similar, sharing, as they do, a Westminster heritage grafted onto federal structures, a written Constitution, and a common law tradition. However, when the layers of each of these institutions are peeled back, obvious differences emerge. These differences are significant enough to alter the nature of the POS available to feminists operating in each country. As outlined in Table 7.1, the variations in the POS occur at a number of levels. Most obviously, they occur between different institutions within the same polity. Differences also occur between similar institutions within the two polities. A third level of variation relates to the interaction between institutions in each polity.

Differences between Institutions and across Polities

Australian and Canadian feminists have chosen to pursue particular political strategies because of the nature of the POS available to them across the institutional spectrum. These POSs have differed between institutions within the same polity. In Australia, feminists have been able to make gains through the bureaucracy and, at times, have been able to use federalism to good effect. They have been less successful in pursing their aims through political parties and the legislature, and they have been frustrated within the legal and constitutional realms. In Canada, a similar pattern emerges in that feminists have experienced variations in the POS between institutions; however, in their case, they have found the legal and constitutional realms more amenable to their demands than have their Australian counterparts.

Variations have also been obvious between ostensibly similar institutions within the two polities, and these have shaped the available POSs. Feminists in both countries have faced a variety of constraints within the parliamentary realm. As Table 7.1 indicates, these have stemmed from the electoral and party systems and from within the legislature itself. Although the nature of the party and electoral systems differs in each country, they have had the same effect, discouraging feminists from engaging in an electoral project. In neither country has these constraints resulted in feminists avoiding an electoral strategy completely; however, in both cases they have found that the rewards of this strategy – in terms of gaining a winnable seat and exercising influence within the legislature – have been incommensurate with the effort needed to enter Parliament. At the same time, they have discovered that external lobbying strategies can bring about some positive outcomes, including making legislation more gender sensitive. As a result, it has made sense for them to continue to put effort into operating as 'outside agitators' vis-à-vis the legislature.

Because of the constraints within the electoral and parliamentary realms, feminists in both countries have been encouraged to look elsewhere to advance their goals. In Australia, feminists have discovered that the bureaucracy, at least under ALP governments, offers them a relatively positive POS. Not only have they been able to bring about favourable policy outcomes through this strategy, but they have also managed to secure a place within the hub of the public service, thus strengthening their institutional position. However, the experience of Canadian feminists with regard to the bureaucratic realm suggests that similar institutions will not always provide the same POS. Faced with structural and normative barriers, they have found it difficult to use the public service to influence policy outcomes or to achieve an entrenched institutional position.

Again, as a result of these constraints, Anglo-Canadian feminists have shifted their focus elsewhere. Their experience has shown that lobbying politicians through traditional and radical means can sometimes be effective. They have had input into a range of royal commissions as well as into the crucial charter debates. Most positively, Anglo-feminists have found that, once the charter was put in place, they have been able to use it to bring about a range of reforms under the broad heading of equality rights. However, during the past ten years it has become obvious to these activists that having access to a bill of rights does not guarantee success. Nevertheless, it does provide them with an additional avenue through which to pursue their objectives, something that is especially important when a conservative government is in office at the federal level. The experience of Anglo-Canadian feminists provides an important lesson to Australian feminists. The latter, who have adopted an ambivalent attitude towards entrenched rights protection, find themselves at a distinct disadvantage when a conservative Commonwealth government, with a weak commitment to existing legislative and executive rights guarantees, is in office. Were Australian feminists able to gain access to a bill of rights (with sex equality guarantees), they too would be better able to work across the institutional spectrum and enjoy an enhanced capacity to make advances through the courts when blocked by other institutions.

Table 7.1

The political opportunity structure in Australia and Canada

	Australia	Canada
Parliamentary institutions	*Structures* **Negative** Class-based party system Majoritarian, single-member electoral system for lower house	*Structures* **Negative** Brokerage/regional party system Multi-party system Majoritarian, single-member electoral system for lower house
	Norms **Negative** Masculine, adversarial parliamentary culture	*Norms* **Negative** Masculine, adversarial parliamentary culture
Bureaucratic institutions	*Structures* **Positive** Centralized women's policy agencies Political support of the ALP	*Structures* **Negative** Decentralized women's policy agencies
	Norms **Positive** Weak neutrality norms/tolerance for internal advocates	*Norms* **Negative** Strong neutrality norms/intolerance for internal advocates
Constitutional and legal institutions	*Structures* **Negative** No bill of rights instrument Limited court challenges funding Restrictive standing and *amicus curiae* provisions	*Structures* **Positive** Charter of Rights and Freedoms, including sex equality guarantees Funding for court challenges Generous standing and *amicus curiae* provisions
	Norms **Negative** Continuing application 'male standard' No rights culture No outwardly feminist judges	*Norms* **Positive** Substantive, contextualized definition of equality Emerging rights culture Feminist judges

▶

◀

Table 7.1

___

The political opportunity structure in Australia and Canada

	Australia	Canada
Federalism	*Structures* **Positive** High federal fiscal and political capacity combined with moderate state political capacity	*Structures* **Negative** Moderate federal fiscal and political capacity combined with high provincial fiscal political capacity
	Positive Intergovernmental machinery Intervening party system	**Negative/moderate** Intergovernmental machinery **Positive** Intervening constitutional charter
	Norms **Moderate** Territoriality relatively weak, ameliorated by party system	*Norms* **Negative** Territoriality strong, only partially ameliorated by charter

___

Institutional Interaction

A key argument of this book, which is in line with arguments developed by neo-institutionalists such as Hall (1986) and Thelen and Steinmo (1992), is that the unique configuration of institutions within each polity has an independent effect on the behaviour of social actors. The interplay between institutions can create new openings that can enable feminists to engage in a particular arena, and, just as easily, it can cause alterations in the interaction of institutions that will foreclose these opportunities. The importance of institutional interaction has been clearly illustrated with regard to Australian feminists. The presence (or absence) of an ALP government, a relatively progressive political force, has had a profound influence on the extent to which feminists have been able to use the bureaucracy to advance their agenda. When the ALP has been in office, it has supported the femocrat project by providing it with a central institutional position and other resources. It has done this at both the federal and state levels, with the result that federal structures have also been open to Australian feminists. The importance of parties has been demonstrated in a less dramatic way in Canada. Because of the electoral system, the NDP is relegated to the provincial sphere, but when it has been elected to office at this level it has helped to create a favourable POS for feminists within the bureaucratic arena and, to a lesser extent, within the legislature.

What these examples have demonstrated is that when certain institutional variables – in this case, bureaucracy, the party system, and federalism – are configured in a particular pattern at a certain point in time, they can help to bring about a positive POS within a specific institutional realm. However, as the story of Canadian and Australian feminists' engagement has demonstrated, these intersections are neither certain nor stable. When one of the institutional variables moves 'out of alignment' (e.g., when a conservative government is elected to office) openings can be quickly replaced by constraints. The instability in the pattern of institutional interaction draws attention to the temporal dimension of institutions. As the neo-institutional and political opportunity literature suggests, institutions, and the openings or closures that they afford, are neither permanent nor fixed (see Thelen and Steinmo 1992; Tarrow 1998). Institutions are dynamic and, as they change, they provide new openings for social actors. However, these openings can soon be closed, sending these actors to look elsewhere to advance their claims. The Australian femocrat strategy is not a story of unbounded success; rather, it has ebbed and flowed over time depending on the alignment of institutional forces. Similarly, in the case of Canadian feminist litigation strategy, a favourable POS emerged only after the entrenchment of equality clauses in the charter and, more particularly, after the *Andrews* decision. Should the *Andrews* decision be successfully challenged and the existing charter jurisprudence overturned, the potential for feminists to use this arena would be severely curtailed.

Importance of Institutional Norms

It is clear from the above discussion that the structural features within, between, and among various institutions have played a significant role in shaping the POS open to feminists in Australia and Canada. Yet these structures tell only half the story with regard to factors shaping the prevailing POS. As discussed in the previous chapters, and as illustrated in Table 7.1, institutional norms have operated alongside structures to create both obstacles and openings for feminists.

According to March and Olsen (1989), institutional norms operate to define a 'logic of appropriateness': they constrain certain types of behaviour while encouraging others. What March and Olsen do not account for is the fact that these norms are often imbued with a gender dimension, proscribing different forms of behaviour and values for men and women within institutions and for those outside institutions. The extent to which these gender norms are entrenched within an institution is central to understanding the POS open to feminists. Katzenstein's (1998, 166) point in relation to the Church and the military in the US is apposite here: 'It is not opportunities by themselves, but their interactive relationship with norms, beliefs, and values that drives feminist protest within institutions.' By intervening in institutions, feminists are involving themselves in a subversive act. Essentially, what they are attempting to do is to unsettle the norms that underpin institutions in order to advance a new 'logic of appropriateness' – one that is more sensitive to women's lives as well as to masculine and feminine modes of behaviour. The extent to which feminists in each country have been able to reveal the gendered aspects of seemingly neutral institutional norms has been crucial to shaping the POS at their disposal.

Chapter 3 highlights the difficulty feminists have experienced in trying to challenge the existing gender norms in the party, electoral, and parliamentary spheres. In both countries, women remain outsiders within the highly masculinized world of pre-selection contests. Although they have attempted to break this mould by lobbying for affirmative action and other reforms to party structures, progress has been slow. The continuing preference for men as candidates and the privileging of male standards within parties continue to thwart the long-awaited 'feminization' of politics. Even for those women who make it into the legislature, the story is one of working against the grain. In both Australia and Canada, the parliamentary culture continues to be adversarial as opposed to consensual. Participants within this arena need toughness, loudness, and, at times, coarseness. While there is plenty of evidence to suggest that women can adopt these skills, many feminists find the culture alien and frustrating. As a result, many have chosen to look elsewhere to pursue their goals. Moreover, gender norms within the legislature have operated to trivialize the contribution of individual women and 'women's issues.' In short, the constraints faced by Australian and Canadian feminists within the parliamentary realm are related as much to the fixity of gender norms within the legislature as they are to structural problems within the electoral and party systems.

The operation of gender norms within the two bureaucracies is a more varied story, providing different POSs for feminists in each country. While the Australian bureaucracy was initially established to reflect Weber's ideal type, some of these traditional features have been challenged over time. An expectation within Australian political culture that groups will use the state to achieve 'syndical satisfaction' has helped to disrupt the strict adherence to certain traditional norms, something that was further encouraged in the 1970s by the reformist Coombs Commission. These shifts have been central to Australian feminist engagement with the bureaucracy. The reforms helped to bring about a new 'logic of appropriateness' and, albeit inadvertently, challenged gender norms that were embedded within such traditional practices as the career public service and the commitment to a neutral public servant model. Feminists found that, because of these normative changes, they were accepted within the bureaucracy alongside other syndical groups and were able, indeed were expected, to use their position to pursue gender-sensitive policy initiatives. Through these activities, femocrats themselves were able to shape the POS within the bureaucracy, inscribing new normative parameters that viewed as 'appropriate' a gender perspective in policy debates. For a time at least, Australian femocrats were able to unsettle existing gender norms and to use the bureaucracy to advance their equity goals.

By contrast, majoritarian Canadian feminists have found it much more difficult to challenge certain traditional bureaucratic norms that are imbued with masculine assumptions. One of the important norms confounding feminists at the federal level, and in most of the provinces, is the expectation that public servants will remain neutral, operating without any overt political bias or favouritism. Within such an environment, the very notion of having advocates operating inside the bureaucracy is anathema, never mind having those who seek to unravel and challenge the existing gender norms that lie at the foundation of these traditional practices. The fact that the federal government has supported affirmative action programs in order to recruit more Aboriginal, Francophone, and female public servants has done little to overturn the neutral public servant model. These programs have been used to improve the nominal representation of individuals from these groups, but they have done nothing to enhance the substantive representation of collective identities that could then use the bureaucracy to advance their own political agenda.

Anglo-Canadian feminists have had much greater success challenging traditional gender norms in the constitutional and legal realms than have Australian feminists. Through a charter litigation strategy and the presence of feminists on the bench, Canadian feminists have been able to unsettle existing norms, including those that underpinned discrimination against women in employment and reproduction and, perhaps most profoundly, the very notion of equality itself. Especially after the *Andrews* decision, which found that women as a group were disadvantaged, feminists have been able to challenge the male standard that for so long justified different, usually unequal, treatment for women. Without a charter or other tools with which to challenge these norms, Australian feminists have been faced with a legal system that continues to reproduce masculine norms in that it upholds men as the standard by which women should be judged.

Norms, like institutional structures, have played an important part in shaping the POS open to feminists in the two countries. The extent to which feminists have been able to challenge these norms has varied between different institutions within each polity as well as across polities.

This reinforces the point that the state needs to be viewed as a differentiated entity. In other words, as with structures, norms will not operate in the same way across all institutions, nor will they manifest themselves in the same way within similar institutions within different political environments. As has been shown in relation to constitutional and bureaucratic realms, feminists in each country have had quite different experiences trying to unsettle gender norms within similar institutional settings.

Institutions and Feminists: A Two-Way Street

A final argument advanced throughout *Gendering Government* is that the relationship between institutions and feminist activists does not occur in a top-down direction but, rather, is co-constitutive. The interaction between agents and institutions can, in and of itself, make a crucial difference to the available POS. One of the benefits of adopting a historical neo-institutional approach to studying the engagement of feminists with the state is that it encourages study not only of how institutions shape the behaviour of political actors, but also of how these agents shape political structures (Peters 1999, 143). To use Cairns's (1995a) phrase, it enables us to understand how institutions are embedded within society. As is illustrated in the foregoing analysis, political institutions have not been fixed and pre-formed entities proscribing the actions of feminists. Through their interaction with these institutions, feminists have themselves been able to shape these institutions and to help create the openings available within them. The best example of this relates to the case of Canadian feminists and the legal and constitutional arenas. Through lobbying tactics, feminists were able to influence the direction of charter debates and eventually ensure the entrenchment of equality clauses within it. Having achieved this much, they were then able to engage in charter litigation and to introduce a gender perspective to charter jurisprudence. Over time, the charter has come to bear the hallmarks of feminist engagement. A similar two-way street can be seen operating within the Australian bureaucracy. Having taken advantage of opportunities to enter the state, once inside feminists have been able to prise open new avenues for reform, including policy agencies in central and line departments. They have also been able to expand the focus of 'women's policy' into mainstream economic policy areas.

In adopting a position that considers political institutions to be embedded within society, this book distances itself from some feminist accounts of women's engagement with the state. It strongly refutes the argument advanced by radical and socialist feminists who, while differing from each other in important respects, both argue that women activists will always be co-opted when they engage with state institutions and that these institutions can never operate to advance women's interests. Instead, it suggests that feminists do have some agency and that they can sometimes achieve their objectives by engaging with political institutions. However, to reject these functionalist accounts of the state is not to endorse a liberal feminist argument. It does not follow that by merely increasing the number of women in an organization, or by relying on 're-education' strategies, feminists will always achieve their aims; nor does it imply support for the naive view that feminists are on an unswerving trajectory towards progress. Clearly, as the experiences of Australian and Canadian feminists have shown, changes can come about only when there is an alignment between institutional and political forces. And there is never any guarantee that the steps towards progress will be permanent. All of these steps are open to challenge at any time and are easily dismantled, as both Australian and Canadian feminists have discovered under conservative governments. Nonetheless, even if gains are incremental and vulnerable, they are not illusory.

Notes

Chapter 1: Gender and Political Institutions in Australia and Canada

1 In the POS literature an 'increased opportunity' implies that actors have more space for manoeuvre and fewer constraints (Gamson and Meyer 1996, 277).

Chapter 2: Feminist Actors in Australia and Canada

1 The movements are so diverse, in fact, that it may be a mistake to refer to either of them in the singular. However, for the sake of clarity it is necessary to use the term 'movement' throughout the following discussion. Where possible differentiation between the segments of each movement is made and the more nuanced term, 'feminist activists,' is used.

2 For a discussion of the Francophone movement, see Dumont (1992).

3 In a riposte to the Mejane leaflet, Mavis Robertson, writing in another WLM journal, argued: 'We cannot assume that a woman in power will sell out; all we can assume is that she may have no choice but to sell out if she is not backed by a strong and independent movement.' Furthermore, 'the movement, like the woman adviser, might be bought off by a few reforms, but it is more likely that each gain can raise our expectations' (cited in Wills 1981, 138).

4 In the early 1980s NAC received approximately 90 percent of its funding from government sources. However, by 1995 government funding had been drastically reduced to 27 percent of its total revenue, with the remainder being made up through NAC's own fundraising activities (NAC, *Action Now*, vol. 5, no. 2, 1995).

Chapter 3: The Feminist Electoral Project

1 Support for AD in lower house contests swings widely between elections. In 1990 it attracted its highest vote, capturing 11.3 percent of first preferences, but support fell in the 1993 election to 3.7 percent. In the 1998 election it achieved 5.1 percent of the vote (AEC 1999, 70-1). One Nation support appears to have peaked at the 1998 election. In the federal election of 2001 the party reduced its vote by more than half, receiving 412,485 votes (4.29 percent) of the total vote (<http://www.aec.gov.au>).

2 In a comparative study of levels of party identification in Australia, Canada, and other Western countries, Bean (1996, 140) shows that party identification in Canada has varied between elections between 79 percent in the early 1960s, to a peak of 84 percent in 1970, and back to 78 percent in 1990. By contrast, Australian party identification levels have been relatively consistent over time and are at least 10 percentage points higher than they are in Canada.

3 Interestingly, as Curtin (1997, 8) notes, 'there was no obvious translation of such efforts into votes for the ALP from women.'

4 The AWP has had limited success in pursuing its electoral strategy. It ran candidates for the Senate in the 1996 election in a number of states but failed to achieve a quota in any of them (a quota is approximately 7 percent of the total state vote). AWPs highest vote was in Western Australia, where it received 1 percent of the total state vote.

5 For instance, in the 1990 federal election the ALP relied heavily on the distribution of second preferences from the Democrats and Green candidates in order to retain office (preferences flowed two to one in favour of the ALP). The effect of the electoral system on minor parties was clearly demonstrated in this election. While these alternative parties had a combined first preference vote of over 11 percent, they were nevertheless unable to secure one lower house seat (see Papadakis 1993, 22).

6 In 1993 the percentage of all women Senate candidates was 31.5 percent. In 1996 the figure had increased to 34.9 percent, and in 1998 it had dropped to 30 percent. By contrast, female candidates for the House of Representatives remained at 27 percent for the 1996 and 1998 elections, and many of these women had stood in 'unsafe' seats. (See <http://www.aec.gov.au>).

7 After the 1990 election women held five of the nine minor party and independent Senate positions; after the 1993 election women held five of the ten minor party Senate positions, increasing to six out of ten minor party positions after the 1996 election. As of June 2002 there were thirteen senators who were from minor parties and/or were independents, four of whom were women.

8 Between 1901 and 1990, the ALP elected only eleven women to the House of Representatives.

9 The number of women ALP candidates endorsed for the House of Representatives has grown from four in 1972 to thirty in 1998 (20 percent of the total).

10 Recent election results demonstrate this point. In the 1996 federal election, Liberal women won seventeen seats in the House of Representatives, ten of which were seats that were previously held by another political party and that the Liberal Party never expected to win (Phillips 1996, 6). In the 1998 election, Liberal women lost two of these seats.

11 As we shall see in relation to Canada, parties using this system do not tend to seek out women candidates or support their nomination (see Brodie 1994a, 79; for a discussion of the impact of local pre-selection processes, see Lovenduski and Norris 1993, 324-6).

12 Although vigorously opposed to the ALP quota system, some branches of the Liberal Party have in fact had some affirmative action measures in place since the formation of the party in 1944. On joining forces with the Liberal Party, the Australian Women's National League in Victoria insisted that there be equal representation of men and women at all levels of the party structure. Other states have designated positions for women within the internal structure (see Brennan 1997).

13 Erickson's (1993, 76) research on the effect of local level pre-selection on women candidates tends to support this argument. The party with the most interventionist selection process, the NDP, had the best record with regard to selecting women for safe ridings.

14 In the 1993 election 38 percent of all female candidates (113 in total) ran for the NDP, only one of whom was elected to office (see Young 1997, 84; Brooks 1996, 330-1).

15 Female representation follows a similar pattern in Australian and Canadian subnational governments. In 1996 women held an average of 18 percent of seats in all state/provincial governments. This increased to approximately 20 percent by 2000. In both cases there have been significant variations between subnational governments. For instance, in 1996 in Australia the lowest rate of female representation was in Queensland, where women held 14.6 percent of seats, while in Tasmania women held 28.6 percent of seats. At the same time, in Canada Nova Scotia had the lowest level of female representation, with 9.6 percent, while British Columbia and Prince Edward Island shared the highest level with 25 percent (for Australia, see Swain 1997; for Canada, see Arscott and Trimble 1997).

16 For instance, in the 1996 election, the Liberal Party of Australia stood a total of thirty-four candidates, seventeen of whom were elected. Of those who won seats, only three held safe seats, nine won marginal seats (i.e., seats requiring a 5 percent swing to win or lose), and six won hard-to-win seats (i.e., requiring over a 5 percent swing) (Sawer, cited in Brennan 1997, 283).

17 For instance, Section 1 of the charter subjects rights to such limitations as are 'demonstrably justified in a free and democratic society,' and Section 33 provides a legislative override for important clauses in the charter (see Simeon 1994, 33).

18 The argument made here rests on a matter of degree. It is true that Australian royal commissions have been used extensively and that they have a wide scope. Like their Canadian counterparts, they have undertaken research that has been fed back into the policy-making process (Prasser 1994, 18). Where they differ most from their Canadian counterparts is in their representative function. As Prasser notes, in Australia 'producer representatives had a clear dominance of all inquiries, sometimes spectacularly so' (19). In Australia, members of the women's movement have participated in royal commissions, including the 1974 Royal Commission on Human Relationships (See RCHR 1974-5; RCAGA 1976). Within the context of this discussion, it is interesting to note that the WEL submission to RCAGA related to the further development of women's policy machinery within the federal bureaucracy. A number of WEL's suggestions were taken up by the commission and were included in its final report (see RCAGA 1976, 370-87). The difference between Canadian and Australian royal commissions is that in Australia there has never been a royal commission established for the express purpose of addressing 'women's issues.' Nor have feminist experts played a prominent role in any Australian royal commission (on this topic, see Arscott 1995a).

19 For example, Monique Begin in the RCSW; and Janine Brodie and Jane Arscott in the Royal Commission on Electoral Reform and Party Financing (RCERPF).

Chapter 4: The Femocrat Strategy

1 Women in the Aboriginal community were also ambivalent about this strategy. Some saw this as an opportunity to work with the government to bring about the dual aims of gender and race reforms, and joined the bureaucracy to work in designated Aboriginal policy units and within the Aboriginal and Torres Strait Islander Commission (ATSIC). Others were hostile to the strategy, arguing that it reflected the biases of White, educated, middle-class women and resulted in, if not racist, then at least inappropriate policy responses for the Aboriginal community.

2 Other than the women's bureau, which had existed in the Department of Labour since the 1950s.

3 In 1975 there were eight women in senior levels of the Australian Public Service out of a possible 1,267 (Conroy 1994, 99).

4 Miller (1964, 65) defines a syndicate as 'organizations of people whose economic and vocational interests have induced them to band together for action to their common advantage.'

5 The number of women in senior levels of the service increased from 2 percent in 1974, to 11 percent in 1990, to 13 percent in 1993 (see Conroy 1994, 94).

6 State ALP governments were elected in South Australia in 1970, in Tasmania in 1975, in New South Wales in 1976, in Victoria in 1982, in Western Australia in 1983, and in Queensland in 1988. Femocrats first entered the bureaucracy in South Australia in 1976, in Tasmania in 1976, in Victoria in 1976, in New South Wales in 1977, in Western Australia in 1983, in the Northern Territory in 1982, and in Queensland in 1990.

Chapter 5: Feminists and the Constitutional and Legal Realms

1 One obvious recent exception here is Alexandra Dobrowolsky's (2000) detailed study of women, representation, and constitutionalism in Canada.

2 *Bliss* v. *Canada* (Attorney General) [1979] 1 S.C.R. 183 (hereinafter *Bliss*).

3 In later years many feminists felt vindicated in their support for the charter, when the Supreme Court overruled *Bliss* in the *Brooks* v. *Canada Safeway Ltd.* [1989] 1 S.C.R. 1252 (hereinafter *Brooks*) decision, which found that discrimination on the basis of pregnancy is sex discrimination and, therefore, unlawful under Section 15 of the charter (CACSW 1992, 1).

4 For instance, in 1994 the Australian Senate Standing Committee into Gender Bias and the Judiciary found that men of Anglo-Saxon or Celtic backgrounds hold 90 percent of federal judicial offices. Most are privately educated and are appointed in their early fifties (Senate Standing Committee on Legal and Constitutional Affairs 1994).

5 Canada's justice Bertha Wilson is a prime example here. In her judgments she often

applied feminist principles that challenged the public/private distinction and the male standard that is applied in the law (see Wilson 1993). See also see Canadian justice Donna Hackett (1998).

6 *Lavell* v. *Attorney General of Canada* (1971), 22 D.L.R. (3rd) (Ont. Co. Ct.).

7 The override clause, Section 33 of the charter, allowed the federal and provincial parliaments to pass laws notwithstanding the provisions of the charter.

8 It should be noted that due to internal disputes, NAC itself did not play a large part in this campaign. However, organizers drew heavily on NAC networks, and many NAC members were involved in the mass effort (see Vickers 1993, 274-5).

9 In the first three years of charter litigation, of the 601 court decisions involving Section 15, only forty-four involved sex equality and only seven were initiated on behalf of women (LEAF 1989a, 1).

10 An *amicus curiae,* or friend of the court, is invited into court to provide information on the case at hand. His or her role is to 'help ensure that courts are properly informed on matters which ought to be taken into account when reaching their decisions' (ALRC 1995, 65).

11 *Morgentaler* v. *The Queen* [1988] 3 S.C.R. 30 (hereinafter *Morgentaler*).

12 *R.* v. *Butler* [1992] 1 S.C.R. 342 (hereinafter *Butler*).

13 *Moge* v. *Moge* [1992] 3 S.C.R. 813.

14 *Schachter* v. *Canada* [1992] 2 S.C.R. 3.

15 *Egan* v. *Canada* [1995] 2 S.C.R. 513 (hereinafter *Egan*) related to equality for gays and lesbians; *Miron* v. *Trudel* [1995] 2 S.C.R. 418 related to equality of married persons under the law; *R.* v. *Thibaudeau* [1995] 2 S.C.R. 627 (hereinafter *Thibaudeau*) related to post-divorce child payments.

16 *Vriend* v. *Alberta* [1998] 1 S.C.R. 493 (hereinafter *Vriend*).

17 *R.* v. *Lavalee* [1990] 1 S.C.R. 853 (hereinafter *Lavalee*).

18 *R.* v. *Seaboyer* [1991] 2 S.C.R. 577 (hereinafter *Seaboyer*).

19 It is important to note that the analysis is based on charter experiences prior to the groundbreaking *Andrews* decision that, as noted above, changed the tide in relation to feminist litigation in Canada.

20 *Australian Iron and Steel Pty. Ltd.* v. *Banovic* (1989) 168 C.L.R. 165, Federal Court 89/1052.

21 In 1993 the Public Interest Advocacy Centre (PIAC) was granted leave to appear before the federal court in a case concerning women's employment in the lead industry (ALRC 1994, 117). In 1994 a group known as Women Lawyers against Female Genital Mutilation intervened before the Children's Court of Victoria to put 'information that would otherwise not have come before the court' (ALRC 1994, 118).

22 *Brandy* v. *Human Rights and Equal Opportunity Commission and ORS* C3/1994 (1994) (hereinafter *Brandy*).

23 The ALRC and the Public Interest Advocacy Centre have also called for reform to these laws (ALRC 1985, 1994, 1995; PIAC 1995). To date (2002), no legislative changes have affected standing laws or the extension of *amicus* intervention. In 1995 the federal ALP government's Women's Justice Strategy provided for additional funding so that 'women could run test cases to challenge a particular area of the law' (Attorney General's Department 1995, 92). As it happened, the ALP was removed from office before the funding became available and the incoming coalition government has not implemented the Women's Justice Strategy.

24 *Superclinics Australia Pty. Ltd* v. *CES and ORS,* s. 88/1996 (hereinafter *Superclinics*). The case involved a woman, known as CES, who was suing her doctor for damages for failure to diagnose her pregnancy in time for her to have an abortion. After losing her case in the NSW Supreme Court, the woman appealed to the NSW Appellate Court, where she won her case. The doctor and the clinic, the defendants in the case, appealed the appeal and it went before the High Court in September 1996 (see Wainer 1997, 135-6).

25 Space does not permit a discussion of each of these campaigns. The point to note is that, instead of looking for constitutional solutions to these problems, women's groups lobbying from outside the state, and femocrats working from inside the state, have sought reforms in the area of statute law. See Graycar (1990) for the campaign for changes to

matrimonial property law; CAPOW! Bulletin, November 1995 for lobbying related to reforms to the Family Law Act; and, O'Donnell and Hall 1988 for legislation to address discrimination in the workforce.

26 For instance, in 1995 a coalition of women's organizations was brought together by the newly formed National Women's Justice Coalition (NWJC) to lobby the government to withdraw the 'Anti-Teoh Bill.' The bill, which eventually lapsed, sought to override the High Court's decision, potentially extending the application of international covenants to domestic law (CAPOW! Bulletin, November 1995).

27 In recent years the move away from centralized wage-fixing structures towards an increased emphasis on enterprise-level bargaining has alarmed many feminists and others concerned with wage equity (Rimmer 1994). They see the shift towards enterprise-level bargaining as a retrograde step as far as women are concerned. This is due to the fact that women continue hold a marginalized position in the labour force, and this diminishes their individual bargaining capacity.

28 In 1990-1 the HREOC heard 803 complaints under the act, the majority of which came from women (House of Representatives Committee 1992, 217).

29 That the sex discrimination commissioners position was saved largely due to the lobbying efforts of two Liberal women senators, Marise Payne and Helen Coonan, indicates the importance of having supportive women inside Parliament.

30 The CEDAW Optional Protocol is aimed at giving individual women the right to appeal directly to the UN for breaches of the convention. The NWJC and other women's organizations have been active in lobbying the federal government to become a signatory to the Optional Protocol. It appears that this lobbying has been unsuccessful, with the Howard coalition government stating that it will not sign the protocol until the entire UN committee system is reformed.

31 During the 1980s two former ALP attorneys general, Lionel Bowen and Gareth Evans, both unsuccessfully attempted to introduce a statutory bill of rights. Neither proposal had strong support in Parliament and both eventually lapsed.

32 Section 51 (xxxi) provides for just terms for the acquisition of property; Section 80 provides the right to trial by jury; Section 116 denies federal legislative power with respect to religion; and Section 117 protects against discrimination by states on the grounds of residence.

33 There are some signs that suggest this is changing. In the past decade, the High Court of Australia has shown a willingness to question the adequacy of parliamentary and common law rights protections and has increasingly cast itself in the role of the guardian of fundamental rights (see Walker 1995, 251).

34 A 1994 study undertaken by Legal Aid and Family Services found that women make up only 33 percent of successful legal aid applications.

35 *Dietrich v. The Queen* (1992) 177 C.L.R. 292 (hereinafter *Dietrich*).

36 In 1996 the Howard government announced that it would cut $33.16 million from the Legal Aid Program and would no longer provide funding for matters arising under state or territory law (Troup 1997, 153).

37 In that they do not become a party to the proceedings, *amici curiae* have a more limited role than do intervenors.

38 Gaudron (1997, 4) notes that in 1996-7 women represented only 2.5 percent of all advocates appearing before the High Court.

39 Later, an appeal overruled Justice Bollen's judgment (Senate Standing Committee on Legal and Constitutional Affairs 1994, 5).

40 Another example of a biased judgment concerned a Victorian judge, Justice O'Bryan, who, in passing sentence in a rape trial, argued that 'fortunately, due to the ferocity of your attack, your victim has no memory of the sexual violation of her body.' In his reasoning this meant that the victim 'was not traumatised by the event' and that, therefore, 'a sentence significantly less than the maximum is deemed appropriate' (Senate Standing Committee on Legal and Constitutional Affairs 1994, 6). An appellate court also overturned this ruling.

Chapter 6: Feminists and Federalism

1 Queensland did not create a women's unit until after the election of the Goss ALP government in the early 1990s.

2 Niland has also been credited with achieving a similar outcome in the women's health field (see Smith 1984).

3 The 1987 Meech Lake Accord was devised by the federal and provincial governments with the intention of bringing Quebec into the 'constitutional fold.' Although supported by Quebec, it failed to be ratified by provincial legislatures and eventually foundered. The Charlottetown Accord represented another try at incorporating Quebec as well as a response to Aboriginal demands for constitutional recognition. It also failed when it was rejected in a national referendum in 1992.

4 Anglo-feminists' fear of women having uneven rights across the country was not new. They had made this point in their campaign in 1978 against the transfer of divorce to subnational governments (Burt 1988, 76).

5 The states collect between 15 and 20 percent of their revenue, while being responsible for approximately 40 percent of total government outlays. Federal government transfers cover the rest.

6 The use of SPPs increased dramatically under the Whitlam government. Between 1972-3 and 1975-6 SPP assistance to the states increased from 26 percent of total funding to the states to 48 percent. In 1995-6 SPPs accounted for 53 percent of total payments to the states (see Joint Committee of Public Accounts 1995).

7 In this case, the federal government was able to invoke the UN Convention on the Elimination of All Forms of Discrimination against Women, to which it was a signatory, to intervene in an area of state jurisdiction.

8 In the late 1980s, under the Hawke government, the Commonwealth was able to enter the women's health field, despite many of the services being the responsibility of the states. It did this through the development of the National Women's Health Program, which was a joint Commonwealth/state program in which the Commonwealth was the dominant financial partner. In the first four years of the program the Commonwealth provided 50 percent of the total $36 million budget, and in the second four-year phase of the program it committed itself to $30 million of the $60 million budget. Canberra has also been able to play the dominant role in the development of childcare policy, despite the fact that it holds the responsibility for this area jointly with the states. In 1994-5, of the $1 billion spent on childcare services, the Commonwealth contributed 90 percent, with the balance provided by the states (OSW 1994, n.p.; Council of Australian Governments Child Care Working Group 1995, 10).

9 In 1994-5, provinces received on average only 18.7 percent of their income through federal government transfers. The rest was made up of a combination of income tax, consumption taxes, licence fees, and government levies. According to Watts's (1996, 71) survey of federation, Canada is second only to Switzerland with regard to the extent of provincial autonomous revenue-raising capacity.

10 In 1994-5 the four wealthiest provinces received between 11 percent and 20 percent of their total revenue from federal transfers, whereas the four Atlantic provinces received between 36 percent and 43 percent (White 1997, 169).

11 It must be noted, however, that the charter contains a major compromise for the provinces. Section 33 allows provincial governments to introduce legislation 'notwithstanding' most charter provisions.

12 In 1985-6 the Women's Program provided $10.8 million in funding for 650 groups across Canada: 37 percent of the funds were allocated to national groups while 63 percent went to local, regional, or provincial groups (House of Commons Standing Committee on the Secretary of State 1987, 7, 12). In 1990-1, only 39 of the 457 women's groups funded by the Women's Program were nationally based groups. The remainder were provincially based. Interestingly, Quebec had the largest number of groups – 117 – funded by the program. The most populated province, Ontario, followed with a total of 76 groups (Phillips 1991, 200).

13 The Women's Program suffered a further cut of 5 percent when it was merged with Status of Women Canada in 1995 *(Action Now* vol. 5, no. 2, 1995).

14 In Australia there have been only two female ALP state premiers, Carmen Lawrence (Western Australia) and Joan Kirner (Victoria), both of whom were appointed to office for brief periods of time. A similar pattern has emerged in Canada. In June 1993 Kim Campbell was appointed prime minister. She lost office at the December 1996 election. In April 1991 the Social Credit Party in British Columbia appointed Rita Johnson as premier, a position she lost in the election of October 1991. Canada's second female premier, Catherine Callbeck, headed the Prince Edward Island government for three years, beginning in 1993.

15 A widespread critique of the move towards executive federalism focuses on its undemocratic nature. Opponents argue that intergovernmental institutions are elitist and bypass democratically elected parliaments (see Painter 1998; Watts 1996).

References

Ad Hoc Committee of Canadian Women Conference on Canadian Women and the Constitution. 1981. 'Resolutions Adopted at the Conference on Canadian Women and the Constitution.' *Atlantis* 6, 2.

Alexander, Malcolm, and Brian Galligan. 1992. 'Australian and Canadian Comparative Political Studies.' In Alexander Malcolm and Brian Galligan, eds. *Comparative Political Studies: Australia and Canada*. Melbourne: Pitman Publishing.

Allen, Avril, and F.L. Morton. 1997. 'Feminists and the Courts: Measuring Success in Interest Group Litigation.' Conference Paper. Canadian Political Science Association, St. John's, NF.

Altman, Carol. 2000. 'Labor's Emily Moves to Save Female Quota.' *The Australian*, 26 April: 6.

Anderson, Jill. 1994. 'Iron and Steel.' *Alternative Law Journal* 193: 107-10.

Andrew, Caroline, and Sanda Rodgers, eds. 1997. *Women and the Canadian State/Les femmes et l'Etat canadien*. Montreal and Kingston: McGill-Queen's University Press.

Ang, Ien. 1995. 'I'm a feminist but ... "Other" Women and Postnational Feminism.' In Barbara Caine and Rosemary Pringle, eds. *Transitions in New Australian Feminisms*. Sydney: Allen and Unwin.

Arscott, Jane. 1995a. 'Twenty-Five Years and Sixty-Five Minutes after the Royal Commission on the Status of Women.' *International Journal of Canadian Studies* 11 (Spring): 33-55.

–. 1995b. 'A Job Well Begun ... Representation, Electoral Reform, and Women.' In François-Pierre Gingras, ed., *Gender and Politics in Contemporary Canada*. Toronto: Oxford University Press.

Arscott, Jane, and Linda Trimble. 1997. 'In the Presence of Women: Representation and Political Power.' In Arscott and Trimble, eds. *In the Presence of Women: Representation in Canadian Governments*. Toronto: Harcourt Brace and Co.

Arscott, Jane, Pauline L. Rankin, and Jill Vickers. N.d. 'Canadian Experiments with State Feminism: Status-of-Women Machinery in a Federal State.' N.p.

Asher, Louise. 1980. 'The Women's Electoral Lobby: An Historical Inquiry.' MA thesis, Department of History, University of Melbourne.

Attorney General's Department. 1994. *Gender Bias in Litigation Legal Aid Issues Paper*. Canberra: Attorney General's Department, Commonwealth of Australia.

–. 1995. *Justice Statement*. May. Canberra: Attorney General's Department, Commonwealth of Australia.

Aucoin, Peter. 1988. 'Contraction, Managerialism and Decentralization in Canadian Government.' *Governance: An International Journal of Policy and Administration* 1, 2 (April): 144-61.

Australian Electoral Commission. 1999. *Electoral Pocketbook*. Canberra: AEC.

Australian Law Reform Commission. 1985. *Standing in Public Interest Litigation*. Discussion Paper 27. Canberra: AGPS.

–. 1993. *Equality before the Law*. Discussion Paper 54. July. Sydney: ALRC.

–. 1994. *Equality before the Law: Justice for Women*. Report No. 67. Canberra: AGPS.

–. 1995. *Beyond the Door Keeper: Standing to Sue for Public Remedies*. Report No. 78. Canberra: AGPS.

Australian Women's Party. 1996. 'The Australian Women's Party: Sharing the Power.' *CAPOW! Bulletin* (Autumn): 20-1.

Bacchi, Carol, and Vicky Marquis. 1994. 'Women and the Republic: "Rights" and Wrongs.' *Australian Feminist Studies* 19 (Autumn): 93-113.

Backhouse, Constance. 1988. 'If I Can't Dance.' *Broadside: A Feminist Review* 9, 9 (July).

Bakvis, Herman. 1978. 'French Canada and the "Bureaucratic Phenomenon."' *Canadian Public Administration* 21, 1: 101-24.

Bakvis, Herman, and William M. Chandler, eds. 1987. *Federalism and the Role of the State*. Toronto: Toronto University Press.

Banaszak, Lee Ann. 1996. *Why Movements Succeed or Fail: Opportunity, Culture, and the Struggle for Woman Suffrage*. Princeton: Princeton University Press.

Bashevkin, Sylvia. 1993. *Toeing the Lines: Women and Party Politics in English Canada*. 2nd ed. Toronto: Oxford University Press.

–. 1996. 'Losing Common Ground: Feminists, Conservatives and Public Policy in Canada during the Mulroney Years.' *Canadian Journal of Political Science* 29, 2 (June): 211-42.

–. 1998. *Women on the Defensive: Living through Conservative Times*. Chicago: University of Chicago Press.

Bean, Clive. 1996. 'Partisanship and Electoral Behaviour in Comparative Perspective.' In Marian Simms, ed. *The Paradox of Parties: Australian Political Parties in the 1990s*. Sydney: Allen and Unwin.

–. 1997. 'Parties and Elections.' In Brian Galligan, Ian McAllister, and John Ravenhill, eds. *New Developments in Australian Politics*. Melbourne: Macmillan.

Begin, Monique. 1992. 'The Royal Commission on the Status of Women: Twenty Years Later.' In Constance Backhouse and David H. Flaherty, eds. *Challenging Times: The Women's Movement in Canada and the United States*. Montreal and Kingston: McGill-Queen's University Press.

Beilharz, Peter, Mark Considine, and Rob Watts. 1992. *Arguing about the Welfare State: The Australian Experience*. Sydney: Allen and Unwin.

Bird, Florence. 1990. 'Introduction.' *Ottawa Law Review* 22: 3.

Black, Naomi. 1993. 'The Canadian Women's Movement: The Second Wave.' In Sandra Burt, Lorraine Code, and Lindsay Dorney, eds. *Changing Patterns: Women in Canada*. 2nd ed. Toronto: McClelland and Stewart.

Bourgault, Jacques, and Barbara Wake Carroll. 1997. 'The Canadian Public Service: The Last Vestiges of the Whitehall Model?' In Jacques Bourgault, Maurice Demers, and Cynthia Williams, eds. *Public Administration and Public Management in Canada*. Sainte-Foy, QC: Les Publications du Québec.

Brennan, Deborah. 1994. *The Politics of Australian Childcare: From Philanthropy to Feminism*. Cambridge: Cambridge University Press.

–. 1997. 'Women and Political Representation.' In Dennis Woodward, Andrew Parkin, and John Summers, eds. *Government, Politics, Power and Policy in Australia*. Melbourne: Longman.

Brodie, Janine. 1994a. 'Women and Political Leadership.' In Maureen Maneuso, Richard G. Price, and Ronald Wagenberg, eds. *Leaders and Leadership in Canada*. Toronto: Oxford University Press.

–. 1994b. *Politics on the Boundaries: Restructuring and the Canadian Women's Movement*. Eighth Annual Robarts Memorial Lecture. Toronto: York University Press.

–. 1995. *Politics on the Margins: Restructuring and the Canadian Women's Movement*. Halifax: Fernwood Publishing.

Brodie, Janine, and Jane Jenson. 1990. 'The Party System.' In Michael S. Whittington and Glen Williams, eds. *Canadian Politics in the 1990s*. 3rd ed. Scarborough: Nelson Canada.

Brodsky, Gwen, and Shelagh Day. 1989. *Canadian Charter Equality Rights for Women: One Step Forward or Two Steps Back?* Ottawa: Canadian Advisory Council on the Status of Women.

Brooks, Stephen. 1996. *Canadian Democracy: An Introduction*. Toronto: Oxford University Press.

–. 1998. *Canadian Public Policy: An Introduction.* Toronto: Oxford University Press.

Brooks, Sue. 1984. 'The OSW and the Way Forward.' *Refractory Girl* (May).

Broughton, Sharon, and Di Zetlin. 1996. 'Queensland ALP Women Parliamentarians: Women in Suits and Boys in Factions.' *International Review of Women and Leadership* 2, 1: 47-61.

Brown, Leslie, Cindy Jamieson, and Marg Kovach. 1995. 'Feminism and First Nations: Conflict or Concert.' *Canadian Review of Social Policy* 35 (Spring): 69-74.

Brown, Wendy. 1995. *States of Injury: Power and Freedom in Late Modernity.* Princeton: Princeton University Press.

Bryson, Lois. 1987. 'Women and Management in the Public Sector.' *Australian Journal of Public Administration* 46, 3 (September): 259-72.

Bulbeck, Chilla. 1996. '"His and Hers Australias": National Genders.' In Jeannette Hoorn and David Goodman, eds. *Vox Reipublicae: Feminism and the Republic.* Special edition of the *Journal of Australian Studies* 47: 43-56.

Burgmann, Verity. 1993. *Power and Protest Movements for Change in Australian Society.* Sydney: Allen and Unwin.

Burnstein, Jodi. 1994. 'The Long Wait for Justice.' *Sydney Morning Herald,* 17 March: 12.

Burt, Sandra. 1988. 'The Charter of Rights and the Ad Hoc Lobby: The Limits of Success.' *Atlantis* 141: 78-81.

–. 1990. 'Organised Women's Groups and the State.' In William Colemand and Grace Skogstad, eds. *Policy Communities and Public Policy in Canada: A Structural Approach.* Mississauga, ON: Copp Clark Pitman.

–. 1993. 'The Changing Patterns of Public Policy.' In Sandra Burt, Lorraine Code, and Lindsay Dorney, eds. *Changing Patterns: Women in Canada.* 2nd ed. Toronto: McClelland and Stewart.

Burt, Sandra, and Elizabeth Lorenzin. 1997. 'Taking the Women's Movement to Queen's Park: Women's Interests and the New Democratic Government.' In Jane Arscott and Linda Trimble, eds. *In the Presence of Women: Representation in Canadian Governments.* Toronto: Harcourt Brace and Co.

Burton, Clare. 1991. *The Promise and the Price: The Struggle for Equal Opportunity in Women's Employment.* Sydney: Allen and Unwin.

Busque, Ginette. 1991. 'Why Women Should Care about Constitutional Reform.' In David Schneiderman, ed. *Conversations among Friends: Women and Constitutional Reform.* Edmonton Centre for Constitutional Studies, University of Alberta.

Byrne, Lesley Hyland. 1997. 'Feminists in Power: Women Cabinet Ministers in the New Democratic Party (NDP) Government of Ontario, 1990-1995.' *Policy Studies Journal* 25, 4 (Winter): 601-12.

Cadzow, Jane. 2000. 'Tasmanian Tiger.' *Sydney Morning Herald,* 18 March: 16-23.

Caiden, Gerald. 1990. 'Australia's Changing Administrative Ethos: An Exploration.' In Alexander Kouzmin and Nicholas Scott, eds. *Dynamics in Australian Public Management: Selected Essays.* Melbourne: Macmillan.

Cairns, Alan. 1992. *The Charter versus Federalism: The Dilemmas of Constitutional Reform.* Montreal and Kingston: McGill-Queen's University Press.

–. 1995a. 'The Embedded State: State-Society Relations in Canada.' In Douglas E. Williams, ed. *Reconfigurations: Canadian Citizenship and Constitutional Change: Selected Essays by Alan C Cairns.* Toronto: McClelland and Stewart.

–. 1995b. 'The Political Purposes of the Charter.' In Douglas E. Williams, ed. *Reconfigurations: Canadian Citizenship and Constitutional Change: Selected Essays by Alan C. Cairns.* Toronto: McClelland and Stewart.

Canadian Advisory Council for the Status of Women. 1974. *What's Been Done? Assessment of the Federal Government's Implementation of the Recommendations of the Royal Commission of the Status of Women.* Ottawa: CACSW.

–. 1979. *10 Years Later: The Royal Commission Report.* Ottawa: CACSW.

–. 1980. 'Women, Human Rights and the Constitution.' (Submission to the Special Joint Committee on the Constitution, November 18.) *Atlantis* 6, 2.

–. 1988. *The Equality Game: Women in the Public Service, 1908-1987.* Ottawa: CACSW.

–. 1992. *A Feminist Guide to the Canadian Constitution*. Ottawa: Canadian Advisory Council on the Status of Women.

Canadian Council on Social Development. 1987. *A Guide to the Charter for Equality Seeking Groups*. Ottawa: Canadian Council on Social Development.

Chaples, Ernie. 1997. 'The Australian Voters.' In Rodney Smith, ed. *Politics in Australia*. 3rd ed. Sydney: Allen and Unwin.

Chappell, Louise. 1995. 'Women's Policy.' In Martin Laffin and Martin Painter, eds. *Reform and Reversal: Lessons from the Coalition Government in New South Wales, 1988-1995*. Melbourne: Macmillan.

–. 2001. 'Federalism and Social Policy: The Case of Domestic Violence.' *Australian Journal of Public Administration* 60, 1: 36-46.

Charlesworth, Hilary. 1993. 'The Australian Reluctance About Rights.' *Osgoode Hall Law Journal* 311: 195-232.

Clarke, Harold D., and Allan Kornberg. 1993. 'Public Attitudes toward Federal Political Parties, 1965-1991.' *Canadian Journal of Political Science* 26, 2: 287-311.

Cohen, Marjorie Griffin. 1993. 'The Canadian Women's Movement.' In Marjorie Cohen, Ruth Roach Pierson, and Philinda Masters, eds. *Canadian Women's Issues: Strong Voices*. Vol. 1. Toronto: James Lorimer and Co.

Colebatch, H.K. 1992. 'Theory and the Analysis of Australian Politics.' *Australian Journal of Political Science* 271: 1-11.

Coleman, Marie. 1990. 'Opening Address.' *National Women's Conference Papers*. Canberra: Write People.

Coleman, William D. 1987. 'Federalism and Interest Group Organization.' In Herman Bakvis and William M. Chandler, eds. *Federalism and the Role of the State*. Toronto: University of Toronto Press.

Connolly, Peter. 1994. 'Should the Courts Determine Social Policy?' *Upholding the Constitution*. Vol. 2. Melbourne: Samuel Griffiths Society.

Conroy, Denise. 1994. 'The Glass Ceiling: Illusory or Real?' *Canberra Bulletin of Public Administration* 76: 91-103.

Corbett, David. 1990. 'Australia's States and Canada's Provinces: The Pace and Patterns of Administrative Reform.' In Alexander Kouzmin and Nicholas Scott, eds. *Dynamics in Australian Public Management: Selected Essays*. Melbourne: Macmillan.

Council of Australian Governments Child Care Working Group. 1995. *Discussion Paper on a Proposed National Framework for Children's Services in Australia*. Canberra: Australian Government's Printing Service.

Cox, Eva. 1990. 'Feminism, Bureaucracy and the State: Reclaiming the State.' *Refractory Girl* 34 (January): 43-4.

–. 1995. *A Truly Civil Society: 1995 Boyer Lectures*. Sydney: ABC Books.

Crowley, Rosemary. 1993. *Report to the Prime Minister on the Review of Government Policy Advice Mechanisms on the Status of Women*. Canberra: Department of Prime Minister and Cabinet.

Cullen, Richard. 1992. 'Constitutional Federalism and Natural Resources.' In Malcolm Alexander and Brian Galligan, eds. *Comparative Political Studies: Australia and Canada*. Melbourne: Pitman.

Curthoys, Ann. 1992. 'Doing It for Themselves: The Women's Movement Since the 1970s.' In Kay Saunders and Ray Evans, eds. *Gender Relations in Australia: Domination and Negotiation*. Sydney: Harcourt Brace.

–. 1993. 'Single, White, Male.' *Arena Magazine*, December-January: 27-8.

–. 1994. 'Australian Feminism Since 1970.' In Norma Grieves and Alisa Burns, eds. *Australian Women: Contemporary Feminist Thought*. Oxford: Oxford University Press.

Curtin, Jennifer. 1997. 'The Gender Gap in Australian Elections.' *Research Paper No. 3, 1997-98*. Department of the Parliament Library Information and Research Services.

Curtin, Jennifer, and Marian Sawer. 1995. 'Gender Equity in the Shrinking State.' In Francis Castles, Rolf Gerritsen, and Jack Vowles, eds. *The Great Experiment: Labour Parties and Public Policy Transformation in Australia and New Zealand*. Sydney: Allen and Unwin.

Department for Women. 1996. *Heroines of Fortitude: The Experiences of Women in Court as Victims of Sexual Assault.* Sydney: Department for Women, New South Wales Government.

Dobrowolsky, Alexandra. 2000. *The Politics of Pragmatism: Women, Representation and Constitutionalism in Canada.* Oxford: Oxford University Press.

Doern, G. Bruce. 1983. 'Priorities and Priority Setting.' In G. Bruce Doern and Richard Phidd, eds. *Canadian Public Policy: Ideas, Structure, Process.* Toronto: Methuen.

Dowse, Sara. 1983. 'The Women's Movement's Fandango with the State: The Movement's Role in Public Policy Since 1972.' In Cora Baldock and Bettina Cass, eds. *Women, Social Welfare and the State.* Sydney: Allen and Unwin.

–. 1984. 'The Bureaucrat as Usurer.' In Dorothy Broom, ed. *Unfinished Business: Social Justice for Women in Australia.* Sydney: George Allen and Unwin.

Dumont, Micheline. 1992. 'Origins of the Women's Movement in Quebec.' In Constance Backhouse and David H. Flaherty, eds. *Challenging Times: The Women's Movement in Canada and the United States.* Kingston/Montreal: McGill-Queen's University Press.

Dunleavy, Patrick, and Brendan O'Leary. 1987. *Theories of the State: The Politics of Liberal Democracy.* Houndsmills, Hampshire: Macmillan.

Eade, Susan. 1977. 'And Now We Are Six.' *Refractory Girl* (March).

Eisenstein, Hester. 1996. *Inside Agitators: Australian Femocrats and the State.* Sydney: Allen and Unwin.

Eisenstein, Zillah. 1993. *The Radical Future of Liberal Feminism.* Rev. ed. Boston: Northeastern University Press.

Elkins, David. 1992. 'Electoral Reform and Political Culture.' In Malcolm Alexander and Brian Galligan, eds. *Comparative Political Studies: Australia and Canada.* Melbourne: Pitman Publishing.

Erickson, Linda. 1993. 'Making Her Way In: Women, Parties and Candidacies in Canada.' In Joni Lovenduski and Pippa Norris, eds. *Gender and Party Politics.* London: Sage.

–. 1997. 'Parties, Ideology and Feminist Action: Women and Political Representation in British Columbia Politics.' In Jane Arscott and Linda Trimble, eds. *In the Presence of Women: Representation in Canadian Governments.* Toronto: Harcourt Brace and Co.

Errington, Jane. 1993. 'Pioneers and Suffragists.' In Sandra Burt, Lorraine Code, and Lindsay Dorney, eds. *Changing Patterns: Women in Canada.* 2nd ed. Toronto: McClelland and Stewart.

Ferguson, Kathy E. 1987. 'Male-Ordered Politics: Feminism and Political Science.' In Terence Ball, ed. *Idioms of Inquiry: Critique and Renewal in Political Science.* New York: State University of New York Press.

Findlay, Sue. 1987. 'Facing the State: The Politics of the Women's Movement Reconsidered.' In Heather Jon Maroney and Meg Luxton, eds. *Feminism and Political Economy: Women's Work, Women's Struggles.* Toronto: Methuen.

–. 1995. "Democracy and the Politics of Representation: Feminist Struggles with the Canadian State." PhD diss. Department of Political Science, University of Toronto.

Fitzroy, L. 1999. 'State Responses to Violence against Women.' In Linda Hancock, ed. *Women, Public Policy and the State.* Melbourne: Macmillan.

Flask, Carmel, and Betty Hounslow. N.d. 'Government Intervention and Right-Wing Attacks on Feminist Services.' *Scarlet Woman* 11: 11-21.

Franzway, Suzanne. 1986. 'With Problems of Their Own: Femocrats and the Welfare State.' *Australian Feminist Studies* 3 (Summer): 43-57.

Franzway, Suzanne, Dianne Court, and R.W. Connell. 1989. *Staking a Claim: Feminism, Bureaucracy and the State.* Sydney: Allen and Unwin.

Fudge, Judy. 1987. 'The Public/Private Distinction: The Possibilities of and the Limits to the use of Charter Litigation to Further Feminist Struggles.' *Osgoode Hall Law Journal* 25, 3: 485-554.

–. 1989. 'The Effect of Entrenching a Bill of Rights upon Political Discourse: Feminist Demands and Sexual Violence in Canada.' *International Journal of the Sociology of Law* 17: 445-63.

Fudge, Judy, and Harry Glasbeek. 1992. 'The Politics of Rights: A Politics with Little Class.' *Social and Legal Studies* 1, 1: 45-70.

Gagnon, Alain-G. 1995. 'The Political Uses of Federalism.' In François Rocher and Miriam Smith, eds. *New Trends in Canadian Federalism.* Peterborough: Broadview Press.

Galligan, Brian. 1990. 'The Distinctiveness of Australian Federalism.' In Alexander Kouzmin and Nicholas Scott, eds. *Dynamics in Australian Public Management: Selected Essays*. Melbourne: Macmillan.

–. 1995. *A Federal Republic*. Cambridge: Cambridge University Press.

Gamson, William A., and David S. Meyer. 1996. 'Framing Political Opportunity.' In Doug McAdam, John D. McCarthy, and Mayer N. Zald, eds. *Comparative Perspectives on Social Movements*. Cambridge: Cambridge University Press.

Gaudron, Mary. 1997. Speech to launch Australian Women Lawyers, Hyatt Hotel, Melbourne, 19 September. <http://www.hcourt.gov.au/speeches/gaudronj/gaudronj_wlasp.htm>.

Gelb, Joyce. 1989. *Feminism and Politics: A Comparative Perspective*. Berkeley: University of California Press.

Geller-Schwartz, Linda. 1995. 'An Array of Agencies: Feminism and the State in Canada.' In Dorothy McBride Stetson and Amy G. Mazur, eds. *Comparative State Feminism*. Thousand Oaks: Sage Publications.

Gillespie, James A. 1995. 'New Federalisms.' In J. Brett, J. Gillespie, and M. Goot, eds. *Developments in Australian Politics*. Melbourne: Macmillan.

Goar, Carol. 1989. 'Why Tories Spurn Feminist Group.' *Toronto Star*, 20 May: D4.

Goodsell, Charles T. 1990. 'Australian Public Administration through Foreign Eyes.' In Alexander Kouzmin and Nicholas Scott, eds. *Dynamics in Australian Public Management: Selected Essays*. Melbourne: Macmillan.

Gotell, Lise. 1994. 'Feminism, Equality Rights and the Charter of Rights and Freedoms in English Canada, 1980-1992: The Radical Future of Liberal Feminism?' PhD diss., Department of Political Science, York University.

Gotell, Lise, and Janine Brodie. 1991. 'Women and Parties: More Than an Issue of Numbers.' In Hugh G. Thorburn, ed. *Party Politics in Canada*. 6th ed. Scarborough: Prentice Hall, Canada.

Gow, David John, and Doug Tucker. 1996. 'Electoral Systems, Women's Candidacy and Electoral Success.' Paper presented at the Annual Conference of the Australasian Political Studies Association, University of Western Australia, Perth, WA, October.

Gray, Gwendolyn. 1991. *Federalism and Health Policy: The Development of Health Systems in Canada and Australia*. Toronto: University of Toronto Press.

–. 1998. 'How Australia Came to Have a National Women's Health Policy.' *International Journal of Health Services* 28, 1: 107-25.

Graycar, Regina. 1990. 'Feminism and Law Reform: Matrimonial Property Law and Models of Equality.' In Sophie Watson, ed. *Playing the State: Australian Feminist Interventions*. Sydney: Allen and Unwin.

–. 1995. 'The Gender of Judgments: An Introduction.' In Margaret Thornton, ed. *Public and Private: Feminist Legal Debates*. Oxford: Oxford University Press.

Greaves, Lorraine. 1988. 'Split Resolve.' *Broadside: A Feminist Review* 9, 8 (June).

–. 1991. 'Reorganizing the National Action Committee on the Status of Women 1986-1988.' In Jerri Dawn Wine and Janice L. Ristock, eds. *Women and Social Change: Feminist Activism in Canada*. Toronto: J. Lorimer.

Hackett, Donna. 1998. 'Finding and Following "The Road Less Travelled": Judicial Neutrality and the Protection and Enforcement of Equality Rights in Criminal Trial Courts.' *Canadian Journal of Women and the Law* 10: 129-48.

Haines, Janine. 1992. *Suffrage to Sufferance: 100 Years of Women in Politics*. Sydney: Allen and Unwin.

Hall, Peter A. 1986. *Governing the Economy: The Politics of State Intervention in Britain and France*. Cambridge: Polity Press.

Harford, Sonia. 1996. 'Canberra Cuts Women's Funds.' *The Age*, 17 May, A5.

Hawes, Rachel. 1997. 'Sex Workers Applaud Goward Choice.' *The Australian*, 26 March.

Healy, Judith. 1991. 'Community Service Programs.' In Brian Galligan, Owen Hughes, and Cliff Walsh, eds. *Intergovernmental Relations and Public Policy*. Sydney: Allen and Unwin.

Heitlinger, Alena. 1993. *Women's Equality, Demography and Public Policies*. New York: St. Martin's Press.

Herman, Didi. 1994. 'The Good, the Bad, and the Smugly: Perspectives on the Canadian Charter of Rights and Freedoms.' *Oxford Journal of Legal Studies* 14 (Winter): 589-604.

House of Commons Standing Committee on the Secretary of State. 1987. *Fairness in Funding: Report on the Women's Program*. Ottawa: House of Commons.

House of Representatives Standing Committee on Legal and Constitutional Affairs. 1992. *Half Way to Equal: Report of the Inquiry into Equal Opportunity and Equal Status for Women in Australia*. Canberra: AGPS.

Howe, Adrian. 1995. 'The Constitutional Centenary, Citizenship, the Republic and All That: Absent Feminist Conversationalists.' *Melbourne University Law Review* 20: 218-35.

Huggins, Jackie. 1994. 'A Contemporary View of Aboriginal Women's Relationship to the White Women's Movement.' In Norma Grieve and Alisa Burns, eds. *Australian Women: Contemporary Feminist Thought*. Oxford: Oxford University Press.

Hurley, James Ross. 1997. 'Executive Federalism.' In Jacques Bourgault, Maurice Demers, and Cynthia Williams, eds. *Public Administration and Public Management in Canada*. Sainte-Foy, PQ: Les Publications du Québec.

Irving, Helen. 1994. 'A Gendered Constitution? Women, Federation and Heads of Power.' *Western Australian Law Review* 24 (December): 186-98.

–. 1996. 'The Republic Is a Feminist Issue.' *Feminist Review* 52 (Spring): 87-101.

Jackson, Sue. 1986. 'According to Some.' *Scarlet Woman* 22: 10-12.

Jaensch, Dean. 1994. *Power Politics: Australia's Party System*. 3rd ed. Sydney: Allen and Unwin.

Jamal, Nadia. 1998. 'Government Finally fills Vacancies in Rights Bodies.' *Sydney Morning Herald,* 9 March: 2.

Jamieson, Suzanne. 1995. 'Equity in the Workplace.' In Michael Hogan and Kathy Dempsey, eds. *Equity and Citizenship under Keating*. Sydney: University of Sydney Public Affairs Research Centre.

Jenson, Jane. 1994. 'Commissioning Ideas: Representation and Royal Commissions.' In Susan Phillips, ed. *How Ottawa Spends: Making Change*. Ottawa: Carleton University Press.

Jhappan, Radha. 1998. 'The Equality Pit or Rehabilitation of Justice.' *Canadian Journal of Women and the Law* 10: 60-107.

Joint Committee of Public Accounts. 1995. *The Administration of Specific Purpose Payments: A Focus on Outcomes*. Canberra: Australian Government Printing Service.

Kaplan, Gisela. 1996. *The Meagre Harvest: The Australian Women's Movement, 1950s-1960s*. Sydney: Allen and Unwin.

Karman, Zeynap Erden. 1996. 'Feminist Initiatives to Gender Macro-Economic Policies in Canada.' Paper presented to the United Nations Research Institute for Social Development and Centre for Policy Dialogue Workshop, Rajendrapur, Bangladesh, 26-8 November.

Katzenstein, Mary Fainsod. 1998. *Faithful and Fearless: Moving Feminist Protest Inside the Church and Military*. Princeton: Princeton University Press.

Kaye, Lynn. 1989. 'Retaliation Seen in Cuts to NAC.' *Globe and Mail,* 29 April: A18.

Keman, Hans. 1997. 'Approaches to the Analysis of Institutions.' In B. Steunenberg and F. van Vught, eds. *Political Institutions and Public Policy*. Netherlands: Kluwer Academic Publishers.

Kennett, Geoffrey. 1994. 'Individual Rights, the High Court and the Constitution.' *Melbourne University Law Review* 19: 581-614.

Kernaghan, Kenneth. 1985. 'Representative and Responsive Bureaucracy.' In Peter Aucoin, ed. *Regional Responsiveness and the National Administrative State*. Toronto: University of Toronto Press.

–. 1997. 'Values, Ethics and Public Service.' In Jacques Bourgault, Maurice Demers, and Cynthia Williams, eds. *Public Administration and Public Management in Canada*. Sainte-Foy, QC: Les Publications du Québec.

Kingston, Margo. 1996. 'The Liberal Party and Women.' In Marion Simms, ed. *The Paradox of Parties: Australian political parties in the 1990s*. Sydney: Allen and Unwin.

–. 1997. 'Women on the Verge.' *Sydney Morning Herald,* 8 March: 40.

Kome, Penny. 1983. *The Taking of Twenty-eight: Women Challenge the Constitution*. Toronto: The Women's Educational Press.

Krygier, Martin. 1997. 'A State of "Dangerous Nonsense."' Extract from Boyer Lectures. *Sydney Morning Herald*, 5 December: 19.

Lake, Marilyn. 1999. *Getting Equal: The History of Australian Feminism*. Sydney: Allen and Unwin.

Landes, Ronald G. 1987. *The Canadian Polity: A Comparative Introduction*. 2nd ed. Scarborough: Prentice-Hall Canada.

Larbiestier, Jan, and Denise Russell. 1995. 'Working for Women? Discrimination, Affirmative Action and Equal Opportunity.' Proceedings of the Women and Law Conference, University of Sydney, Women's Studies Centre, Sydney, 22 September.

Lawrence, Carmen. 1994. 'Women and Political Life.' *Canberra Bulletin of Public Administration* 76 (April): 1-6.

Lees, Meg. 1999. 'Tax Cuts and GST-free Food Eminently Achievable Say Democrats.' Press Release 99/53, 14 February.

Legal Education and Action Fund (LEAF). 1988. *LEAFlines* (Newsletter). Vol. 2, no. 6.

–. 1989a. Vol. 2, no. 7.

–. 1989b. Vol. 3, no. 1.

–. 1992. Vol. 5, no. 2.

–. 1993. Vol. 5, no. 3.

–. 1994. Vol. 6, no. 2.

Levan, Andrea. 1996. 'Violence against Women.' In Janine Brodie, ed. *Women and Canadian Public Policy*. Toronto: Harcourt Brace and Co.

Lewis, Julie. 1993. 'Judge Calls for Courts to Hear Women's Groups.' *Sydney Morning Herald*, 11 June: 3.

Lovenduski, Joni, and Pippa Norris, eds. 1993. *Gender and Party Politics*. London: Sage.

–. 1996. *Women in Politics*. Oxford: Oxford University Press.

Lynch, Lesley. 1984. 'Bureaucratic Feminisms: Bossism and Beige Suits.' *Refractory Girl* 27 (May): 38-44.

MacIver, D.N. 1995. 'The Crisis of Canadian Federalism.' *The Round Table* 334: 219-40.

MacKinnon, Catharine. 1989. *Toward a Feminist Theory of the State*. Cambridge: Harvard University Press.

Maddox, Graham. 1996. *Australian Democracy in Theory and Practice*. 3rd ed. Melbourne: Longman.

Makin, Kirk. 1990. 'Supreme Court Decisions Helps Turn Over New LEAF.' *Globe and Mail*, 7 July: D2.

–. 1993. 'NAC Takes Aim at the Tories.' *Globe and Mail*, 11 September: A7.

Malloy, Jonathan. 1999. 'What Makes a State Advocacy Structure Effective? Conflicts Between Bureaucratic and Social Movement Criteria.' *Governance* 12, 3: 267-88.

Mandel, Michael. 1994. *The Charter of Rights and the Legalization of Politics in Canada*. Rev. ed. Toronto: Thompson Educational Publishing.

Manji, Irshad. 1995. 'Contrary to Elite Criticism, NAC Still in the Mainstream.' *Toronto Star*, 15 March: A23.

March, James G., and Johan P. Olsen. 1989. *Rediscovering Institutions: The Organizational Basis of Politics*. New York: The Free Press.

Marsden, Lorna. 1993. 'Women's Contribution to the Senate.' *Canadian Parliamentary Review* (Winter): 45.

Maslove, Allan M. 1992. 'Reconstructing Fiscal Federalism.' In Frances Abele, ed. *How Ottawa Spends: The Politics of Competitiveness 1992-93*. Ottawa: Carleton University Press.

Matthews, Trevor. 1978. 'Implementing the Coombs Report: The First Eight Months.' In R.F.I. Smith and Patrick Weller, eds. *Public Service Inquiries in Australia*. St. Lucia: Queensland University Press.

Matthews, Trevor, and John Warhurst. 1993. 'Australia: Interest Groups in the Shadow of Strong Parties.' In Clive S. Thomas ed. *First World Interest Groups: A Comparative Perspective*. Westwood, CT: Greenwood Press.

McAdam, Doug, John D. McCarthy, and Mayer N. Zald. 1996. 'Introduction: Opportunities, Mobilizing Structures and Framing Processes: Toward a Synthetic, Comparative

Perspective on Social Movements.' In McAdam, McCarthy, and Zald, eds. *Comparative Perspectives on Social Movements*. Cambridge: Cambridge University Press.

McAllister, Ian. 1986. 'Compulsory Voting, Turnout and Party Advantage in Australia.' *Politics* 21, 1: 89-93.

McDiven, Chrisitine. 1996. 'The Liberal Party and Women.' In Marian Simms, ed. *The Paradox of Parties: Australian Political Parties in the 1990s*. Sydney: Allen and Unwin.

McFarland, Janet. 1993. 'New Head of Women's National Action Committee Learns Early Lession in the Public Eye.' *Financial Post*, 10 July.

McFerren, Ludo. 1990. 'Interpretation of a Frontline State: Australian Women's Refuges and the State.' In Sophie Watson, ed. *Playing the State: Australian Feminist Interventions in the State*. Sydney: Allen and Unwin.

McDiven, Christine. 1994. 'Women in Parliament: The Liberal Way.' *Liberal Times* 1, 1: 8.

McLellan, A. Anne. 1991. *Women and the Process of Constitutional Reform*. Edmonton, AB: Advisory Committee on Women's Issues.

Melbourne Women's Liberation Movement. 1974. 'The Halfway House National Women's Conference on Feminism and Socialism Papers.' Melbourne, October.

Miller, J.D.B. 1964. *Australian Government and Politics*. 3rd ed. London: Duckworth and Co.

Mitchell, Susan. 1996. 'Natasha Stott-Despoja, Democrat Senator: At Twenty-Six the Youngest and Newest Woman on the Parliamentary Block.' In *The Scent of Power: On the Trail of Women and Power in Australian Politics*. Pymble: Angus and Robertson.

Morgan, Jenny. 1993. 'Women and the Law.' *Refracting Voices: Feminist Perspectives for Refractory Girl*. Sydney: Refractory Girl Feminist Journal Publication.

Morris, Cerise. 1980. 'Determination and Thoroughness: The Movement for a Royal Commission on the Status of Women in Canada.' *Atlantis* 5, 2 (Spring): 1-21.

–. 1982. 'No More than Simple Justice: The Royal Commission on the Status of Women and Social Change in Canada.' PhD diss., Department of Sociology, McGill University, Montreal.

Mossman, Mary Jane. 1993. 'Gender Equality and Legal Aid Services: A Research Agenda for Institutional Change.' *Sydney Law Review* 15, 1: 30-58.

–. 1995. 'The Paradox of Feminist Engagement with the Law.' In Nancy Mandell, ed. *Feminist Issues: Race, Class, Sexuality*. Scarborough: Prentice Hall Canada.

Nathan, Richard P. 1992. 'Defining Modern Federalism.' In Harry N. Scheiber, ed. Berkeley: University of California Institute for Governmental Studies Press.

National Action Committee on the Status of Women. 1980. 'Presentation to the Senate, House of Commons Special Joint Committee on the Constitution of Canada.' *Atlantis* 6, 1.

–. 1985. Vol. 1, no. 2.

–. 1986. *Feminist Action* Vol. 1, nos. 7 and 8.

–. 1987. *Feminist Action* Vol. 2, no. 5.

–. 1988. *Feminist Action* Vol. 3, nos. 2 and 3.

–. 1991. 'Report on Organizational Change.' Papers from NAC Conference.

–. 1992. *Action Now* Vol. 2, nos. 4 and 7.

–. 1992. 'The Women's Agenda: Declaration of Principles and a Call to Action.' Strategies for Change: Part 2, 20th Anniversary Conference, 5-7 June.

–. 1993. *Action Now* Vol. 3, no. 9.

–. 1994. *Action Now* Vol. 4, no. 5.

–. 1995. *Action Now* Vol. 5, nos. 2 and 4.

–. 1995. *A Very Political Budget*. NAC Press Release.

Neales, Sue. 1989. 'Peak Body Plan to Give Lobbyists More Muscle.' *Australian Financial Review*, 4 July.

Neave, Marcia. 1994. 'One Step Forward, Two Steps Back: Law and Gender Bias.' In *Women, Power and Politics: Conference Proceedings*. Adelaide, South Australia: Women's Suffrage Centenary Steering Committee.

Ng, Roxanna. 1993. "Racism, Sexism, and Immigrant Women." In Sandra Burt, Lorraine Code, and Lindsay Dorney, eds. *Changing Patterns: Women in Canada*. 2nd ed. Toronto: McClelland and Stewart.

Norris, Pippa. 1997. 'Choosing Electoral Systems: Proportional, Majoritarian and Mixed Systems.' *International Political Science Review* 18, 3: 297-312.

Norris, Pippa, and Joni Lovenduski. 1995. *Political Recruitment. Gender, Race and Class and the British Parliament*. Cambridge: Cambridge University Press.

O'Connor, Julia, Ann Shola Orloff, and Sheila Shaver. 1999. *States, Markets, Families: Gender, Liberalism and Social Policy in Australia, Canada, Great Britain and the United States*. Cambridge: Cambridge University Press.

O'Donnell, Carol, and Phillippa Hall. 1988. *Getting Equal: Labour Market Regulation and Women's Work*. Sydney: Allen and Unwin.

Office of the Status of Women. 1989. *OSWomen Newsletter* (July).

–. 1992. *OSWomen Newsletter*, 14 (September); 15 (December).

–. 1994. *OSWomen Newsletter*, 19 (January).

O'Neil, Maureen, and Sharon Sutherland. 1997. 'The Machinery of Women's Policy: Implementing the RCSW.' In Caroline Andrew and Sanda Rodgers, eds. *Women and the Canadian State/Les Femmes et l'Etat canadien*. Montreal and Kingston: McGill-Queens University Press.

Painter, Martin. 1996. 'Federal Theory and Modern Australian Executive Federalism.' In John Halligan, ed. *Public Administration under Scrutiny: Essays in Honour of Roger Wettenhall*. Canberra: Centre for Research in Public Sector Management, University of Canberra, Institute of Public Administration Australia.

–. 1997a. 'Elections.' In Rodney Smith, ed. *Politics in Australia*. 3rd ed. Sydney: Allen and Unwin.

–. 1997b. 'Federalism.' In Rodney Smith, ed. *Politics in Australia*. 3rd ed. Sydney: Allen and Unwin.

–. 1998. *Collaborative Federalism: Economic Reform in Australia in the 1990s*. Cambridge: Cambridge University Press.

Pal, Leslie A. 1993. *Interests of State*. Montreal and Kingston: McGill-Queen's University Press.

Paltiel, Freda L. 1990. 'Status of Women in Canada: Zeitgeist, Process and Personalities.' Paper presented to the Canadian Sociology and Anthropology Association, University of Victoria, British Columbia, 28 May.

–. 1997. 'State Initiatives: Impetus and Effects.' In Caroline Andrew and Sanda Rodgers, eds. *Women and the Canadian State/Les Femmes et l'Etat canadien*. Montreal and Kingston: McGill-Queens University Press.

Papadakis, Elim. 1993. 'New Aspirations: Changing Patterns of Representation and Electoral Behaviour.' In Ian Marsh, ed. *Governing in the 1990s: An Agenda for the Decade*. Melbourne: Longman Cheshire.

Pateman, Carole. 1989. 'Feminist Critiques of the Public/Private Dichotomy.' In *The Disorder of Women*. Cambridge: Polity Press.

Pearlman, Lynne, and Brettel Dawson. 1989. 'The Shaping of Equality.' *Broadside: A Feminist Review* 105: 8-9.

Pellatt, Anna S. 2000. 'Equality Rights Litigation and Social Transformation: A Consideration of the Women's Legal Education and Action Fund's Intervention in *Vriend v. R.*' *Canadian Journal of Women and the Law* 12: 117-44.

Peters, B. Guy. 1999. *Institutional Theory in Political Science: The 'New Institutionalism.'* London: Pinter.

Phillips, Anne. 1991. *Engendering Democracy*. Cambridge: Polity Press.

Phillips, Dennis. 1996. 'Women in Australian and American Politics: Some Contemporary Comparisons.' *Current Affairs Bulletin* 73, 2 (September).

Phillips, Susan D. 1991. 'How Ottawa Blends: Shifting Government Relationships with Interest Groups.' In Frances Abele, ed. *How Ottawa Spends The Politics of Fragmentation*. Ottawa: Carleton University Press.

Pierson, Paul. 1995. 'Fragmented Welfare States: Federal Institutions and the Development of Social Policy.' *Governance* 8: 449-78.

Pierson, Ruth Roach. 1993. 'The Mainstream Women's Movement and the Politics of Difference.' In Ruth Roach Pierson, Marjorie Griffen Cohen, Paula Bourne, and Philinda

Masters, eds. *Canadian Women's Issues.* Vol. 1: *Strong Voices, Twenty-five Years of Women's Activism in English Canada.* Toronto: Lorimer.

Poiner, Gretchen, and Sue Wills. 1991. *The Gifthorse: A Critical Look at Equal Employment Opportunity.* Sydney: Allen and Unwin.

Prasser, Scott. 1994. 'Royal Commissions and Public Inquires.' In Patrick Weller, ed. *Royal Commissions and the Making of Public Policy.* Melbourne: Macmillan.

Pross, A. Paul. 1990. 'Pressure Groups: Talking Chameleons.' In Michael S. Whittington and Glen Williams, eds. *Canadian Politics in the 1990s.* 3rd ed. Toronto: Nelson Canada.

Public Interest Advocacy Centre (PIAC). 1995. *Hearing the People: amicus curiae in Our Courts.* Seminar Papers No. 95/16. Sydney: PIAC.

Raman, Padma. 1997. 'Gendered Justice: Some Feminists Interventions into Law.' In Kate Pritchard Hughes, ed. *Contemporary Australian Feminism 2.* Melbourne: Longman.

Randall, Vicky. 1987. *Women and Politics.* Basingstoke: Macmillan.

Rankin, L. Pauline, and Jill Vickers. 1998. 'Locating Women's Politics.' In Manon Tremblay and Caroline Andrew, eds. *Women and Political Representation in Canada.* Ottawa: Ottawa University Press.

–. 2001. *Women's Movements and State Feminism: Integrating Diversity into Public Policy.* Ottawa: Status of Women Canada.

Razack, Sherene. 1991. *Canadian Feminism and the Law: The Women's Legal Education and Action Fund and the Pursuit of Equality.* Toronto: Second Story Press.

Reade, Katy. 1994. 'Struggling to Be Heard: Tensions between Different Voices in the Australian Women's Movement in the 1970s and 1980s.' In Kate Pritchard Hughes, ed. *Contemporary Australian Feminism.* Melbourne: Longman Cheshire.

Rebick, Judy. 1991. 'Unity Should Be News.' *Globe and Mail,* 28 June: A12.

–. 1993. 'The Charlottetown Accord: A Faulty Framework and a Wrong-Headed Compromise.' In Kenneth McRoberts and Patrick Monahan, eds. *The Charlottetown Accord: The Referendum and the Future of Canada.* Toronto: University of Toronto Press.

Review of New South Wales Government Administration. 1977. *Directions for Change Interim Report.* New South Wales, Government Printer.

Reynolds, Margaret. 1996. 'Women, Pre-selection and Merit: Who Decides?' *Reinventing Political Institutions.* Papers on Parliament No. 27, March. Canberra: Department of the Senate, Parliament House.

Rhinehart, Diane. 1995. 'NAC Members Boo, Hiss at Ministers.' *Montreal Gazette,* 13 June: A8.

Riker, William H. 1964. *Federalism: Origin, Operation, Significance.* Boston: Little, Brown and Company.

Rimmer, Shelia M. 1994. *Australian Labour Market and Microeconomic Reform.* Melbourne: La Trobe University Press.

Roberts, Barbara. 1988. *Smooth Sailing or Storm Waters? Canadian and Quebec Women's Groups and the Meech Lake Accord.* Ottawa: Canadian Research Institute for the Advancement of Women.

Rocher, François, and Miriam Smith. 1995. 'Four Dimensions of the Canadian Constitutional Debate.' In François Rocher and Miriam Smith, eds. *New Trends in Canadian Federalism.* Peterborough: Broadview Press.

Ronalds, Chris. 1990. 'Government Action against Employment Discrimination.' In Sophie Watson, ed. *Playing the State: Australian Feminist Interventions.* Sydney: Allen and Unwin.

Royal Commission on Australian Government Administration. 1976. Appendix, Vol. 3. Canberra: Australian Government Publishing Service.

Royal Commission on Human Relationships. 1974-5. *Transcript of Evidence.* Held in National Library, Canberra.

Royal Commission on the Status of Women. 1970. *Report of the Royal Commission on the Status of Women in Canada.* Ottawa: RSCW.

Ryan, Julia. 1990. 'The Story So Far ...' *Papers from the National Women's Conference 1990.* Canberra: National Women's Conference.

Ryan, Lyndall. 1990. 'Feminism and the Federal Bureaucracy: 1972-1983.' In Sophie Watson, ed. *Playing the State: Australian Feminist Interventions.* Sydney: Allen and Unwin.

Ryan, Susan. 1994. 'Women in Government and Cabinet "Two Steps Forward, One Step Back."' Proceedings of the Women, Power and Politics Conference, Adelaide, South Australia, 8-11 October.

–. 1999. *Catching the Waves: Life In and Out of Politics.* Sydney: Harper Collins Publishers.

Savage, Mike, and Anne Witz, eds. 1992. *Gender and Bureaucracy.* Oxford: Blackwell Publishers/The Sociological Review.

Sawer, Marian. 1990. *Sisters in Suits: Women and Public Policy in Australia.* Sydney: Allen and Unwin.

–. 1991. 'Why Has the Australian Women's Movement Had More Influence on Government in Australia than Elsewhere?' In Francis Castles, ed. *Australia Compared.* Sydney: Allen and Unwin.

–. 1994. 'Feminism and the State: Theory and Practice in Australia and Canada.' *Australian-Canadian Studies* 12, 1: 49-68.

–. 1996a. 'Challenging Politics? Seventy-five Years of Women's Parliamentary Representation in Australia.' *International Review of Women and Leadership.* Special Issue: Women and Politics 2, 1 (July): i-xvi.

–. 1996b. 'Femocrats and Ecocrats: Women's Policy Machinery in Australia, Canada and New Zealand.' UNRISD Occasional Paper, UNRISD, Geneva.

–. 1997a. 'Shooting the Messenger: Australia and CEDAW.' In G. Crowder, H. Manning, D.S. Mathieson, A. Parkin, and L. Seabrooke, eds. *Australian Political Studies 1997: Proceedings of the 1997 APSA Conference.* Department of Politics, Flinders University of South Australia.

–. 1997b. *Women are People Too!* Transcript, Women into Politics Lecture Series, Parliament House, Sydney, 10 June.

–. 1997c. 'Topsy-Turvy Land – Where Women, Children and the Environment Come First.' In John Warhurst, ed. *Keeping the Bastards Honest: The Australian Democrats First 20 Years.* Sydney: Allen and Unwin.

Sawer, Marian, and Abigail Groves. 1994. 'The Women's Lobby: Networks, Coalition Building and the Women of Middle Australia.' *Australian Journal of Political Science* 29: 435-59.

Sawer, Marian, and Marian Simms. 1984. *A Woman's Place: Women and Politics in Australia.* Sydney: George Allen and Unwin.

Sawer, Marian, and Jill Vickers. 2001. 'Women's Constitutional Activism in Australia and Canada.' *Canadian Journal of Women and the Law* 13: 1-36.

Scarlet Woman. 1975. 'Editorial Out of the Shadows ... ??? Our Rave.' *Scarlet Woman* 2 (September): 1-3.

Scott, Sarah. 1994. 'NAC: Strident Radicals or Female Advocates?' *Vancouver Sun,* 18 June.

Scutt, Jocelynne. 1990. *Women and the Law.* Sydney: The Law Book Company Limited.

Self, Peter. 1978. 'The Coombs Commission: An Overview.' In R.F.I. Smith and Patrick Weller, eds. *Public Service Inquiries in Australia.* St. Lucia: Queensland University Press.

–. 1989. 'Federal Institutions and Processes: An Economic Perspective.' In Brian Galligan, ed. *Australian Federalism.* Melbourne: Longman Cheshire.

Senate Standing Committee on Legal and Constitutional Affairs. 1994. *Gender Bias and the Judiciary.* Canberra: Commonwealth of Australia.

Sexton, Mary. 1995. 'Second Thoughts on the WEL ACT: Paper on a Peak Organisation for Women.' N.p.

Sherry, Ann. 1994. 'Twenty-five Years Is Not Long for Catching Up.' *Canberra Bulletin of Public Administration* 76 (April): 84-8.

Simeon, Richard. 1988. 'Meech Lake and Shifting Conceptions of Canadian Federalism.' *Canadian Public Policy: The Meech Lake Supplement* 14 (September):

–. 1994. 'In Search of a Social Contract: Can We Make Hard Decisions as if Democracy Matters?' CD Howe Institute Benefactors Lecture, Toronto, 13 September.

Simms, Marian. 1996. 'Two Steps Forward, One step Back: Women and the Australian Party System.' In Marian Simms, ed. *The Paradox of Parties: Australian Political Parties in the 1990s.* Sydney: Allen and Unwin.

Simms, Marian, and Diane Stone. 1990. 'Women's Policy.' In Christine Jennett and Randall Stewart, eds. *Hawke and Australian Public Policy.* Melbourne: Macmillan.

Skocpol, Theda. 1985. 'Bringing the State Back In: Strategies of Analysis in Current Research.' In Peter B. Evans, Dietrich Rueshemeyer, and Theda Skocpol, eds. *Bringing the State Back In.* Cambridge: Cambridge University Press.

Smith, David E. 1990. 'The Federal Cabinet in Canadian Politics.' In Michael S. Whittington and Glen Williams, eds. *Canadian Politics in the 1990s.* 3rd ed. Scarborough: Nelson Canada.

Smith, Meg. 1984. 'The Struggle for Women's Health Centres in NSW.' *Refractory Girl* (May).

Staggenborg, Suzanne. 1991. *The Pro-Choice Movement: Organization and Activism in the Abortion Conflict.* Oxford: Oxford University Press.

Status of Women Canada. 1987. *Perspectives.* Vol. 1, no. 1.

–. 1988. *Perspectives.* Vol. 1, no. 2.

–. 1995a. *Canada's National Report to the United Nations for the Fourth World Conference on Women.* Ottawa: Status of Women Canada.

—. 1995b. *Fast Facts: 12 Major Issues on the Agenda at Beijing.* Ottawa: Status of Women Canada.

Stetson, Dorothy McBride, and Amy G. Mazur, eds. 1995. 'Introduction,' *Comparative State Feminism.* Thousand Oaks: Sage.

Stivers, Camilla. 1993. *Gender Images in Public Administration: Legitimacy and the Administrative State.* Newbury Park, California: Sage.

Stone, Janey. 1974. 'A Strategy for the Women's Liberation.' In *National Women's Conference on Feminism and Socialism Papers.* Melbourne.

Sullivan, Kathy Martin. 1994. 'Women in Parliament – Yes! But What's It Really Like?' *Views of Parliamentary Democracy Papers on Parliament* 22. Canberra: Department of the Senate.

Summers, Anne. 1973. 'Where's the Women's Movement Moving To?' *Mejane,* 10 March: 6-8.

–. 1986. 'Mandarins or Missionaries: Women in the Federal Bureaucracy.' In Norma Grieve and Alisa Burns, eds. *Australian Women: New Feminist Perspectives.* Melbourne: Oxford University Press.

Swain, Marie. 1997. *Women in Parliament: An Update.* Briefing Paper No. 1/97. Sydney: NSW Parliamentary Library Research Service.

Swayze, Mikael Antony. 1996. 'Continuity and Change in the 1993 Canadian General Election.' *Canadian Journal of Political Science* 29, 3: 555-66.

Tarrow, Sidney. 1998. *Power in Movement: Social Movements and Contentious Politics.* 2nd ed. Cambridge: Cambridge University Press.

Teghtsoonian, Katherine. 2000. 'Gendering Policy Analysis in the Government of British Columbia: Strategies, Possibilities and Constraints.' *Studies in Political Economy* 61: 105-27.

Thelen, Kathleen, and Sven Steinmo. 1992. 'Historical Institutionalism in Comparative Politics.' In Sven Steinmo, Kathleen Thelen, and Frank Longstreth, eds. *Structuring Politics: Historical Institutionalism in Comparative Analysis.* Cambridge: Cambridge University Press.

Thompson, Elaine. 1997. 'The Constitution.' In Rodney Smith, ed. *Politics in Australia.* 3rd ed. Sydney: Allen and Unwin.

Thorburn, Hugh G. 1985. 'Interpretations of the Canadian Party System.' In Hugh Thorburn, ed. *Party Politics in Canada.* Scarborough: Prentice-Hall Canada.

Townsend, Lynn. 1994. *Report to the WESNET Steering Committee: The Establishment of Women's Emergency Service Network (WESNET Inc.).* June.

Tremblay, Manon. 1997. 'Quebec Women in Politics: An Examination of the Research.' In Jane Arscott and Linda Trimble, eds. *In the Presence of Women: Representation in Canadian Governments.* Toronto: Harcourt Brace and Co.

Troup, Maggie. 1997. 'Cuts to Legal Aid: The Impact on Women's Access to Justice.' *Australian Feminist Law Journal* 9: 151-8.

Trudeau, Pierre Elliott. 1968. *Federalism and the French Canadians.* Toronto: Macmillan.

Veilleux, Gérard, and Donald J. Savoie. 1988. 'Kafka's Castle: The Treasury Board of Canada Revisited.' *Canadian Public Administration* 31, 4: 517-38.

Vickers, Jill. 1990. 'Why Should Women Care about Constitutional Reform?' In David Schneiderman, ed. *Among Friends: Women and Constitutional Reform – Proceedings of an Interdisciplinary Conference on Women and Constitutional Reform*. Edmonton: Centre for Constitutional Studies, University of Alberta.

–. 1991. 'Bending the Iron Law of Oligarchy: Debates on the Feminization of Organization and Political Process in the English Canadian Women's Movement, 1970-1988.' In Jeri Dawn Wine and Janice L. Ristock, eds. *Women and Social Change: Feminist Activism in Canada*. Toronto: James Lorimer.

–. 1992. 'The Intellectual Origins of the Women's Movement in Canada.' In Constance Backhouse and David H. Flaherty, eds. *Challenging Times: The Women's Movement in Canada and the United States*. Montreal and Kingston: McGill-Queen's University Press.

–. 1993. 'The Canadian Women's Movement and a Changing Constitutional Order.' *International Journal of Canadian Studies* 7-8 (Spring-Fall): 261-84.

–. 1994. 'Why *Should* Women Care About Federalism?' In Janet Hierbert, ed. *Canada: The State of the Federation*. Kingston: Queen's School of Public Policy.

–. 1997a. 'Toward a Feminist Understanding of Representation.' In Jane Arscott and Linda Trimble, eds. *In the Presence of Women: Representation in Canadian Governments*. Toronto: Harcourt Brace and Co.

–. 1997b. *Reinventing Political Science: A Feminist Approach*. Halifax: Fernwood Publishing.

Vienneau, David. 1992. 'Budget Cuts Undermine Legal Group's Fight for Equality Rights.' *Toronto Star*, 2 March: C1.

Vizard, Steve. 1998. *Two Weeks in Lilliput: Bear-Baiting and Backbiting at the Constitutional Convention*. Melbourne: Penguin.

Wainer, Jo. 1997. 'Abortion Before the High Court.' *Australian Feminist Law Journal* 8: 133-8.

Walker, Kristen. 1995. 'Who's the Boss? The Judiciary, the Executive, the Parliament and the Protection of Human Rights.' *Western Australian Law Review* 25 (December): 238-54.

Watson, Sophie. 1992. 'Femocractic Feminisms.' In Mike Savage and Anne Witz, eds. *Gender and Bureaucracy*. Oxford: Blackwell Publishers/The Sociological Review.

Watts, Ronald L. 1996. *Comparing Federal Systems in the 1990s*. Kingston: Institute of Intergovernmental Relations.

Weaver, Sally. 1993. 'First Nations Women and Government Policy, 1970-92: Discrimination and Conflict.' In Sandra Burt, Lorraine Code, and Lindsay Dorney, eds. *Changing Patterns: Women in Canada*. Toronto: McClelland and Stewart.

Wente, Margaret. 1995. 'The Sad Decline of NAC.' *Globe and Mail*, 4 February: A2.

White, Graham. 1997. 'Provinces and Territories: Characteristics, Roles and Responsibilities.' In Jaques Bourgault, Maurice Demers, and Cynthia Williams, eds. *Public Administration and Public Management: Experiences in Canada*. Sainte-Foy, QC: Les Publications du Québec.

Whitlam, Gough. 1975. 'Address to Women and Politics Conference.' Australian National University, Canberra, 1 September.

Wilcox, Murray R. Justice. 1993. *The Australian Charter of Rights*. North Ryde: The Law Book Company.

Wills, Sue. 1981. 'The Politics of Sexual Liberation.' PhD diss., Department of Government, University of Sydney.

–. 1995. 'Sexual Equality.' In M. Hogan and K. Dempsey, eds. *Equity and Citizenship under Keating*. Sydney: Public Affairs Research Centre, University of Sydney.

Wilson, Bertha. 1993. *Women and the Canadian Charter of Rights and Freedoms*. Ottawa: National Association of Women and the Law.

Women's Electoral Lobby. 1996. "Settlement of CES vs. Superclinics." Media Release. 9 October <http://www.wel.org.au/issues/abortion/med9_10.htm>.

–. 1997. 'Recommendations of National Strategic Planning Group.' Memo, 4 February.

–. 1999. 'Out in Front for Women.' Press Release. 13 October. <http://www.wel.org.au>.

Wright, Tony. 1997. 'Radio Choice Makes Waves.' *Sydney Morning Herald*, 25 March: 13.

Wynhausen, Elisabeth. 1998. 'The Wife Who's Paying for Ending 13 Years of Domestic Cruelty.' *The Australian*, 19 February.

Yeatman, Anna. 1990. *Bureaucrats, Technocrats, Femocrats: Essays on the Contemporary Australian State*. Sydney: Allen and Unwin.

Young, Lisa. 1996. 'Women's Movements and Political Parties: A Canadian-American Comparison.' *Party Politics* 2, 2: 229-50.

–. 1997. 'Fulfilling the Mandate of Difference: Women in the Canadian House of Commons.' In Jane Arscott and Linda Trimble, eds. *In the Presence of Women: Representation in Canadian Governments*. Toronto: Harcourt Brace and Co.

–. 2000. *Feminists and Party Politics*. Vancouver: UBC Press.

Interviews

Former Director of the Women's Program, Department of Secretary of State. 1995. Interview with the author. Toronto, 3 November.

Former Director, Office of the Status of Women, Department of Prime Minister and Cabinet. 1995. Interview with the author. Canberra, 14 July.

Former Director, Office of the Status of Women, Department of Prime Minister and Cabinet. 1995. Interview with the author. Sydney, 18 July.

Former Director, Office of the Status of Women, Department of Prime Minister and Cabinet. 1995. Interview with the author. Canberra, 14 July.

Former Minister Assisting the Prime Minister on Women's Affairs. 1997. Interview with the author. Parliament House, Canberra, 10 February.

Former NAC Executive Assistant. 1995. Interview with the author. Toronto, 6 December.

Former President, National Action Committee. 1995. Interview with the author. Toronto, 6 December.

Legal Officer, Public Interest Advocacy Centre. 1998. Telephone interview with the author. Sydney, 8 March.

Senior Officer, Director, Office of the Status of Women of South Australia. 1998. Interview with the author. Adelaide, 2 October.

Senior Officer, Policy Directorate, Status of Women Canada. 1995. Interview with the author. Ottawa, 4 October.

Senior Women's Program Officer, Status of Women Canada. 1995. Interview with the author. Ottawa, 27 November.

Index